The Weaponizing of Language in the Classroom and Beyond

Language and Social Life

Editors
David Britain
Crispin Thurlow

Volume 28

The Weaponizing of Language in the Classroom and Beyond

Edited by
Kisha C. Bryan and Luis Javier Pentón Herrera

ISBN 978-3-11-221477-0
e-ISBN (PDF) 978-3-11-079952-1
e-ISBN (EPUB) 978-3-11-079954-5
ISSN 2364-4303

Library of Congress Control Number: 2023942413

Bibliographic information published by the Deutsche Nationalbibliothek
The Deutsche Nationalbibliothek lists this publication in the Deutsche Nationalbibliografie; detailed bibliographic data are available on the internet at http://dnb.dnb.de.

© 2025 Walter de Gruyter GmbH, Berlin/Boston
This volume is text- and page-identical with the hardback published in 2024.
Cover image: Tim Perdue/Moment Open/Getty Images
Typesetting: Integra Software Services Pvt. Ltd.
Printing and binding: CPI books GmbH, Leck

www.degruyter.com

Kisha C. Bryan and Luis Javier Pentón Herrera

Preface

In this edited volume, each of the chapters illustrates the serious consequences of language weaponization that often stigmatizes entire groups of people. It is our hope that this book will serve as an important resource for educators, researchers, organizations, and policymakers as they attempt to recognize and combat language weaponization. It is important that society has an awareness of language weaponization in its various forms, including the use of loaded words, book banning, discriminatory language policies, and coded language. Awareness must happen before one can respond to instances of language weaponization when they are encountered. We encourage readers to challenge language weaponization directly. This may involve calling out individuals, policies, or organizations that use language in harmful and/or discriminatory ways. We ask that you educate others about the dangers of language weaponization and the importance of using language responsibly. This may involve discussing these issues with friends, family members, and colleagues, as well as sharing information on social media and other platforms. Finally, we ask that YOU, our reader(s), reflect on your own language ideologies and practice responsible language use in your communications and everyday practices. This involves being mindful of the impact of your words and beliefs about other people's language(s) or language use, avoiding loaded or inflammatory language, and promoting respectful and inclusive communication practices throughout our global society.

Kisha C. Bryan, Tennessee State University
Luis Javier Pentón Herrera, Akademia Ekonomiczno-Humanistyczna w Warszawie

https://doi.org/10.1515/9783110799521-202

Contents

Kisha C. Bryan and Luis Javier Pentón Herrera
Preface —— V

Kisha C. Bryan and Luis Javier Pentón Herrera
Chapter 1
An introduction to the weaponizing of language in the classroom and beyond —— 1

Abu Saleh Mohammad Rafi
Chapter 2
Language weaponization, missed opportunities, and transformational spaces in Bangladeshi English departments: A biographical perspective —— 13

Ming-Hsuan Wu, Ching-Ching Lin, Ming-Yao Hsiung, and Po-Hui Min
Chapter 3
Flipping the script: A collaborative autoethnography of agency and voices in the weaponization of bilingual education in Taiwan —— 35

Kisha C. Bryan, Daphne Germain, Mama Raouf, Susan Githua, and Renee Figuera
Chapter 4
The price we pay: An autobiographical dialogue of linguistic violence in the African diaspora —— 63

Xinyue Zuo and Denise Ives
Chapter 5
"That's easy": An analysis of speech acts in an instance of cross-cultural miscommunication —— 89

Gabriel T. Acevedo Velázquez
Chapter 6
A critical look at 'Pato' y 'Maricón': Puerto Rican Gay teachers' interventions with homophobic language —— 109

Anderson Chebanne and Kemmonye Monaka
Chapter 7
The weaponization of Setswana: Implications for marginalized languages in Botswana —— 127

Jason A. Kemp
Chapter 8
Using your own language against you: Spanish in U.S. classrooms —— 147

Burcu Ates and Benita Brooks
Chapter 9
Banned books in K-12 classrooms: Weaponization of children and young adolescent literature —— 169

Sandra Descourtis
Chapter 10
French variations and language weaponization in US higher education —— 191

Juan A. Ríos Vega
Chapter 11
Dismantling weaponizing language in teacher preparation programs —— 213

Sender Dovchin
Afterword: Language weaponization and its harm —— 231

Editors —— 237

Contributors —— 239

Index —— 243

Kisha C. Bryan and Luis Javier Pentón Herrera

Chapter 1
An introduction to the weaponizing of language in the classroom and beyond

Abstract: In this opening chapter, we establish the groundwork for the edited volume by delving into the intricate interplay between language, discourse, and societal change. Here, we underscore the dual nature of language, recognizing its potential both as a force for positive transformation and as a vehicle for harm and marginalization in the classroom and beyond. Utilizing linguistic theories and discourse analysis as our lens, we illustrate how the choices made in the process of communication possess the power to shape perceptions and foster dialogues, impacting social interactions while also potentially perpetuating harm against marginalized individuals and groups. Moreover, we provide a clear definition of language weaponization, or the weaponizing of language, framing our discussions within the parameters of applied linguistics and social sciences. We end the chapter by recording the origins of this edited volume, which provides a backdrop for introducing the subsequent chapters.

Keywords: weaponizing of language, language weaponization, language and harm, boarding schools

1 Introduction to the weaponization of language

Language[1] is present in every single part of our lives. From thoughts to street signs, and spoken or written messages, language is the vehicle our brain uses to understand its surroundings and make sense of the world. In the field of linguistics, language has been described as a technology packaging "knowledge in radically different ways, facilitating certain means of conceptualizing, naming, and discussing the world" (Harrison, 2010, p. 59). As language learners and speakers,

---

[1] Throughout this manuscript and edited volume, we use the word 'language' to refer to all forms of language including verbal and nonverbal, rhetoric, discourse, signs/writing, as well as the language used in media and other outlets, to name a few.

Kisha C. Bryan, Tennessee State University
Luis Javier Pentón Herrera, Akademia Ekonomiczno-Humanistyczna w Warszawie

https://doi.org/10.1515/9783110799521-001

we understand that words carry meaning. When we learn a language, whether it is our first (L1) or additional language (L2), we attach emotions, imagery, and memories to the vocabulary we acquire. For example, if we hear the phrase "pure love," we may quickly think of someone dear to us, an image representing pure love, or a story that has continuously been portrayed as such (e.g., Romeo and Juliet). Certainly, language is directly connected to human emotions, and the words we use have the power to affect how we act, feel, and understand our existence (Lindquist et al., 2015).

Language, as a mechanism with the power to influence the emotions and actions of humans, has been a topic of interest for many years, especially in the social sciences. The past and present works of scholars concerned with justice and equity shed light on how language and discourse are used to promote conflict and discrimination in our societies. For example, in their book, Young et al. (2018), describe *political fear* as a type of discourse used to gain support by exploiting people's emotions and anxieties. Political fear is often used by those in positions of power (e.g., "build the wall") to capitalize on danger and dangerous situations and influence people's actions through fear. The result is that those affected by political fear replicate this type of discourse through the process of contagion. Discourses such as political fear demonstrate the power that language has in our societies to evoke reactions, garner support in favor of the person/people leading the narrative, and influence how others think and act.

By looking at human history, we can learn that language and discourse can be used to both empower or dehumanize groups of people in societies. For centuries, civilizations around the world have witnessed how language is used to exert ethnic dominance while depriving some groups of positive human qualities and opportunities. McConnell-Ginet (2020) shares various examples in her book about the consequences of using language to dehumanize others. From the "genocidal language games" (McConnell-Ginet, 2020, p. 138) of the 1994 Rwandan massacre, to the vilification of those of Japanese descent during World War II-era in the United States, linguistic patterns of dehumanization (i.e., slurs, labels, hate speech, etc.) often emerge as early indicators of escalations of conflict and harm. Further, in a recent article, Pentón Herrera (2022) asserts that throughout history, language has been used to justify the dehumanization of others in three simple steps: (1) beginning the process of dehumanization by assigning labels to groups, (2) solidifying a culture of dehumanization by solidifying a culture that these groups are *something* (i.e., not human) rather than someone (i.e., *human*), and (3) engaging in physical harm by hurting and eradicating those groups of people who were dehumanized.

In every major event of ethnic domination and racism, we can find language being used as the precursor to physical harm and violence (McConnell–Ginet, 2020; Pentón Herrera, 2022). An example of this is found in apartheid South Africa

(1948–1990s), where language played a major role in the enforcement of white supremacist policies favoring racial segregation. The laws passed during this period restricted the quality and opportunities of Black people in nearly every social sector, including education, health, and community spaces. In addition, signs were planted throughout the country to set racial boundaries (e.g., *Whites area*, or *For use by white persons*, etc.) and to solidify racist fears and attitudes about 'native' people, as shown in Figure 1.1. Eventually, linguistic racism and dehumanization paved the way for overt acts of violence to repress, oppress, torture, and kill Black people in South Africa. Pre-apartheid events, which are reminiscent of other race-based segregation events around the world, such as in the United States (De Costa et al., 2022; Weber, 2015), remind us that language is vital to the dissemination of racist, dehumanizing, and divisive ideologies that create societal conflicts, and influence the minds and actions of people (Clyne, 1995; Wenden, 1995).

Figure 1.1: Sign in South Africa during Apartheid (1948–1990s).
Note: Image retrieved from History.com (https://www.history.com/topics/africa/apartheid#&gid=ci0245618b100025ab&pid=photo-gallery-apartheid-getty-2664162)

In the same way, language is used in societies to privilege or harm groups, it is also used in educational institutions at every level. Schools are microcosms of our societies and, as such, the discourse allowed and used in communities naturally percolates into educational settings. Language weaponization in educational contexts occurs when the majority of the population allows the use of discourse with the purpose of dehumanizing a group of people in the community. Thus, language weaponization in education occurs organically in societies where discourse is already being used to reproduce dehumanization and harm toward groups of people deemed undesired. History shows that language weaponization in education has traditionally resulted in policies and/or practices favoring the monolingualism of the ruling class and, in some cases, forbidding or deeming as less important the language(s) of diverse populations and Indigenous Peoples.

One of the most well-recorded reminders of language weaponization in educational contexts is the internment or boarding schools for Indigenous Peoples. These practices of forced colonization in educational settings occurred all around the world, including the Americas, Australia (Perpitch, 2018; Welch, 1988), New Zealand, Scandinavia, Russian Federation, Asia, Africa, and the Middle East (Smith, 2009). In most, if not all, of these historical events of internment/boarding schools, a similar pattern occurred: Indigenous children were forcefully taken away from their parents to be colonized into the morality of the ruling group, usually the white man and the white culture (Smith, 2009; Welch, 1988). Missionaries (e.g., Catholics, Christians, Lutherans) indoctrinated children into forced Christianity (i.e., forced evangelization), punished the use of Indigenous languages inside of school, and imposed the colonial language, perpetuating a monolingual mindset and promoting the erasure of Indigenous cultures, traditions, and languages (Lomawaima, 1994; Smith, 2009). It has been recorded that Indigenous children at these schools were often used as display or living exhibits to the white public (Fear-Segal, 2010), and were also victims of physical and sexual abuse. Many Indigenous children around the world died in internment/boarding schools due to poor sanitary and physical conditions (Dawson, 2012; Smith, 2009).

Figure 1.2 shows an image of Catholic nuns and Mapuche children in a historical event known as "La campaña al desierto" (Campaign to the Desert), in which the Argentine military sought to establish dominance over the Patagonian Desert and its Indigenous Peoples, the Mapuche. The figure has written on it: "¿Dónde estás nuestrxs desaparecidxs de 'La Campaña al Desierto?' Nunca más van a ocultar este genocidio." (Where are our missing from 'The Campaign to the Desert?' They [the colonizers] will never hide this genocide again). Figure 1.3 shows an image of the Qu'Appelle Indian Residential School, in Saskatchewan, Canada, circa 1885, where Indigenous parents camped outside of the gates of the school to visit their children since they were forbidden by law to remove their children from the school.

Figure 1.2: Mapuche children in forceful evangelization.
Note: Image retrieved from Mapuchememe: (https://www.facebook.com/mapumemes/photos/a.113723863579879/119154933036772/?type=3&theater)

2 What do we mean by language weaponization?

The field of applied linguistics has been interested in exploring the effects of language all around the world. From this interest, different fields, such as critical discourse studies (CDS), language ideologies, linguistic racism, and more recently, raciolinguistics, have emerged to explore how language can be used to benefit or harm individuals and societies. Each of these fields, however, approaches the conversation of language, social justice, and inequality in society from different, albeit

Figure 1.3: Indigenous parents camping outside of the gates of Qu'Appelle Indian Residential School.
Note: Image retrieved from Library and Archives Canada: (https://data2.archives.ca/ap/a/a182246.jpg)

related, standpoints. For example, the field of critical discourse studies has largely focused on "the substantively linguistic and discursive nature of social relations of power in contemporary societies" (Fairclough & Wodak, 1997, p. 272). As such, scholars in the field of CDS have looked at how discourse controls, influences, and shapes contemporary society (Krzyżanowski & Forchtner, 2016). On the other hand, the field of language ideologies has been interested in conceptualizations about discursive practices in specific cultures and contexts. More specifically, scholars in the field of language ideologies have been interested in exploring the role of language in moral interests, political discourses, and the connection between language and inequality (Woolard & Schieffelin, 1994).

In this edited volume, we use the term *language weaponization*—or the *weaponization of language*—to describe the process in which words, discourse, and language in any form have been used/are being used to inflict harm on others (Bryan & Gerald, 2020; Pascale, 2019; Rafael, 2016). In this definition, the term *harm* is of vital importance because it refers to how minoritized individuals, as well as their cultures and languages, are affected by ideologies and practices that normalize inequity and injustice in their environments. Further, we are interested in advancing the knowledge of how language weaponization affects the well-being of individuals and communities (i.e., people's quality of life, health, and happiness, opportunities), perpetuating inequality and injustice in society.

This definition arises from our awareness that language is a human-made social and political object (Otheguy et al., 2015), and factor (Wenden, 1995), that has been used to (re)position the prestige, prominence, and realities of groups of people and events in society. From this standpoint, language can also be viewed as a form of currency benefiting those in positions of power leading the narrative, and influencing the minds and lives of the community.

3 Origins and overview of this volume

The idea for this project emerged from a 2021 collaborative panel presented at the TESOL International Association organized by Dr. Anita Bright, Dr. Anastasia J. Khawaja, and Ms. Liana Smith. In this panel titled *Weaponizing language: Making counternarratives the new narratives for the marginalized*, each of the panelists explored the ramifications of language use and narratives in societies around the world. From this initial collaboration, a second collaboration was organized by Dr. Anita Bright for the 2021 Language Education for Social Justice Conference in Applied Language Studies in Finland. This colloquium, titled *Words as weapons in the US and Palestine: Towards restoration and reconciliation*, explored the weaponization of language in the US and Palestinian contexts, calling for a reversal of damaging narratives, and for a dismantling of systematic, hierarchical oppressions which control language. After these initial panels, we (Kisha and Luis) proposed to continue this conversation in a different space, resulting in this edited volume.

The chapters included in this edited volume were carefully selected after we disseminated a Call for Proposals welcoming abstracts from scholars from around the world interested in exploring the weaponizing of language in education and beyond. As such, the authors and contributions included in this edited volume broadly represent the fields of applied linguistics and language education, and explore the weaponization of language in education in the contexts of Benin, Taiwan, Trinidad and Tobago, Kenya, Botswana, and the United States. Thus, the geo-cultural coverage of this edited book primarily includes the United States (including Puerto Rico), the Caribbean (Trinidad and Tobago), Asia (Taiwan), and Africa (Kenya, Benin, and Botswana), with a primary focus on English, including Trinidadian English Creole and African-American Vernacular English, Spanish languages, Haitian Creole, French, and the languages of Benin, Botswana, and Kenya.

Inspired by our previous work on language weaponization (see Pentón Herrera & Bryan, 2022), we expand our conversation on the use of languages as weapons in this edited volume. Our purpose with this edited book is to provide an international scholarly platform where we can continue advancing the knowledge of how language has been—and continues to be—weaponized in societies, and foment its relationship to social justice. Furthermore, in this edited volume, we hope to explore the growing conversation of how language use and weaponization directly affect (both positively and negatively) the well-being of individuals—a topic still limited in scholarly conversations.

For this chapter, Chapter 1, our goal is to provide a broad overview of language weaponization so as to set the stage for this volume that spans geographical contexts. In Chapter 2, Abu Saleh Mohammad Rafi employs an autobiographical approach to examine the ways that Bangladeshi English departments promote Anglo-normative practices by weaponizing the English language. He further highlights the ways in which teachers and students in Bangladesh are affected by the linguistic, cultural, and ideological dimensions of weaponization. Utilizing a collaborative autoethnographic approach, Ming-Hsuan Wu, Ching-Ching Lin, Ming-Yao Hsiung, and Po-Hui Min explore in Chapter 3 the rollout of Taiwan's Bilingual 2030 Policy and the neoliberalist discourse that has been weaponized to mobilize public support for or against the policy. The authors discuss how they have navigated and resisted the discourses of neoliberal educational reform, describing how they create opportunities for student empowerment that successfully challenges and rejects oppressive and weaponized language policies and/or educational reform. In Chapter 4, Kisha C. Bryan, Susan Githua, Daphne Germain, Raouf Mama, and Renee Figuera discuss the legacy of colonization and racism from West Africa to the United States to the islands of the Caribbean, reflecting on the linguistic, social, economic, and cultural price that Blacks across the African diaspora have paid. They critique the role of racism, colonization, and standard language ideologies in their personal, social, and professional lives in the United States, Kenya, Benin, and Trinidad. Chapter 4 concludes with a discussion of the common characteristics of linguistic violence across the diaspora and a call to action for policymakers, educational and civil rights leaders.

Xinyue Zuo and Denise Ives highlight the interpretive nature of discourse in Chapter 5. Through a pragmatic perspective, they examine the speech acts of an instructor's utterance "that's easy!" and students' interpretations and responses, alongside the interrelations between language, identity, and power. They show the importance of raising higher education practitioners' awareness of pragmatic competence and microaggression, and identifying feasible solutions to minimize communication conflicts. An interrogation of how interventions against homophobic slurs in Puerto Rico are thought of and understood by gay teachers is the focus of Chapter 6. In this chapter, Gabriel Acevedo employs a dual critical discourse analysis-narrative framework to highlight and critique discourses that show gay Puerto Rican teachers' understanding of their relationship with *Pato* y and *Maricón* (i.e., homophobic slurs in Spanish), their expressed interventions, and their lack thereof. He highlights both the experiences of addressing homophobic language and the permissive attitudes that assault gay students' and teachers' identities to go unchecked. In Chapter 7, Andersen Chebanne and Kemmonya Monaka share the situation that has led to the predominance and weaponization of Setswana in the Botswanan context. This chapter takes the view that the actions of the state (i.e., the elevation of English and Setswana above minoritized Indigenous languages) are a form of weaponization as they are undemocratic, oppressive, and violate the language and cultural rights of a sizable portion of the population. Ethnic groups whose languages are marginalized quickly get assimilated, leading to acute language and ethnic endangerment across Botswana.

In Chapter 8, Jason Kemp explores language weaponization in U.S. classrooms in which Spanish is the language of communication. He argues that ideologies and practices that frame students and their Spanish as deficient or broken are harmful, and they ignore the rich cultural knowledge and linguistic practices Spanish-speaking Latinx students bring to the classroom. After providing a history of linguistic violence in U.S. schools, Kemp concludes that educators at all levels of instruction should strive to reduce harm by employing humanizing pedagogies that uplift students' languaging practices. Continuing with the U.S. context, Burcu Ates and Benita Brooks, contend that book banning is a form of language weaponization in Chapter 9. They utilize critical discourse analysis (Fairclough, 1995) to examine how supporters of banned books have used Pascale's (2019) four interlocking components of weaponized language to have books removed from school libraries and curricula to serve their own personal, social, and political agendas. Ates and Brooks provide implications for students, school staff, teacher education programs, and community partners to continue the fight against book banning.

In Chapter 10, Sandra Descourtis addresses the perceptions and use of slang (e.g., verlan and argot) by undergraduate students in the U.S. who are learning French. Online surveys and interviews reveal that students' perceptions of French slang are influenced by their primary language and by French language clichés. The findings of the study suggest that although students feel it important to learn formal and informal varieties of French, standard language ideologies, perpetuated by society, institutions, and media, have served as weapons to stigmatize French slang users and discourage learners from acquiring those less formal, but equally important French language varieties. In the final chapter, Chapter 11, Juan A. Ríos Vega argues that the language of weaponization in teacher education programs results in pre-service and in-service teachers not being as prepared to teach students of color, especially English language learners (ELLs). As such, the author encourages teacher educators, pre-and in-service teachers, and school administrators to treat students of color as cultural and linguistic assets in the classroom. Ríos Vega concludes that chapter with his reflection on education as "an ethic of love."

References

Bryan, Kisha C., & J. P. B. Gerald. 2020. The weaponization of English. *Language Magazine*, 1–8. https://www.languagemagazine.com/2020/08/17/the-weaponization-of-english/

Clyne, Michael. 1995. Establishing linguistic markers of racist discourse. In Christina Schäffner & Anita L. Wenden (eds.), *Language and peace*, 111–118. Amsterdam: Harwood Academic Publishers.

De Costa, Peter I., Lee Her & Vashti Lee. 2022. Weaponizing and de-weaponizing antiracist discourse: Some things for language educators to consider. *International Journal of Literacy, Culture, and Language Education 2*. 98–107. https://doi.org/10.14434/ijlcle.v2iMay.34393

Dawson, Alexander S. 2012. Histories and memories of the Indian Boarding schools in Mexico, Canada, and the United States. *Latin American Perspectives 39*(5). 80–99. https://doi.org/10.1177/0094582X12447274

Fairclough, Norman &Ruth Wodak. 1997. Critical discourse analysis. In Teun A. Van Dijk (ed.), *Discourse as a social interaction*, 258–284. Thousand Oaks, CA: SAGE.

Fear-Segal, Jacqueline. 2010. Institutional death and ceremonial healing far from home: The Carlisle Indian school cemetery. *Museum Anthropology 33*(2). 157–171. https://doi.org/10.1111/j.1548-1379.2010.01093.x

Harrison, K. David. 2010. *The last speakers. The quest to save the world's most endangered languages*. Washington D.C.: National Geographic.

Krzyżanowski, Michał, & Berhard Forchtner. 2016. Theories and concepts in critical discourse studies. *Discourse & Society 27*(3). 253–261. https://doi.org/10.1177/0957926516630900

Lomawaima, K. Tsianina. 1994. *They called it prairie light. The story of Chilocco Indian school*. Lincoln, NE: University of Nebraska Press.

Lindquist, Kristen A., Jennifer K. MacCormack, & Holly Shablack. 2015. The role of language in emotion: Predictions from psychological construction. *Frontiers in Psychology 6*(444). 1–17. https://doi.org/10.3389/fpsyg.2015.00444

McConnell-Ginet, Sally. 2020. *Words matter. Meaning and power*. Cambridge, UK: Cambridge University Press.

Otheguy, Ricardo, Ofelia García, & Wallis Reid. 2015. Clarifying translanguaging and deconstructing names languages: A perspective from linguistics. *Applied Linguistics Review 6*(3). 281–307. https://doi.org/10.1515/applirev-2015-0014

Pascale, Celine-Marie. 2019. The weaponization of language: Discourses of rising right-wing authoritarianism. *Current Sociology Review 67*(6). 898–917. https://doi.org/10.1177/0011392119869963

Pentón Herrera, Luis Javier. 2022. Is the language you teach racist? Reflections and considerations for English and Spanish (teacher) educators. *International Journal of Literacy, Culture, and Language Education 2*. 58–70. https://doi.org/10.14434/ijlcle.v2iMay.34390

Pentón Herrera, Luis Javier & Kisha C. Bryan. 2022. Language weaponization in society and education: Introduction to the special issue. *International Journal of Literacy, Culture, and Language Education 2*. 1–5. https://doi.org/10.14434/ijlcle.v2iMay.34380

Perpitch, Nicolas. 2018. A journey into 'hell on Earth'. *ABC News*. https://www.abc.net.au/news/2018-05-26/moore-river-aboriginal-settlement-journey-into-hell-on-earth/9790658?nw=0

Rafael, Vicente L. 2016. *Motherless tongues: The insurgency of language amid wars of translation*. Durham, NC: Duke University Press.

Smith, Andrea. 2009. *Indigenous Peoples and boarding schools: A comparative study*. Secretariat of the United Nations Permanent Forum on Indigenous Issues.

Weber, Jean-Jacques. 2015. *Language racism*. London: Palgrave Macmillan.

Welch, A. R. 1988. Aboriginal education as internal colonialism: The schooling of an Indigenous minority in Australia. *Comparative Education 24*(2). 203–215. https://doi.org/10.1080/0305006880240205

Wenden, Anita L. 1995. Critical language education. In Christina Schäffner & Anita L. Wenden (eds.), *Language and peace*, 211–227. Amsterdam: Harwood Academic Publishers.

Woolard, Kathryn, A., & Bambi B. Schieffelin. 1994. Language ideology. *Annual Review of Anthropology 23*. 55–82.

Young, Lynne, Michael Fitzgerald & Saira Fitzgerald. 2018. *The power of language: How discourse influences society* (2nd ed.). UK: Equinox Publishing.

Abu Saleh Mohammad Rafi

Chapter 2
Language weaponization, missed opportunities, and transformational spaces in Bangladeshi English departments: A biographical perspective

Abstract: This chapter examines how Bangladeshi English departments promote Anglo-normative practices by weaponizing the English language, and how they could benefit from the shifting paradigms of English departments in England. I employ a biographical perspective to draw on my experience as an English major, English teacher, and critical applied linguist. I also provide a retrospective analysis of the linguistic, economic, and political factors that led me to enroll in an English department in Bangladesh and, later, England. Next, I discuss how my expectations and accomplishments as an English department student and teacher were met and denied. Throughout the chapter, I point out the ways in which teachers and students in Bangladesh are affected by the linguistic, cultural, and ideological dimensions of weaponization. I conclude this chapter by recommending changes to improve linguistic and cultural inclusivity in Bangladeshi English departments.

Keywords: Language weaponization, English studies, translanguaging, Bangladesh

1 Introduction

Unlike many students in the highly regimented structures of Bangladeshi education, I had a non-linear academic journey. Starting out as a science student in secondary school, I ended up in the English department, a top-tier humanities department at Bangladeshi universities. This was largely due to my desire to learn to speak English like so-called native speakers of English. While the bachelor's degree in my department includes both English linguistics and English (language) literature as course requirements, the master's program requires students to graduate in one of the two streams. Like most graduate students in the department, I gravitated toward the literature stream because I was fascinated by stories of kings and queens, glitter and

---

Abu Saleh Mohammad Rafi, University of Liberal Arts, Bangladesh; James Cook University, Australia

https://doi.org/10.1515/9783110799521-002

glamour, and the tremendous wordplay that came with deep analysis of the soul-searching journeys of fictitious characters in English literary works, as opposed to the rather ordinary, everyday communication in the humdrum realm (*sic*) of language and linguistics that remain largely limited to English language teaching (ELT) in Bangladeshi universities. After completing my bachelor's and master's degrees with a concentration in literature, I eagerly anticipated entering academia and teaching literature courses to students.

My career as a university teacher exposed me to the competing realities set by the new generation of Bangladeshi private universities that focus on marketable skills such as English proficiency and outcome-based education. Such priorities did not quite match the illusory world of literature, nor did my literature training enable me to help close the gap, compelling me to change my track from English literature to linguistics. The location for the second phase of my academic training was intriguing because I was determined to study linguistics in England, the land of former colonizers and the birthplace of the English literature and linguistics disciplines. While specializing in sociolinguistics at a British University, I had the privilege of observing how English departments functioned in the territories of colonizers and colonized. While the former apparently embraced multilingualism and de-eliticized English, accepting language variation and change alongside protection of minority languages and language revitalization, the latter in Bangladesh continued to weaponize the use of the English language while ghettoizing local languages, cultures, and literature written in those languages.

Language weaponization, in the context of this chapter, entails the conscious and emotional manipulation of words, discourse, and language in any form, including but not limited to national language policy, language in education policies, programs, and curricula to harm people, cultures, and languages while normalizing inequality and injustice in their surroundings (Bryan & Gerald, 2020; Pascale, 2019; Rafael, 2012; Rafi & Morgan, 2022e). In this chapter, I examine the weaponization of English and Bangla in my personal experiences and knowledge, against the backdrop of multiple English departments and a nexus of socio-historical events that occurred in colonial and postcolonial times in Bangladesh. While themes of language weaponization overlap through flashbacks and flashforwards, I demonstrate how the weaponization of English from the colonial period to the present has supplanted other languages and ways of knowing and being in the normative practices of English departments in Bangladesh. As tangential themes, I also discuss how the weaponization of Urdu-based language policy compelled the separation of East and West Pakistan, paving the way for Bangla to assert Bangla-based nationalism to liberate East Pakistan as a sovereign nation, today known as Bangladesh. Nonetheless, Bangla has also been weaponized in the newly independent country, rendering all Indigenous languages invisible to promote *one nation, one language* ideologies (Rafi, 2023b). Weaving through these historical accounts of language weaponization, I explore how my experiences in different English departments in Bangladesh and the United Kingdom have altered, shifted, and transformed my perspective on language and identity.

While I observe that differences in English departments across countries are caused by the ideologies, requirements, and constraints of each environment, I believe Bangladeshi English departments would benefit greatly from England's welcoming attitude toward multilingualism, de-eliticized English, language variation, and change. These encounters collectively broadened my perspective as a teacher leading me to pursue a doctorate in Applied Linguistics carried out at two Australian universities, focusing on the potential of translanguaging pedagogies —a cutting-edge method of teaching and learning for bilinguals that makes use of all available linguistic and semiotic resources while disrupting and decolonizing anglo-normative knowledge structures and inequalities that have persisted and prevailed in non-English speaking contexts (García & Kleyn, 2016; Rafi & Morgan, 2022a, 2022b, 2022c, 2022d). In light of such transcontinental academic and research experiences, I adopted 'biography' as a methodology in this chapter, focusing on how the use of language as a weapon has contributed to the further stratification of social experiences of students and thus threatened linguistic and cultural diversity in the teaching practices, policies, programs, and curricula of Bangladeshi English departments.

In theory, "biography" is a social format of self-construction and a process of sense-making that situates the individual within a nexus of socio-historical events and life experiences and represents "the self" in a temporalized narration (Hahn, 2000; O'Neill et al., 2014). This current biographic work is based on phenomenological approaches that allowed me a first-person perspective for exploring my lived experiences, feelings, emotions, and reflections that centered time on the present and incorporated memories of the past and anticipations of the future (Husserl, 1989). While writing this biography, I draw on pre-existing literature and datasets from my doctoral research, but I also include my personal memories, which I believe are just as valuable as field notes, recorded interviews, or any other data a researcher might have gathered (Winkler, 2018). The strength of this memory-based narrative, I realize, is not in its precision or accuracy, but in my ability to relate to the (re)construction of my past, which I hope, on both an intellectual and an emotional level, strikes a chord with many members of Bangladeshi English departments (See more on the power of memory-based narrative in Hayler, 2010). In phenomenological terms, my biography also aligns with Fabel-Lamla and Wiezorek (2008), who showed how deeply teachers' biographies are rooted in family contexts and how closely professional orientation, interpretation, and action patterns, as well as professional identity, are entwined with biographical identity.

To this end, I divide my biography into three parts. The first part is a retrospective analysis of the linguistic, economic, and political influences that led me to enroll in an English department in Bangladesh and, later, in England. By doing this, I established a connection between my own self and the postcolonial ecology of Bangladesh and contemporary England. In part two, I look at how my expectations and accomplishments were met and denied during my time as an English department student and teacher in Bangladeshi universities. While these are strictly personal experiences, they coincide with those of many English department graduates and teachers in Bangladesh. In the third part, I identify linguistic, cultural, and ideological dimensions of weaponization that shape teachers' and students' identity positions in Bangladesh, necessitating changes to create linguistically and culturally equitable spaces within English departments. I conclude this narrative with an investigation of how translanguaging scholarship can help with the required adjustments through the reforming and redesigning of curricula and pedagogies, as well as transforming the academic and ideological structures of English departments to make them culturally relevant, expansive, and responsive to the global trans-movement in language, culture, and education.

2 Part 1: Retrospective analysis

2.1 Weaponizing languages against the historical backdrop of Bangladesh

Bangladesh is home to more than 39 languages; among them, I particularly focus in this chapter on how two dominant languages, Bangla and English, are weaponized in the construction of Bangladeshi identity, drawing on the colonial history of the subcontinent and how the relationship and role of two languages shape the overall linguistic ecology of Bangladesh. People in the Indian subcontinent first encountered English through British colonizers, and English was widely used in political discourse as well as all formal domains, such as administration and education (Farida et al., 2022). On August 15, 1947, the subcontinent was divided into India and the Islamic Republic of Pakistan following the collapse of the British Empire. The Islamic Republic at the time was also divided into East Pakistan and West Pakistan, due to their geographical distance and stark sociocultural and linguistic differences. In Figure 2.1, I show a map of the Indian subcontinent for more context.

Chapter 2 Language weaponization, missed opportunities, and transformational spaces — 17

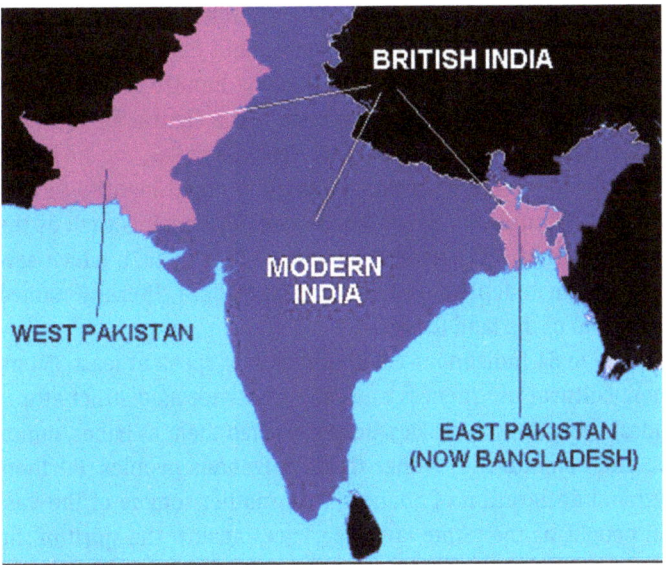

Figure 2.1: Map of the Indian subcontinent.
Note: Source is Oocities.org (n.d.)

The majority of West Pakistanis speak Panjabi, Pashtu, Sindhi, and Balochi. whereas the majority of East Pakistanis (also known as Bangalis) speak Bangla. As part of the nation-building project, India adopted Hindi as the official language, whereas Pakistan's central leaders surprisingly wanted Urdu to be the only official language of the entire country, despite the fact that only 7% of Pakistan's population spoke it and 54% spoke Bangla (Fathema, 2019). On his only visit to East Pakistan in 1948, the governor-general of Pakistan, Muhammad Ali Jinnah, declared:

> Let me make it very clear to you that the state language of Pakistan is going to be Urdu and no other language. Anyone who tries to mislead you is really the enemy of Pakistan. Without one state language, no nation can remain tied up solidly together and function. Look at the history of other countries. Therefore, so far as the state language is concerned, Pakistan's shall be Urdu (Jinnah in Racecourse, Dhaka 1948, in Fathema, 2019).

Jinnah's Urdu-only policy was strongly opposed by the people of East Pakistan. Students at the University of Dacca (now the University of Dhaka) organized the 1952 Bangla Language Movement, widely known as Bhasha Andolan, demanding that Bangla become the country's official language. This movement was precipitated by the economic disparity between the two regions of Pakistan, the dominance of the West Pakistani ruling elite over Pakistan, martial law, and a demeaning attitude toward Bangali culture and population. As part of the protest, students from

Dhaka University, Jagannath College, and Dhaka Medical College marched on February 21, 1952. Police opened fire, killing Abdus Salam, Abul Barkat, Rafiq Uddin Ahmed, Abdul Jabbar, and Shafiur Rahman and injuring hundreds. The deaths sparked widespread civil unrest. After years of conflict, the central government relented and granted Bangla official status in 1956. Needless to say, the 1952 Language Movement ignited the assertion of Bangla-based national identity in East Pakistan and served as a precursor to Bangali nationalist movements such as the 6-Point Movement and, later, the Bangladesh Liberation War in 1971, which saw East Pakistan emerge as an independent country, Bangladesh, literally named after the language (Bangla) of the land (desh).

Bangladesh is home to 54 Indigenous communities that speak at least 35 languages. Despite their cultural uniqueness and long existence as distinct ethnic groups, the Bangladeshi constitution makers have classified them as tribes, minor races, ethnic sects, and communities rather than Indigenous peoples. Furthermore, the constitutional declaration of "Bangla," the mother tongue of the vast majority of Bangali people, as the "State language," goes against the spirit of the 1952 language movement since it ignores languages of other communities, especially those of indigenous ethnicities (Azad, 2020). English was also demoted from being a second to a foreign language in Bangladesh, elevating Bangla's status in all facets of society, particularly education, as an effort to decolonize curriculum, a move that ultimately proved ineffective due to a decline in English proficiency among the learner community (Hamid & Baldauf, 2014).

Since the turn of the 21st century, Bangladesh has been influenced by a variety of powerful economic forces. More than half of the population was affected by pervasive poverty and crises involving food, shelter, and clean water. Furthermore, the Bangladeshi economy is extremely susceptible to weather, floods, and periodic food supply crises, and international aid agencies, the majority of which operate in English, play a significant role in supporting affected populations and developing the country's infrastructure. Bangladesh's participation in the global economy has grown in recent years, and globalization is now directly impacting the language-in-education policy in Bangladeshi educational institutions (Tsui & Tollefson, 2017). For instance, the 2010 National Education Policy recommended that all secondary education streams include English language writing and speaking from the start of primary education. Since English has emerged as a fashion statement for internationalizing higher education, private universities, which account for 67% of the Bangladeshi higher education sector, have adopted English as the medium of instruction to compete in both domestic and international markets (Rafi & Morgan, 2022c). Even further, the elite private universities promoted North American curricula and course structures, delegitimizing Bangla and other local languages, cultures, and epistemologies in teaching, learning, and assessment practices (Rafi & Morgan, 2022a, 2022d). In non-English speaking contexts, the decision to use English as the medium of instruction in higher education institutions has significant symbolic and practical implications, given that the English language benefits from teaching, research, innovation, and subsequent monetization, whereas Bangla and other languages could thrive.

In terms of Indigenous languages, the Bangladeshi Constitution's failure to recognize the "existence of different peoples within the country" has been weaponized against them, excluding Indigenous language speakers from the mainstream and making them the poorest members of society (Borchgrevink & McNeish, 2007, p.16). As a result, their languages have not made it into the educational sector. Since most previous research has focused on the country as a whole or on the mainstream population, little is known about Indigenous people's educational status. According to the 1991 census, which is widely regarded as inaccurate, the adult literacy rate among Indigenous peoples was 26.1% (Sarker & Davey, 2009). As a result, minority teachers are in short supply. Despite this, Bangladesh's commitment to achieving the Education for All (EFA) goals provides a ray of hope. Several non-governmental organizations are currently constructing and operating informal schools across the nation. Several of them participate in literacy and education programs for indigenous children. The majority of these use the minority learners' mother tongues as the medium of instruction (Cavallaro & Rahman, 2009).

2.2 Weaponizing language in personal history

If you ask anyone who grew up in the 1990s in Bangladesh what their parents wanted them to be, they will respond, "a doctor or an engineer." According to my understanding of Bangladesh's developmental phase, the country required a sizable number of engineers and doctors to build the infrastructure of the newly born nation and provide free or inexpensive medical care to the impoverished population. These fundamentals might have provided these professions with financial security and social prestige. As a result, almost all Bangladeshi parents wanted their kids to pursue careers in engineering or medicine. The next tier of subjects involved Mathematics and English; as the very popular saying goes in Bangladesh, "if you study mathematics or English, you will never be unemployed." This euphoria stems from the proliferation of primary, secondary, and higher secondary educational institutions in the country, where these subjects were made mandatory to educate the country's mass population. This trend was followed by the limited number of public universities prior to the introduction of the private university act of 1992, which spawned private universities in and around Dhaka, the capital city. Regardless, every public or private university has an English department, though Mathematics could not maintain its legacy and became part of the general education department in private universities.

My father was a renowned mathematics teacher, and I started out as a top-scoring student in every elementary and secondary school grade. As a result, it was clear that I was destined for a career in medicine or engineering. However, math and other science classes have never held my interest like language, culture, religion, and the social sciences have. I did well in math and science when I lived with my parents, but in comparison to other subjects, I always felt I had to work twice as hard to achieve the same results in these subjects. For my higher secondary education, I moved to the capital city and managed to get admission to science at Dhaka College, the country's most prestigious and selective institution, and a historical powerhouse known for producing most of the leaders in the country. As a government college, Dhaka College provides almost absolute freedom and flexibility like a Bangladeshi public university does, where everyone is on their own. With this newfound freedom, I mostly chose to roam around Dhaka city, exploring arts, culture, museums, libraries, and public talks over sitting in classrooms listening to science lectures. There is a popular myth in Bangladesh that science students are not good at English, and humanities students are not good at science. At a very early age, I realized that that myth is not absolutely untrue. My science-nerd friends were terribly bad at English grammar and language in general. I tutored my classmates in English, and they tutored me in science. I was able to pass all of the in-course exams. However, this trade-off with my friends did not help me much in the centralized public exams as I ended up with good grades in only English subjects but barely passing in the science ones.

My parents abandoned their dreams of having their only son become a doctor or engineer. They did not foresee me gaining admission in other subjects, including English, due to my low Cumulative Grade Point Average (CGPA). Furthermore, they were hesitant about the idea of me studying in English due to its foreignness in Bangladesh as an academic discipline. As previously discussed, the weaponization of Bangla in post-independent Bangladesh to decolonize education demoted English from second language status to a foreign language, resulting in a decline in English language proficiency among Bangladeshis. In addition, stories of other Bangladeshi students barely completing a degree in English made it a particularly challenging subject in the arts, humanities, and social sciences. Surprise! Despite my poor grades, I was accepted into the English department of one of the four largest and most competitive public universities in Bangladesh. My parents were probably happy or mostly confused, or mostly happy and confused! Nevertheless, they unquestionably supported my decision to study English because I had no other better choice.

3 Part 2: Expectations and accomplishments

3.1 Weaponizing English in colonial and postcolonial English departments

Thomas Babington Macaulay, a British historian, and politician, is credited with introducing the British educational system to India. He advocated for the replacement of Arabic, Sanskrit, and Persian with English in colonial schools in India in his "Minute on Indian Education" on February 2, 1835. The British rulers believed that English education would "civilize" (*sic*) the native population in India (Eaglestone, 2000). The English department of the University of Dhaka, the first in East Bengal and founded in 1921, can trace its origins to Macaulay's minutes (Farida et al., 2022). The Education Act was first passed in 1835 as a product of Macaulay's "Minutes," which aimed to create "a class of persons Indian in blood and color, but English in tastes, in opinions, in morals, and in intellect" (para. 34). English literature dominated English teaching at that time because British administrators believed it would help students learn the target language and culture and humanize (*sic*) the local population (Macaulay, 1835). One way or another, the British maintained control over the natives under the guise of a liberal education (Viswanathan, 1987). They wanted Indian universities to produce English-speaking civil servants and educators who could serve as "good intermediaries between the British and the people they ruled" (Professor Fakrul Alam, in Farida et al., 2022). Since English was the official language, graduates from the Department of English could easily find employment in administrative, judicial, or academic fields. In addition, people in colonial India spoke a variety of languages, and English quickly became the lingua franca. Therefore, it was not surprising that English graduates became highly esteemed and prestigious (Farida et al., 2022).

The English department of Dhaka University modeled and remodeled most English departments in independent Bangladesh. Almost all public and private universities in Bangladesh have an English department or at least an English language center. However, except for a few private universities, Bangla departments can only be found at public universities. Students who gain admission to the English department through the highly competitive admission tests will almost never be interested in studying in the Bangla departments. As a result, very few private universities house Bangla departments because private universities depend on students' tuition fees, and Bangla departments do not generate revenue. In essence, the global demand for English as a lingua franca has allowed English departments to maintain their hegemony in postcolonial Bangladesh, promoting the legacy of colonial masters while demoting Bangla departments and their graduates, lowering their status in Bangladeshi universities as well as in job markets.

While it is true that English departments have produced graduates with literary and liberal inclinations for generations and have played a pivotal role in the dissemination of English learning and teaching alongside producing writers, poets, journalists, and artists, it is worth considering how the spirit of the 1952 Bangla language movement manifested in socio-academic categorization, prestige, and preferences in Bangladeshi universities.

3.2 My journey as an English major

There is no formal medium of instruction (MOI) policy in place for Bangladeshi universities. As a result of the lack of clarity in the policy framework, public universities have resorted to translanguaging practices under the guise of Bangla, while private universities have become English-medium institutions, as discussed above (Rafi & Morgan, 2022c). However, both public and private university English departments assume English as the medium of instruction, lingua franca, or natural condition in and out of the classroom. English literature and linguistics are taught in all English departments. While the former is primarily concerned with the creative work of prominent English-speaking writers, the latter is primarily concerned with English language teaching (ELT). English departments, whether they focus on literature or linguistics, tend to favor Anglo-normative approaches to teaching and learning. For instance, all public and private universities with an English department offer a freshman-level course titled "Introduction to Poetry," which covers canonical works by major English-language poets such as William Shakespeare, John Keats, Percy Bysshe Shelley, T.S. Eliot, and Seamus Heaney, spanning the early modern era to the present day. These content materials do not resonate with students' cultures and do not correspond to their linguistic proficiency for access.

Studies also show that the linguistics stream devoted all its time and energy to teaching students "proper" or native variety of academic English while actively discouraging the use of students' native languages and limiting the use of localized varieties of the language (Rafi & Morgan, 2021; 2022d). In my experience as a student, only six or seven students with adequate proficiency would interact with the teachers in a class of sixty, while the rest barely spoke a word. Students majoring in English were disadvantaged by the requirement of fast-paced proficiency in the English language and pedagogical practices because they lacked the required linguistic depth and cultural contexts of English and English texts. Although the English language itself is not harmful and fluency in it is made crucial for participating in discussion tasks in English department classrooms, the weaponization of English continues to be felt by the majority of students in the form of confusion, frustration, discomfort, and pain (Kiyota, 2022).

Half a decade later, I returned to Bangladesh to observe linguistic practices in four Bangladeshi English departments as part of my doctoral research, only to discover that nothing had changed. Most students still struggle in English medium instruction classes, need sufficient proficiency to understand the English lecture, and are too shy to ask questions. Furthermore, teachers are under-trained in how to use students' bilingual (or multilingual) abilities to create interactive, learner-centered, and activity-based classrooms (Rafi, 2020; Rafi & Morgan, 2021, 2022a, 2023). I had the opportunity to discuss the syllabus for an "Introduction to Poetry" course with Heidi Byrnes, Professor Emeritus at Georgetown University, and her response was as follows:

> How curriculum developers for an Introduction to Poetry course in Bangladesh can believe that working with Shakespeare's sonnets is a good entry into the subject matter (i.e., content) while also fostering English language learning (SFL connections!?) is difficult for me to follow" (Byrnes, personal communication, 27 March 2021).

My thesis supervisor, Professor Anne-Marie Morgan (currently the Dean of Programs at the University of South Australia), commented on my thesis draft on this topic by stating that texts written in Early modern English chosen for first-year students will be inaccessible "frankly, for any but specialist English language scholars" (Morgan, personal communication, 21 March 2021). I do not know if the situation has changed, but during my time, students found ways to overcome these linguistic obstacles to pass exams. For instance, they relied more on guidebooks written by Indian authors than on class lectures or scholarly articles written by western authors. The primary reason was that these guides offered linguistic support such as word meanings, definitions, paraphrases, and explanations of major plot points and characters in various works of literature, as well as explanations of ELT concepts in an adapted version of the language and culturally relevant examples. Intriguingly, the majority of teachers discouraged or shamed students for reading these guidebooks, whereas they had no such reservations regarding western equivalents such as Cliffs notes, Coles notes, York notes, SparkNotes, etc. The only reason I understood at the time was that the quality of the Indian guidebooks was likely inferior to those of the West, and in some cases, this was the case. However, looking back, I can see how mental colonization maintained the hierarchy of producing knowledge favoring the West, thereby preventing the localization of that knowledge in our own contexts.

Furthermore, nurturing students' 'individualism' (agency) is a strong educational focus of Bangladeshi English departments, which they promote through themes of individualism in the literary works chosen as curricular content. These contents are meant to give students a deeper understanding of the fictional characters' inner lives, both psychologically and socially, which also affects students' individual growth as an educational outcome (Harish, 2012). However, the weaponization of English medium instruction and English-only content does not correspond to the various individual repertoires present in Bangladeshi English department classrooms. These repertoires, known linguistically as "idiolects," are unique and personal to everyone (Otheguy et al., 2019). English-only instruction and texts fail to address the idiolects of bilingual students and, ironically, work against the core principles of individualism that English departments strive to promote (also discussed in Rafi, 2023b).

This may be an unpopular opinion, but English literature has a higher status in Bangladeshi departments than its junior stream, ELT. Numerous prominent figures in Bangladesh's history have studied English literature and contributed to its legacy. I cannot speak for others, but in my senior years, my English literature degree expanded to include Indian literature, African literature, Australian literature, and American literature until and unless the texts were written in English. While ELT remained the primary focus of linguists, other fields like sociolinguistics and psycholinguistics were stunted in Bangladesh. Along with literature, the master's degree in English included film and media studies as well as gender and cultural studies, which could not essentially be classified as English literature or English studies. However, I was a big fan of Jacques Derrida's "Deconstruction," Laura Mulvey's "Visual Pleasure and Narrative Cinema," Sean Nixon's "Exhibiting Masculinity," and Fredric Jameson's magisterial work, "Postmodernism" and I have always wanted to teach these topics to my students if I ever became an English teacher.

3.3 . . . And as a teacher

In my undergraduate term paper, I investigated "Lady Brett Ashley," one of Ernest Hemingway's famous "bitch" characters, in relation to the Bangladeshi queer communities on the newly introduced social media Facebook and received an "A" for it. One of my professors not only nudged me in the direction of submitting the paper to a journal, but also provided editorial support beyond what I expected. Regardless, the reviewer corrected the manuscript's English using the so-called native English variety throughout. The reviewer's only memorable comment on the substance of the paper was that I was comparing apples to oranges. They did, however, graciously recommend the publication of the paper, which was published in Bangladesh's oldest English studies journal while I was a master's student (Rafi, 2012). This single factor strengthened my desire to enter academia and gave me an advantage over my contemporaries in launching my teaching career. After finishing my master's degree, I began teaching at a small private university, where, as the most junior faculty member, I was assigned only English language learning classes.

I was not properly trained or prepared to teach these courses. I did well at one thing I learned as an English major, though, and that was to bring the department's Anglo-normative practices into my classroom and foster an English-only, monocultural atmosphere for my students. I used to write "English only" on the whiteboard before starting any lesson because I believed that using only English was the best way to teach English. Bangladeshi private universities at the time primarily attracted students who were unable to gain admission to highly competitive public universities. During my Ph.D. research on the language education of Bangladeshi students, I realized that my lack of sociolinguistic awareness disempowered my students by disapproving of their multilingual resources in the process of learning English. During the collection of doctoral research data, I observed similar practices among my colleagues and in universities. For instance, I observed a university with "English please" signs in its classrooms, and a teacher participant who said, "I will not tell you the rule unless you ask the question in English" when a student asked in Bangla about the correct use of prepositions (Rafi & Morgan, 2021, page 25). I documented how the weaponization of English-only requirements and expectations of English departments negatively impacted students' psychological well-being and socio-cultural identification as English majors in a recently published study (See more, Rafi, 2023). These findings collectively contribute to the literature on the feeling of regret frequently associated with language teachers realizing that their past practices were insufficient for a variety of reasons, such as not receiving adequate professional development, particularly in the case of effectively teaching multiple languages to the emerging multilingual youth in Bangladesh (Mercer & Gregersen, 2020; Humphries, 2020; Pentón Herrera & Martínez-Alba, 2022; Tomlinson, 2018).

At the start of my teaching career, most private universities preferred Linguistics/ELT graduates, but I was able to teach at three universities simultaneously (at two as an adjunct faculty and at one as a full-time faculty) in a year and a half before settling at another university where I was given the opportunity to teach advanced literature subjects such as literary theories as well as design my own subject on media studies. Surprisingly, these topics did not resonate with my students as much as they did with me. Either the subject matter was beyond their intellectual or emotional capabilities, or it was insensitive to their culture. For example, while teaching Freudian theories of the Oedipus complex that dealt with the issues of a symbolic incestuous relationship between mother and son, my students said: "Nauzubillah" (apostasy), or students could not look at my eyes during my lecture on Picola's rape by her father in Tony Morrison's *The Bluest Eye*. Despite consistently receiving high evaluation scores from my students, those reactions, the cultural inappropriacy of materials, my lack of expertise in teaching the English language, and the demands of Linguistics/ELT in the private sector of higher education prompted me to change my path and study Linguistics. It was a difficult decision for a passionate literature student/teacher, but funding for advanced studies for English literature majors was nearly non-existent. Then I realized why literature streams in Bangladeshi English departments were gradually blending with non-literature subjects like media studies, cultural studies, gender studies, film studies, and so on. Interestingly, I decided that if I had to switch from literature to linguistics, I wanted to do so in England, where these disciplines were born. There are two main reasons for this: first, the culture in which I was raised continues to place a higher value on a degree from a British university than a degree from any other university, and second, going to England is almost like a pilgrimage for English literature graduates in Bangladesh.

3.4 My journey as a linguistics postgraduate in my former colonizer's land

Linguistically, my first impression of the United Kingdom was largely limited to two sentences: "Are these white people really speaking English?" or "Did I learn incorrect English in Bangladesh?" I lived and studied in Liverpool, which has its own dialect of English known as "scouse," which has nothing in common with the English taught in Bangladesh. My Bangladeshi education took a prescriptive approach to language teaching, with no room for different varieties of English. Our English language learning was mostly limited to reading and writing, with little emphasis on speaking. There was not any pressure to speak in standard British or American English, but anybody who managed to acquire that skill would be treated with high regard by teachers and peers with compliments such as "oh my God! His/her English is so good." In other words, students and teachers alike would be praised for abandoning their Bangladeshi ways of speaking English, and thus their Bangla accent and identity, in favor of assuming those of their former colonial masters.

After enrolling in the linguistics program at my British university, I became conscious for the first time in my life of the differences between varieties of Englishes, as well as how they affect society. This program was housed in the English department, which, like its Bangladeshi counterpart, has an English literature stream. However, there were significant differences in the program design, course structure, and overall teaching philosophy. The linguistics streams, for example, were proud of their linguistically and culturally diverse faculty: six faculty members from six different ethnolinguistic backgrounds, including Bangladesh, Sri Lanka, Germany, England, France, and Italy. The program was sociolinguistics focused, with modules such as language variation and change, language, identity, and migration, language and education, world Englishes, and so on. This program provided me with such a solid foundation in sociolinguistics that I have never had to look back.

Since my degree did not focus on English literature at my British university, I cannot offer any insightful recollections or observations on this track. In any case, I was aware that the student satisfaction rate for this track had once reached a perfect 100. The student populations were a fundamental difference between English departments in the United Kingdom and Bangladesh when it came to offering English literature courses. A nearly homogeneous group of English students studied English literature at the British university, whereas Bangladeshi students who study English literature in the Bangladeshi English department share little or no background knowledge of English literary texts. Interestingly, the linguistics stream attracted a large group of multiracial, multiethnic both domestic and international student populations. However, a stereotype I often heard from my international peers was that British universities and tutors already think less of you when you are not a native speaker of English, and grade you accordingly. While such perceptual weaponization of so-called native English may exacerbate stratification and marginalization for international students in British classrooms, I probably did not experience this because I scored nearly as well as my British classmates. However, a particular parameter focused on English literacy in the grading criteria always made me wonder how I would ever achieve such native English-like literacy as a Bangladeshi. I also remember some of my tutors advised us to get our assignments proofread by a native English speaker. Some were meticulous about seeking help, particularly from Arts and Humanities graduates giving an impression that the English of science students were probably as bad as ours.

4 Part 3: Linguistic, cultural, and ideological dimensions of weaponization

4.1 My academic vagaries in Australian universities

I am extremely grateful for my British education, which not only introduced me to language differences in society and their implications for human life and psychosocial well-being, but also prepared me for the next adventure of my academic journey. I was offered Ph.D. fellowships at several prestigious universities right away. I chose an Australian university because of its generous scholarship package and the length of the program. Perhaps most importantly, what piqued my interest was translanguaging theory, which my prospective supervisor at that university suggested I use as a theoretical framework rather than some traditional theories that I included in my research proposal as part of my application. Although I transferred to a new university in the middle of my candidature, I was able to keep working with the supervisors from my old university all the way through graduation. I investigated the promises of translanguaging pedagogical approaches in the context of Bangladeshi higher education, with the goal of providing a culturally and linguistically responsive medium of instruction policy and closing the English language proficiency gap between tertiary and pre-tertiary education (Rafi, 2022).

From the beginning to the end of my candidacy, my research progressed smoothly, answering all my questions and teaching me how the ontology of the world shifted, changed, and was ultimately transformed by powerful forces like colonization and neoliberalism. It also sparked some ideas for how translanguaging can function as a counterforce to systems that favor the already privileged and marginalize the already marginalized. For instance, the weaponization of English as a global lingua franca and the language of internationalizing research and education in non-English speaking contexts frustrates and confines bilingual researchers from non-English backgrounds as deficient English learners and detaches them from their own social realities and theoretical resources (Shen, 2017). Furthermore, against the predominance of Euro-American theories, these researchers are often labeled as having "substandard" English and a lack of critical thinking, and they struggle to be recognized as theory generators rather than consumers in research (Singh & Meng, 2013). Such deficit views about them connect to the experiences of my classmates at the British university and become a source of pain and struggle for many bilingual researchers from non-English backgrounds (Shen, 2017). Against this weaponization of English and Euro-American theories, translanguaging scholarship endorses the languaging practices of bilinguals in education and research, as the researchers are capable of selecting the most appropriate expressions to make meanings following the most appropriate way of interaction from their entire linguistic repertoire, which includes all linguistic and societal features from two or more languages (García & Wei, 2014; Rafi, 2023b).

I only had a small number of interactions that would qualify as sociolinguistically significant because completing the Ph.D. itself was a solitary (though intellectually stimulating) process. When I returned to Bangladesh to collect data from a university there, I noticed that a few of my colleagues and students were avoiding speaking Bangla with me in favor of English. I could be wrong, but I wondered if returning from Australia gave them the impression that they should speak in English with me. Interestingly in Australia, my supervisor advised me to write my thesis in Australian English since the awarding institution was an Australian one. It is worth noting how these two incidents demonstrate striking differences in the attitudes people developed toward their languages. While the second incident expects a non-Australian researcher to conform to Standard Australian English and promote that variety rather than his own in international academia, the first incident in Bangladesh depicts a clash between English and local languages as the former encroaches on the latter's functions and spaces.

Aside from these, perhaps the most illuminating experience for me was being invited to teach preservice teachers (teacher education students) after completing the pre-completion milestone of my Ph.D. candidature. I taught two subjects to Australian pre-service teachers that made significant progress in the curriculum in terms of appreciating and embracing cultural and linguistic diversity, respectively, for Australian teaching contexts and included topics such as white privilege, white supremacy, sexism, place-based education, multicultural education, linguistic diversity, language shift, and language loss in the context of Australia's monolingual mindset (Clyne, 2008).

While teaching these subjects, I was constantly at war with myself. When I was engaging White Australian students in social justice and equity issues and encouraging them to dislodge their white privilege and bring about systemic change for empowering minority languages and cultures in Australia, I often found myself wondering how much I did for minority languages and cultures in my own country as an advocate for social justice and equity. Instead, I (we) have become the stereotypical "whites," in Bangladesh, whose language, culture, religion, and knowledge structure have contributed to the exclusion of minority communities. In this context, English departments took linguistic and cultural weaponization a step further by promoting colonial practices in their curricula and marginalizing Bangladeshi cultures, languages, and pedagogical modalities. Based on my multi-country educational and research experience in both colonizers' and colonized' countries, I would humbly make some recommendations for Bangladeshi English departments that can help spark a paradigm shift.

4.2 Transformational spaces

Translanguaging is the full range of linguistic performances of multilingual language users' (Wei, 2011, p. 1224) as well as a pedagogical approach in which such practices are utilized systematically in education (Cenoz & Gorter, 2022; Duarte, 2016). Wei (2011) expands the meaning of the prefix "trans" by combining concepts from a variety of theoretical perspectives: i) "trans" means moving between and beyond (linguistic) systems and structures and communicative contexts, ii) the act of "trans" in translanguaging is transformative in that it brings together different aspects of the multilingual speakers' linguistic, cognitive, and social skills, their knowledge and experience of the social world, as well as their attitudes and values, iii) "trans" in translanguaging is transdisciplinary and is used to accept multilingual practices as a lens to holistically view human sociality, cognition, social relations, and social structures. Considering these theoretical dimensions, I recommend three major changes:

First, as previously discussed, Bangladeshi English departments promote Anglo-normative practices via the native-speaker English mode. However, contrary to what is commonly taught in English department classrooms, in English as a lingua franca (ELF) interaction, adherence to English speaker norms is not crucial for effective communication (Sato et al., 2019). Since new linguistic forms, functions, and meanings of English are constantly evolving in an international context, I recommend that Bangladeshi English departments reconsider English as a resource that can be appropriated and exploited without much allegiance and embrace localized versions of English as a crucial part of Bangladeshi identity (Wei, 2016).

Second, English departments can employ translanguaging pedagogies to personalize and streamline instruction while empowering students to "cognitively engage with learning and to act on learning" (García & Wei, 2014, p. 79). Such pedagogies would necessitate that these departments select materials that are culturally relevant to students and sequence them according to their English proficiency levels. Additionally, they can help students understand texts written in complex or archaic English through the use of multilingual vocabulary scaffolding, translation, paraphrasing, and guided multilingual readings. Translanguaging pedagogies can foster greater linguistic integration, open the door to cross-linguistic analysis, and improve students' comprehension of course material (Rafi & Morgan, 2022a, 2022b, 2022c, 2022d).

Finally, English departments can choose literature from various cultures and languages alongside English literary texts, allowing students to examine the same topic from various linguistic and cultural vantage points. Such a curriculum will not only foster future English language and literature experts, but also "culturally literate" citizens who are fluent in and familiar with the linguistic and cultural norms of their local community and other communities (Zhaoxiang, 2002). By doing so, English departments can break away from Anglo-normativity and create a canon that focuses on transdisciplinary spaces within curricula and practice, encourages culturally sustainable teaching methods, and strengthens ties to the local community.

5 Concluding remarks

To conclude, I drew on my transcontinental academic and research experiences in this biographical piece to examine various forms of language weaponization that threatened linguistic and cultural diversity in the teaching practices, policies, programs, and curricula of Bangladeshi English departments in the context of their socio-political backgrounds. I also made recommendations based on translanguaging scholarship that can potentially eliminate the effects of such weaponization through reforming and redesigning curricula and pedagogies as well as transforming the academic and ideological structures of English departments. Several universities in Bangladesh have already begun to diversify their English departments by changing their names from traditional "Department of English" to more inclusive titles like "Department of English & Humanities" or "Department of English and Modern Languages," (as are the cases at University of Liberal Arts and North South University, respectively). They also incorporate continental and world literature into their syllabi, as long as the texts are written in English. Other English departments, I hope, will follow suit. Most importantly, I wish for the English departments to be as linguistically expansive as feasible in terms of embracing other languages, cultures, and knowledge frameworks as opposed to catering only to Euro-American ones and perpetuating colonial legacies. In that scenario, I hope this piece serves as inspiration for a critical paradigm shift toward developing linguistically and culturally equitable spaces inside Bangladeshi English departments.

References

Azad, Emraan. 2020. Language and the constitution of Bangladesh–In Memory of Professor Anisuzzaman. *The Daily Star*. https://www.thedailystar.net/law-our-rights/professor-anisuzzaman-language-and-bangladesh-constitution-1364716

Borchgrevink, Axel & John-Andrew McNeish. 2007. *Review of Bistandsnemda's (Norwegian Missions in Development) work with indigenous peoples*. Bergen: Chr. Michelsen Institute.

Bryan, Kisha C. & J. P. B. Gerald. 2020. The Weaponization of English. *Language Magazine*, 1–8. https://www.languagemagazine.com/2020/08/17/the-weaponization-of-english/

Cavallaro, Francesco & Tania Rahman. 2009. The Santals of Bangladesh. *Linguistics Journal 4*. 192–220.

Cenoz, Jasone & Durk Gorter. 2022. *Pedagogical translanguaging*. Cambridge, UK: Cambridge University Press. https://doi.org/10.1017/9781009029384

Clyne, Michael. 2008. The monolingual mindset as an impediment to the development of plurilingual potential in Australia. *Sociolinguistic Studies 2*(3). 347–366. https://doi.org/10.1558/sols.v2i3.347

Duarte, Joana. 2016. Translanguaging in mainstream education: A socio-cultural approach. *International Journal of Bilingual Education and Bilingualism 22*(2). 150–164. https://doi.org/10.1080/13670050.2016.1231774

Eaglestone, Robert. 2000. *Doing English: A guide for literature students*. New York, NY: Routledge.

Fabel-Lamla, Melanie &Christine Wiezorek. 2008. Schulentwicklung im Transformationsprozess – Zum Verhältnis von Biographie und schulischen Reformprozessen. In Georg Breidenstein & Fritz Schütze (eds.), *Paradoxien in der Reform der Schule: Ergebnisse qualitativer Sozialforschung*, 327–345. The Netherlands: Springer.

Farida, Nevin, Qumrul Hasan Chowdhury, Begum Shahnaz Sinha, Ahmed Bashir & Bijoy Lal Basu. 2022. History of the Department of English (1921–2021): An academic overview. *Spectrum* 16. 3–23. https://doi.org/10.3329/spectrum.v16i100.61062

Fathema, Kaniz. 2019. Why was there a battle of Urdu-Bangla? *New Age*. https://www.newagebd.net/article/65472/why-was-there-a-battle-of-urdu-bangla

García, Ofelia & Tatyana Kleyn (eds.). 2016. *Translanguaging with multilingual students: Learning from classroom moments*. New York, NY: Routledge.

Hamid, M. Obaidul & Richard B. Baldauf. 2014. Public-private domain distinction as an aspect of LPP frameworks: A case study of Bangladesh. *Language Problems and Language Planning 38*(2). 192–210. https://doi.org/10.1075/lplp.38.2.05ham

Harish, Janani. 2012. Study of individuality & social evolution in literature. *Eruditio* 1(1). 44–52.

Hayler, Mike. 2010. Autoethnography: Making memory methodology. *Research in Education* 3(1). 5–9.

Humphries, Simon. 2020. 'Please teach me how to teach': The emotional impact of educational change. In Christina Gkonou, Jean-Marc Dewaele & Jim King (eds.), *The emotional rollercoaster of language teaching*, 150–172. Bristol, UK: Multilingual Matters.

Husserl, Edmund. 1989. *Ideas pertaining to a pure phenomenology and to a phenomenological philosophy: Second book studies in the phenomenology of constitution* (HUCO 3). Dordrecht: Springer Science & Business Media.

Kiyota, Akiko. 2022. Problematizing fluent speakers' unintentional exclusion of emergent bilinguals: A case study of an English-medium instruction classroom in Japan. *International Journal of Literacy, Culture, and Language Education 2*. 6–19. https://doi.org/10.14434/ijlcle.v2iMay.34385

Macaulay, T. B. 1835. Minute on education. In Henry Sharp (ed.), *Selections from Educational Records, Part I (1781–1839)*, 107–117. Calcutta, India: Superintendent, Government Printing.

Mercer, Sarah & Tammy Gregersen. 2020. *Teacher wellbeing*. Oxford: Oxford University Press.

O'Neill, Maggie, Brian Roberts & Andrew Sparkes (eds.). 2014. *Advances in biographical methods: Creative applications*. New York, NY: Routledge.

Otheguy, Ricardo, Ofelia García & Wallis Reid. 2015. Clarifying translanguaging and deconstructing names languages: A perspective from linguistics. *Applied Linguistics Review 6*(3). 281–307. https://doi.org/10.1515/applirev-2015-0014

Oocities.org. (n.d.). Map of the Indian subcontinent. http://www.oocities.org/thalsena

Pascale, Celine-Marie. 2019. The weaponization of language: Discourses of rising right-wing authoritarianism. *Current Sociology Review 67*(6). 898–917. https://doi.org/10.1177/0011392119869963

Pentón Herrera, Luis Javier & Gilda Martínez-Alba. 2022. Emotions, well-being, and language teacher identity development in an EFL teacher preparation program. *Korea TESOL Journal 18*(1). 3–25.

Rafael, Vicente L. 2012. Targeting translation: Counterinsurgency and the weaponization of language. *Social Text 30*(4). 55–80. https://doi.org/10.1215/01642472-1725793

Rafi, Abu S. M. 2012. The "lost generation" now and then: An analysis of Lady Brett Ashley in The Sun Also Rises in conjunction with "facebook" case-studies. *Harvest: Jahangirnagar University Studies in Language and Literature 27*. 22–42.

Rafi, Abu S. M. 2022. *Pedagogical benefits, ideological and practical challenges and implementational spaces of a translanguaging education policy: the case of Bangladeshi higher education*. James Cook University dissertation. https://doi.org/10.25903/k2bf-7s18

Rafi, Abu S. M. 2023. Students' uptake of translanguaging pedagogies and translanguaging- oriented assessment in an ELT classroom at a Bangladeshi university. In Rubina Khan, Ahmed Bashir, Lal B. Basu & Elias Uddin (eds.), *Local research and glocal perspectives in English language teaching: Teaching in changing times*. Singapore: Springer Nature.

Rafi, A. S. M. 2023b. Creativity, criticality and translanguaging in assessment design: Perspectives from Bangladeshi higher education. *Applied Linguistics Review*.

Rafi, Abu S. M. &Anne-Marie Morgan. 2021. Translanguaging and academic writing in English- only classrooms: Possibilities and challenges in English-only classrooms. In W. Ordeman (ed.), *Creating a transnational space in the first year writing classroom*, 17–40. Wilmington, DE: Vernon Press.

Rafi, Abu S. M. & Anne-Marie Morgan. 2022a. A pedagogical perspective on the connection between translingual practices and transcultural dispositions in an Anthropology classroom in Bangladesh. *International Journal of Multilingualism*. https://doi.org/10.1080/14790718.2022.2026360

Rafi, Abu S. M. & Anne-Marie Morgan. 2022b. Linguistic ecology of Bangladeshi higher education: A translanguaging perspective. *Teaching in Higher Education 27*(4). 1–18. https://doi.org/10.1080/13562517.2022.2045579

Rafi, Abu S. M. & Anne-Marie Morgan. 2022c. Translanguaging as a transformative act in a reading classroom: Perspectives from a Bangladeshi private university. *Journal of Language, Identity & Education*. https://doi.org/10.1080/15348458.2021.2004894

Rafi, Abu S. M. & Anne-Marie Morgan. 2022d. Blending translanguaging and CLIL: Pedagogical benefits and ideological challenges in a Bangladeshi classroom. *Critical Inquiries in Language Studies*. https://doi.org/10.1080/15427587.2022.2090361

Rafi, Abu S. M. & Anne-Marie Morgan. 2022e. Translanguaging and power in academic writing discourse. *Classroom Discourse*. https://doi.org/10.1080/19463014.2022.2046721

Sarker, Profulla & Gareth Davey. 2009. Exclusion of indigenous children from primary education in the Rajshahi Division of northwestern Bangladesh. *International Journal of Inclusive Education 13*(1). 1–11. https://doi.org/10.1080/13603110701201775

Sato, Takanori, Yuri Jody Yujobo, Tricia Okada & Ethel Ogane. 2019. Communication strategies employed by low-proficiency users: Possibilities for ELF-informed pedagogy. *Journal of English as a Lingua Franca 8*(1). 9–35. https://doi.org/10.1515/jelf-2019-2003

Shen, Haibo. 2017. *Translanguaging for bilingual educational theorising in higher degree researcher education: a case study of using Chinese funds of theoretical knowledge for research*. Western Sydney University dissertation.

Singh, Michael & Hui Meng. 2013. Democratising western research using non-western theories: Rancière and mute Chinese theoretical tools. *Studies in Higher Education 38*(6). 907–920.

Tomlinson, Brian. 2018. Emotional dilemmas faced by teachers in ELT materials selection and adaptation: Implications for teacher education. In Juan de Dios Martínez Agudo (ed.), *Emotions in second language teaching: Theory, research, and teacher education*, 165–182. Singapore: Springer.

Tsui, Amy B. M. & James W. Tollefson (eds.). 2017. *Language policy, culture, and identity in Asian contexts*. New York. NY: Routledge.
Viswanathan, Gauri. 1987. The beginnings of English literary study in British India. *Oxford Literary Review* 9(1 & 2). 2–26.
Wei, Li. 2011. Moment Analysis and translanguaging space: Discursive construction of identities by multilingual Chinese youth in Britain. *Journal of Pragmatics 43*(5). 1222–1235. https://doi.org/10.1016/j.pragma.2010.07.035
Winkler, Ingo. 2018. Doing autoethnography: Facing challenges, taking choices, accepting responsibilities. *Qualitative Inquiry 24*(4). 236–247. https://doi.org/10.1177/1077800417728956
Zhaoxiang, Cheng. 2002. English departments in Chinese universities: Purpose and function. *World Englishes 21*(2). 257–267. https://doi.org/10.1111/1467-971X.00246

Ming-Hsuan Wu, Ching-Ching Lin, Ming-Yao Hsiung, and Po-Hui Min

Chapter 3
Flipping the script: A collaborative autoethnography of agency and voices in the weaponization of bilingual education in Taiwan

Abstract: In this collaborative autoethnography, we examined how language is weaponized in ideological warfare in Taiwan's bilingual education policy, a nation aspiring to become bilingual English-Mandarin Chinese by 2030. In particular, we explored how in the rollout of Taiwan's Bilingual 2030 Policy, neoliberalist discourse has been weaponized to mobilize public support for or against the policy and how two local teachers navigated and resisted the neoliberal "educational reform." Data were collected through a sequential approach that enabled two Taiwan-based practitioners and two US-based researchers to explore voices, experiences, and memories most salient to this bilingual policy and analyzed through thematic analysis. With a focus on how local practitioners engaged students in challenging neoliberalist ideologies through civic engagement and activism, we argue that participants' understanding and critical engagement with neoliberal language ideologies illustrated the need to explicitly address these dynamics within Taiwan's bilingual education reform. Furthermore, these findings demonstrated teachers' and students' agency and creativity toward language and its use in complex and dynamic global contexts. We also discuss the intended and unintended harmful consequences of the policy for various stakeholders.

Keywords: Taiwan bilingual policy, neoliberalism, the hegemony of English, weaponization

---

Ming-Hsuan Wu, Ching-Ching Lin, Adelphi University
Ming-Yao Hsiung, Taipei Wanfu Elementary School
Po-Hui Min, Taichung Shang Shih Elementary School

1 Introduction

As a small island that has been historically controlled by superpowers surrounding it, Taiwan's aspiration to become a bilingual nation by 2030 was a quest rooted at the intersection of colonialism, neoliberalism, and self-determination. Driven by the belief that Taiwan's major trading role in the global economy is linked to local talents' bilingual proficiency, the goal of Taiwan's Bilingual 2030 plan is to "boost the competitiveness of Taiwan's young people and enable them to gain better job opportunities and higher salaries" (National Development Council, 2021, p. 1). In Taiwan's new quest for greater participation in the international community in today's globalized world, the promotion of English language proficiency has thus become Taiwan's top education priority. Since the policy's launch in 2018, Taiwan's government has actively sought to restructure teacher education by redesigning curriculum, instruction, and assessments, while using stimulus funding to increase the government's monitoring of the education system for the purpose of improving English proficiency in the island.

The current reform, which is highly centralized, has varying effects on the quality of education, student and teacher agency, and equity and inclusion of Taiwan's student population. As the first conscious and most articulated effort to promote English education in Taiwan, it is also an important case to study how local teachers and students navigate and make sense of a bilingual policy at the nexus of globalization, neoliberalism, and linguistic imperialism. In this chapter, we examine the discursive development and practices based on Taiwan's recent bilingual education policy through the lens of weaponization as it enables us to capture a fuller picture of the impacts of the policy on different stakeholders' struggle for agency and voice. In this collaborative autoethnographic (CAE) study, the four of us collectively and individually reflect upon our own stances and experiences as local educational professionals in Taiwan and/or US-based language educators as we navigate the bilingual policy.

2 Literature review

2.1 Neoliberalism and the power and geopolitics of English

Since the 1980s, neoliberalism, as a prevalent Western ideology that positions the free market and global capitalist expansion as the key to a nation's economic growth, has become a dominant paradigm of nation-building for countries like Taiwan, which has been struggling for living space under the threat of imperialist powers. As the most dominant ideology of the current world order, neoliberalism has profoundly influenced Taiwan's policy development in all domains, including its educational policies and practices (Huang, 2012). As a result, an integral part of Taiwan's policy development is to effectively align education policies with workforce development and economic growth. The official government paper "Blueprint for Developing Taiwan into a Bilingual Nation by 2030" manifested this mindset clearly. The document starts out with a sentence that strongly suggests the direct link between English proficiency and economic growth: "how to raise citizens' English ability to a more internationally competitive level has become a vital issue common to all non-English speaking countries. Taiwan certainly cannot except itself from this" (p. 1).

In view of the relationship between neoliberalism and education, numerous authors note that the dominant status of English as a global language is intricately intertwined with the West's neoliberalist agenda. The West's effort to pursue its political and economic interests and maintain control over the English language often comes with the support of national and international organizations in the English language teaching (ELT) industry (Al Hosni, 2015; Ciprianová & Vanco, 2010). The ubiquitous presence of English is further heightened by the fact that today's information and knowledge industry is primarily coded in English. Consequently, learning English is the *sine qua non* of global and individual success in every sphere of life, including politics, culture, business, and education. Such considerations strengthen the argument that English should be prioritized as part of the commercial and geopolitical strategies for nations to gain an advantage in today's global era.

2.2 The weaponization of English education & linguistic imperialism

Authors such as David Crystal (2003) attributed the global status quo of English to "the expansion of the British colonial power which peaked towards the end of the nineteenth century, and the emergence of the United States as the leading economic power of the twentieth century" (p. 59). Throughout history, colonial empires have maintained power over their former subjects through language, which is an essential aspect of colonial governance. The role of linguistic imperialism in colonial power dynamics and strategies of domination cannot be regarded as unintentional by-products. The effects the hegemony of English has had on the culture of the colonized in the colonial era, and particularly the fact that they still live on today in such concrete ways, are indicative of the "use of language as a weapon for oppression" (Flores-Rodríguez, 2012, p. 28).

In this study, we follow Pentón Herrera and Bryan (2022) to use the term *language weaponization* to describe "the process by which words, discourse, and language in any form have been used or are being used to inflict harm on others, and how language education practices, policies, programs, and curricula are weaponized" (p. 3). It is important to note that the harms inflicted on individuals may not always be explicit. In particular, oppression and resistance should not be imagined as discrete categories, nor should their cultural expressions be dichotomized. Instead, we approach and view language use and praxis as interlinked, taking place in a dynamic system as different groups use strategic influences to promote social changes. Throughout the history of the world, while the cultures and languages of colonized countries were affected by ideologies and practices of colonizing countries that normalized inequity and injustice in fundamental ways, the weaponization of language is often exerted through both macro and micromechanisms put in place by colonial powers and the effects of different levels of colonialism on the colonized countries' development can be diffused, heterogeneous and implicit.

Phillipson (1992) aptly defined the linguistic imperialism of the English language as "the dominance of English is asserted and maintained by the establishment and continuous reconstitution of structural and cultural inequalities between English and other languages" (Phillipson, 1992, p. 47). Linguistic imperialism today may not exist in the same ways which we tend to imagine. It has adapted and morphed into new forms. The power dynamics developed through linguistic assimilation continue to manifest in multiple aspects of our existence. According to Akiko Kiyota, the popularity of English-Medium Instruction (EMI) classrooms in non-English speaking countries such as Japan often creates unintentional exclusion and marginalization for emerging bilinguals and as such. Furthermore, EMI may help perpetuate the socioeconomic hierarchy since it can make the school curriculum less accessible or less interesting for children who are underprivileged and have limited access to the resources for learning English (Kiyota, 2022). On the other hand, the feeling of speaking a 'common' language contributes to some feeling of equality. Many countries have intentionally chosen to use English as a lingua franca or a de facto working language to facilitate communication between citizens who speak different languages, and as such, English is not learned as a form of resistance and anti-colonial gesture. Rather, adopting English as an additional language allows learners to experience a sense of freedom and masks the feeling of inferiority. We should not deny that speaking a colonial language can be a form of resistance and agency. On the contrary, by engaging in powerful language practices that speak to their histories, cultures, and identities, people from formerly colonized countries can crack the systems of colonial power and, in doing so, bring about meaningful social changes within them.

While the influence of neoliberalism and linguistic imperialism has been prevalent through the process of globalization, it may reveal different impacts, depending on particular different socio-cultural contexts. To understand the influence of neoliberalism in Taiwan, thus, it is necessary to take into account how different socio-cultural contexts have contributed to the construction of social practice, in particular, the agency and voice of the people who are affected by the weaponization of (English) language education.

2.3 Contextualizing Taiwan's educational reform in the era of neoliberalism

The elevation of English education in Taiwan's most recent educational reform reflects the influence of neoliberalism on Taiwan's educational reform, which aims to transform English language learning into a matter of neoliberal anticipation. In past decades, the language policy orientation has gradually moved from "Mandarin-only" to "Mandarin plus," with some local languages, such as Holo, Hakka, and Austronesian languages making their initial appearance in the elementary school curriculum in 2001 due to the mother tongue education requirement (Wu, 2011). It was also the time when nationwide English education was implemented at the elementary level to address the growing disparity in students' access to English education. However, due to the hegemony of English, mother tongue education rarely went beyond the one session per week requirement, whereas the role of English has made its historical importance in the educational system in Taiwan. An example of this is that Taiwan is now undergoing an educational reform that demands local teachers use English to teach English and/or other subjects. Part of the bilingual policy is to enhance the country's global competitiveness by making Taiwan a Mandarin-English bilingual country by 2030. Specifically, first to 12th-grade students are expected to move beyond learning English as an academic subject, and English is to be used as a medium of instruction through which English and other subjects would be taught (and learned). By 2024, sixty percent of primary and secondary schools nationwide are expected to adopt all-English teaching in English classes, and one in every seven schools is expected to implement bilingual teaching in some fields and subjects (National Development Council, 2018).

Taiwan is fully committed to leaping from its multilingual past and present into a bilingual future where local languages, except Mandarin, are superseded by English in the educational sector. Chang (2022) provided a detailed text analysis of keywords and content in the policy documents and identified the following three prevalent ideologies in this 10-year national bilingual policy: "English supremacy," "neoliberalism," and "linguistic instrumentalism." While it is clear that the Bilingual Nation 2030 policy is situated within a neoliberalism and globalization discourse that positions English education as a means for Taiwanese students to reach upward mobility, it did not come without resistance. Several problems have been identified about the policy, including many bilingual teachers finding it difficult to teach different subjects in English; students' difficulty in understanding subject matters in English; neglect or ignorance of the urban-rural education gap; and the lack of adequate co-teaching context for foreign and local teachers to work together (Hioe, 2022; Lee, 2022). The pushback from academics and teachers has resulted in the policy being recently rebranded as "Bilingual 2030." The change from "Bilingual Nation 2030" to "Bilingual 2030" in the public discourse to refer to the bilingual policy is noteworthy. This change can be seen as a form of resistance from the locals. It is the government's response to the public's disapproval of the ambitious goal of making Taiwan into an English-Mandarin bilingual country by 2030.

3 Methodology

In this CAE, drawing from our personal experiences and stories, we employed a sequential approach to collect data that would allow u to examine how language is weaponized in ideological warfare through a case study of Taiwan's bilingual education policy, where Taiwan expresses its ambition to become a bilingual English-Mandarin nation by 2030, with a particular focus on primary and secondary students and their civic engagement. A closer collaboration between local practitioners in Taiwan (Ming-Yao and Po-Hui) and U.S. university-based researchers (Ming-Hsuan and Ching-Ching) has led to a more productive insight into the contextual dynamics of language weaponization as a social practice developing within social-cultural, political, and historical contexts.

3.1 Research questions

While the neoliberal dream has increasingly saturated the world view of non-English speaking countries like Taiwan, the effects of English are often more diffused, more subtle, and more indirect. To understand the collusion of neoliberalism, globalization, and the power of the English language in the context of Taiwan, we need to understand the aspects of agency, culture, and creativity. Hence, we engaged in a CAE to understand:

1) How has, in the rollout of Taiwan's "bilingual nation" policy, neoliberalist ideology been weaponized to mobilize public support for or against the policy?
2) How did Taiwanese teachers resist the neoliberal "educational reform," and how did they engage students in challenging neoliberalist ideologies through civic engagement and activism?

3.2 Data sources

Following VanLier (1988) and Kiyota (2022), the study gathered multiple data sources for triangulation and various perspectives. Data included the following:

3.2.1 Participant positionality

The first source of data was collected through participant positionality, which allows four participating authors in this study to explore their own English learning and teaching experiences to construct a narrative interpretation of the new bilingual policy in Taiwan. As a qualitative approach where two or more participants use their own life stories and lived experiences to unpack, problematize, and/or explore a sociocultural phenomenon (Chang, 2008), CAE allows us to situate our collective experiences as life stories to develop a more holistic perspective on a complex social phenomenon.

We each reflected on our positionalities and how our positionalities were linked to our identities and life journeys as we navigated our careers as practitioners in the ELT field. All the participating authors in this study were born and educated in Taiwan and have struggled in their English language learning journeys. These lived experiences have made us sensitive and attuned to issues related to Taiwan's current educational reform. Through an interrogation of our own experiences, first as English learners in Taiwan and later as English language educators in Taiwan or the US, we gain a deeper understanding of how English education in Taiwan has evolved over the years and reached its status. More information about our positionality is shared in the section below.

3.2.2 Interviews

The second source of data includes interviews among ourselves; more specifically, Ming-Hsuan's interview with Po-Hui and Ching-Ching's interview with Ming-Yao. Since Po-Hui and Ming-Yao work directly with students in public schools in Taiwan, they possess tremendous local knowledge and live through the new bilingual policy on a daily basis. As a result, Ming-Hsuan and Ching-Ching, both currently based in the US, developed the interview questions for this study and adopted the role of interviewers and listeners to learn about Ming-Yao and Po-Hui's practitioner experiences, perspectives, and insights relating to the policy interpretation and implementation. See the Appendix for the interview questions.

3.2.3 Student work and classroom activities snapshots

In addition to the interview data described above, we also draw on self-reported posts from Ming-Yao's and Po-Hui's Facebook pages. As many teachers have used Facebook to share ideas and resources and engage in informal professional development that is "participant driven, practical, collaborative" (Rutherford, 2010, p. 60), Facebook has gradually become a valuable data collection tool for researchers. Facebook posts often include self-reported information, photos, and others' comments. These data used as an additional data source, can help researchers address the shortcomings of participants' memories and potential biases (Kosinski et al., 2015). As the four of us have previously collaborated on various projects related to English education in Taiwan, we have become friends on Facebook. Ming-Yao and Po-Hui are both active on Facebook and often posted snapshots of student activities and classroom scenarios, which presented a rich source of data to support and triangulate their perspectives about the unfolding of Taiwan's Bilingual 2030 Policy.

3.3 Data collection and analysis

We began collecting data by first engaging in a series of conversations in which we shared critical experiences. All the conversations took place in Zoom and were recorded. In the next phase of data collection, Ming-Hsuan and Ching-Ching switched to the role of researchers and interviewed Po-Hui and Ming-Yao, respectively. Ming-Hsuan and Ching-Ching listened to the recordings of their interviews independently for further reflection and analysis. Next, Ming-Hsuan and Ching-Ching shared their reflections from those conversations on a shared Google Document and engaged in sequential writing, responding to each other's comments, asking probing questions, and facilitating each other's reflection. After several iterations of this data collection and meaning-making analysis, several major themes were identified.

Using Braun and Clarke's (2006) approach to thematic analysis in which the researcher plays an active role in identifying themes, Ming-Husuan and Ching-Ching followed the six steps to thematic analysis outlined by Braun and Clarke to proceed with their analysis: familiarization with data, generating initial codes, identifying themes that reflect collections of codes, reviewing data to understand and explain the meaning and dynamics of themes, maintaining rigor through inter-coder agreement and producing the final report.

Ming-Hsuan and Ching-Ching began their analysis by first reading through the data set together and taking notes of potential codes, themes, and connections to the research questions and relevant literature. Ming-Hsuan and Ching-Ching helped each other attend to both latent and semantic meaning as they recursively examined specific patterns and interactions among patterns with each recursion. Although the stages used in the analysis of the data looked sequential, Braun and Clarke's dynamic analysis tool allowed Ming-Hsuan and Ching-Ching to explore, understand, and examine the meaning in their data systematically and yet interactively. We summarize our positionalities as follows and discuss the major themes that emerged from the analysis in the next section.

4 Who we are: Our positionality

In this study, participating authors' (i.e., participants) full-circle experiences as multilingual learners, academics, teachers, and administrators played a critical role in understanding and analyzing the effects of Taiwan's bilingual education policy as a weapon of a neoliberalist agenda for both students and teachers. Our experiences and insights allowed us to take an insider view of the hegemony of English throughout our life journeys as well as across diverse global contexts. This CAE draws on our experiences and voices as we navigate our career paths as English teaching professionals in Taiwan and the US and explore complex issues pertinent to our understanding of language weaponization as well as the challenges and opportunities it affords to stakeholders affected by the recent reform in Taiwan.

4.1 Ming-Hsuan

Ming-Hsuan went through the *buxiban* (after-school paid services that provide additional education to students) culture and the test-driven English education in Taiwan. As a result, she is keenly aware of the social and economic costs and benefits of English education. As a core subject on the high school and college entrance exams, English was the subject that she spent the most time studying. She did not learn about linguistic imperialism and English hegemony until she came to the US for graduate degrees in Teaching English to Speakers of Other Languages (TESOL) and educational policy. Since then, her teaching and research have always been guided by a critical sociolinguistic lens to explore students' and educators' agentive roles in advancing their educational surroundings.

As a speaker of Mandarin, Holo, and Hakka, Ming-Hsuan often has to grapple with positionality as a US-based TESOL teacher educator. On one hand, she teaches culturally relevant and sustaining pedagogy in her teacher preparation courses in New York that highlight the importance of including students' cultures and languages in the curriculum. On the other hand, when she met teachers and parents in Taiwan, she noticed that they were skeptical about this approach, causing her to wonder how English education in Taiwan has changed, evolved, and adapted according to Taiwan's unique history and positioning in the world. Her experiences of working with local teachers and parents in Taiwan provide her with local insights as she examines English education and policies through the weaponization framework.

4.2 Ching-Ching

Ching-Ching's struggle as a former English learner has shaped her personal and professional identities, teaching philosophy, and research agenda. Her interest in participating in this study stems from her desire to reckon with her own full circle experience as an English learner, from its aspiring devotee to today's discontent rebel. Reflecting on her own language learning experiences and identity development led Ching-Ching to realize the extent to which her language journey has been shaped and continues to be shaped by her discontent and disenchantment with the neoliberalist discourse and the colonial gaze she has internalized and yet struggled against throughout the entire journey of her language learning. She was her own worst enemy and was once an avid supporter of monolingual ideologies during her years as a graduate student. There was a period of time when she intentionally shunned away from her culture so that she could immerse herself in an English-only environment. She once looked upon her language through a deficit lens amidst a culture of shame and silence. Then to her deepest regret, in the early stage of her career as an English as a second language (ESL) teacher, she aligned with the English-only policy and blindly reinforced the monolingual policy without realizing the harm it had inflicted on her students.

She wrote her part of this paper with the intention of exposing the complexity and nuances of the weaponization of English for non-English speakers in Taiwan. Through examining her own complex relationship with English language learning, she has sought to bring to light the hegemony of English in the global context. She hopes her experience serves to bear witness to the nexus of neoliberalism, the globalized spread of English, and the role it plays in reinforcing the colonial divide and racial inequity when examined from a sociohistorical lens.

4.3 Ming-Yao

Ming-Yao currently works as Director of the Resource Center for English teaching and learning housed at Taipei Wanfu Elementary School, a school district on the outskirt of Taipei, where student populations are culturally and linguistically diverse, including children of foreign parents who are international exchange scholars in Taiwan. English was her favorite subject during school, and through reading English literature, she understood the multicultural nature of the world. While she was not accepted into an English program in college as she had hoped, her enthusiasm for English learning and her English skills helped her forge an academic and career path as a journalism major. In fact, her journalism background and knowledge of English played an instrumental role in her landing a job in a foreign trading company. The job and traveling abroad experience exposed her to diverse cultures and, later, inspired her to further her study to become an ESL teacher. She believes English teaching and learning should be authentic and meaningful, and people should cherish and value their own cultures and identities. That is why at her job, one of her cherished projects is to develop an SDG (Sustainable Development Goals) focus in the school curriculum to foster children's environmental awareness in global–local contexts.

4.4 Po-Hui

Po-Hui is currently the Director of Academic Affairs at a public elementary school in Taichung city. She has completed an initiative program provided by the Ministry of Education (MOE), the "International Education 2.0," and became an instructor for international education. She plays a key role in developing a bilingual and international education curriculum at her school and often shares her experiences with other schools in Taiwan. Her passion for providing all students in her school with the opportunity to learn about different cultures and interact with people from different countries stems from her lack of access to English education growing up in Taiwan in the 70s and 80s. She aspires to make English learning available to all students, especially those from families that can't afford to send them to *buxiban* for English enrichment experiences. She has won several teaching awards, and is now taking on a leadership role in helping her school strengthen its connections with schools in Japan, South Korea, Nepal, and beyond.

5 Findings

We present our findings under the following three themes: 1) Our perception of Taiwan's Bilingual 2030 policy and experience navigating the weaponization of the policy; 2) opportunities the policy offered for student and teacher agency and voices; and 3) the intended and unintended harmful, negative consequences of the policy for stakeholders.

5.1 Our perception of Taiwan's bilingual 2030 policy and experience navigating the weaponization of the policy

While both Ming-Yao and Po-Hui support the goals and broad outlines of the bilingual mandate, they also perceived the bilingual policy as representing a top-down approach to education reform that is confusing, inchoate, and not well thought out. For example, in discussing the rollout of the bilingual education policy, Ming-Yao commented:

> "政府其實沒有很強的雙語教學概念, 起初他一直跟我們講什麼叫 CLIL, 後來定調為content language integrated learning. 剛開始的想法是從所謂的藝能, 比較操作型的科目開始著手, 再慢慢推入natural sciences. 但是不同的教授就會一直給我們意見說: 專業英文太難, 孩子們聽不懂. 政府然後改變步調說, 不一定完全都要講英文喔! 政策方向的一再調整, 甚至充滿矛盾讓我們現場的老師很為難!" ("As of now, we still don't have a clear idea of what is "bilingual teaching." The government kept referring us to CLIL [Content and Language Integrated Learning] as a teaching guideline, though what it actually entails is still open to interpretation. For example, the method requires teachers to teach subjects in English. When teachers aimed to implement the policy, we also heard from different professors who criticized that we are losing the children since content-based English is too difficult. The government then changed the tone by saying that if it is too difficult for students to understand, then teachers don't need to teach in English. For teachers who work on the frontline, the government's directory is constantly shifting and sometimes can seem to be full of contradiction!")

As a result, the government's lack of clear direction has created a climate of uncertainty or even fear for both school teachers and principals as to how to comply with rules they do not fully understand. Teachers' adopting a CLIC approach to English learning and other subjects often neglects the cognitive, social, and emotional needs of learners by insisting on an English-only ideology and rigid language compartments. The plan masks major inconsistency, relating to different goals, visions, and interpretations of a bilingual policy, and more fundamentally, a hidden agenda of neoliberal education policy with often a lopsided emphasis on English education while paying only lip service to mother tongue education.

Limited resources have compelled teachers to think outside of the box as they strive toward a more equitable bilingual education and classroom practices. Ming-Yao, for example, has worked to engage students' learning through meaningful activities. The resource center she supervises created an "English-friendly living environment" (National Development Council, 2018, p. 1) where students can practice everyday English language in an authentic way, such as ordering food in the cafeteria or checking out books in the libraries. To expand students' exposure to English and find the use of English, students engage in virtual exchange with English language learners in other countries, where they introduce their cultures to each other. For example, her students researched about Taiwan's endangered species and taught their international peers the importance of protecting nature and the environment. She wanted her students to see themselves as cultural ambassadors of their country.

As for Po-Hui, her leadership role in her school and district puts her at the forefront of the policy implementation. Working with teachers directly made her especially aware of teachers' resistance to the bilingual policy. To reach out to those who are uncomfortable using English to teach in class or skeptical about bilingual education policy, she made a concerted effort to ensure that the school will not leave policy implementation to individual teachers and that bilingual education, as required by the government does not equate with English only education. For example, she encouraged the physical education teachers to view themselves as the "guardians of bilingual and health education" (雙語和健康的守護者) if they are willing to teach their classes in "70% Mandarin and 30% English." Below, she further explained the important role that administrators play in implementing the bilingual policy.

> 一個政策出來,我不會去逼迫老師說你一定要做。但是其實任何政策,都會有鼓勵的措施。像我們就可以去申請一些新的計劃。拿到錢後,我們就可以去push老師,或者是鼓勵老師。我身為行政人員,我必須努力滿足老師教材方面的需求。比如說,老師們可能會很想要聽某個教授的分享,那我就來邀請。所以我覺得老師們可以負面解讀,也可以正面解讀這個政策。但很重要的就是看行政人員怎麼去經營。(When a policy comes out, it is not my role to tell teachers what to do. Policies often come with reward initiatives. This provides us with opportunities to apply for grants. Once we get the funds, we can encourage the teachers to take advantage of it creatively. As an administrator, I have to work hard to support teachers' curricular needs. For

example, I will invite professors to give a talk, upon teachers' requests. It is up to us to interpret a policy positively and creatively. It is quite important as to how the administrators and teachers would navigate the policy.)

Po-Hui's words suggested that there was some resistance from teachers in her school. She had to interpret the policy for the teachers and make it into something manageable for them to implement. As an administrator, she looks for ways to empower teacher agency for creativity and innovation and to support them through English-imbedded international education. She has learned from her own experiences that building a relationship with schools in non-English speaking countries often has created more successful and mutually beneficial results than with schools in English-speaking countries. As a result, she purposely chose not to apply for the government fundings that required local Taiwanese schools to collaborate with schools in English-speaking countries. Instead, she applied for funding for innovative curriculum development and received funding for her to purchase tablets for her teachers. Po-Hui's tactical strategy to navigate the bilingual policy enables her to crave space for different interpretations and implementations that minimize the negative impacts that the policy might have created.

5.2 Opportunities for student and teacher agency and voices

While teachers' perceptions and perspectives on Taiwan's Bilingual 2030 policy pointed to the confusion and inconsistency in the policy, the implementation of the policy with an aim toward globalization also provides opportunities for teachers to rethink directions and goals in language teaching and learning, and to engage more actively and creatively with content and pedagogical practices. The themes that emerged in this study highlight ways in which local teachers navigated the tensions of bilingual teaching within the school settings in complex global contexts, and how they navigate the government mandates through innovative curricular designs, and regional and international collaboration and partnerships. Understanding teachers' perceptions and navigation of policy requirements to meet students' diverse needs provides insight to contextualize implementation decisions and highlights local teachers' voice and agency.

5.2.1 Example 1: SDG curriculum

In order to inspire the next generation of environmental advocates, teachers at Taipei Wanfu Elementary School developed a school project titled "Rivers in our Community," through which children learned about the importance of nature and the potential harm humans can do to its life. Foreign English teachers researched and learned about the important roles of rivers in Taiwan's history and how cities' developments are linked along the rivers. They then incorporated what they learned in developing a learning unit, which included a field trip to the river. Activities included: teachers, students with parents' and teachers' help moved their hand-made canoes to the river (Figure 3.1); as a class, they discussed how rivers can affect people, animals, and plants (Figure 3.2); and explored the habitat of the river in their canoes (Figure 3.3). The project incorporated English learning in the environmental study as well as successfully galvanized community support to increase awareness of rivers and the surrounding environment. This learning unit is also an apt example of how teachers in Taiwan sought to navigate the tides of globalization and neoliberalism and instead engage students in meaningful and authentic learning with active, fun elements in the problem-based learning approach. All pictures in this chapter are used with permission.

Figure 3.1: Students proudly posing pictures in front of their DIY canoes.

5.2.2 Example 2: Global quarantine conversation clubs for kids

To expand children's opportunities to develop students' intercultural competence and communication skills, teachers at Taipei Wanfu Elementary School utilized digital resources to transform their classroom into a global learning opportunity

Figure 3.2: Discussing the ecology of the river.

and young learners into global citizens. With virtual exchanges, teachers and their students joined the Global Quarantine Conversation Clubs for Kids and met friends from around the world. Through the process of getting to know each other (Figure 3.4) and sharing daily routines and personal life via video or a medley of asynchronous tools, students were given an intimate glimpse into the routines, habits, and cultures of their global peers who lived thousands of miles away (Figure 3.5). These unique classroom experiences were not just fun, but also provided an escape from the straight jacket of neoliberalist schooling. Virtual exchanges increase students' understanding and acceptance of other cultures, diversify student's academic repertoire, and help them explore their perspectives of the world.

5.2.3 Example 3: Lunch around the world project

The English education in Po-Hui's school, Shan Shi Elementary School is embedded in its international and cross-curricular education. Teachers of different subjects work closely with English specialists to create lessons in which English mediates students' learning. A series of lessons on lunch around the world consists of students learning about lunch in different countries through videos re-

Figure 3.3: Exploring the habitat of the river.

corded from various countries (Figure 3.6), making some dishes at school (mac and cheese, panini making in Figure 3.7), setting tables for serving western food, and talking to a sushi chef and a retired diplomat from Taiwan. During the conversation with the diplomat, some students asked him which Taiwanese dish he often introduced at an international event. In the end, this project is integrated with art, social studies, health education, and language arts. The students have the opportunity to not only learn about different cultures, but share their school lunches with their sister schools in Japan, Korea, and Israel through videos. The school also welcomes international students from a nearby university to come to interact with students during lunch time. The school started the curriculum with a few classes, but strives to make this into a school-wide event. This is an example of how teachers utilize the local community resources to help students find some relevance to learning English and feel connected to the world.

Figure 3.4: Getting to know each other.

Figure 3.5: A journey into each other's cultures.

Figure 3.6: My school lunch project with video recordings around the world.

5.2.4 Example 4: Treasure box exchange project

Po-Hui's school has a history of putting together a box of treasures from Taiwan and mailing it to their sister schools abroad. In return, they often also receive something similar from abroad. Students and teachers work together to decide what to put in the treasure box that can best showcase their lives in Taiwan, which includes students' letters written in English, stationery that is made in Taiwan, or local sweets made by students at school. During the peak of the pandemic, when many countries suffered from a lack of medical supplies, the school decided to put some Made in Taiwan medical masks in the package. To make a more personal connection, the school had the local factories produce medical masks with their sister schools' logos on them. From time to time, the school also showcased their students' medical masks with a Thank you note and flags of countries that donated Covid vaccines to Taiwan, or masks that marked important diplomatic visits in Taiwan (e.g., Pompeo's and Pelosi's visits to Taiwan). See a collage of these Made in Taiwan medical masks in Figure 3.8. There is no doubt that English education in Taiwan is often embedded in the "economic competitiveness and advancement" type of neoliberal discourse, and parents often are worried about their children's English proficiency lagging behind and not being able to get a head start in the world economy as Taiwanese citizens who speak

Figure 3.7: Panini and Mac and Cheese cooking classes.

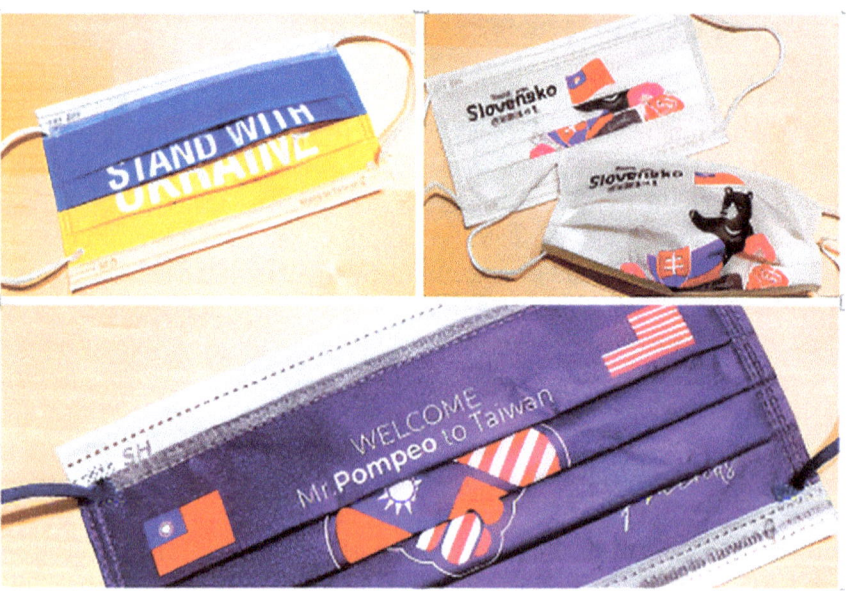

Figure 3.8: Made in Taiwan medical masks with diplomatic messages.

predominantly in Mandarin. However, teachers at Po-Hui's school tried to flip the script and create opportunities for the students to cultivate a sense of caring and pride through international education.

5.3 The intended and unintended harmful consequences of the policy for stakeholders

Taiwan's 2030 Bilingual plan as an educational policy remains controversial, especially toward linguistic justice and diversity. As a theoretical framework, language weaponization provides a critical lens for us to examine the outcomes of bilingual education for language development, academic achievement, and equity for children with diverse needs. Although the data shows that two focal Taiwanese teachers have overall supported the provision of the government's bilingual policy, their experience with the policy implementation also has borne witness to the intended and unintended harmful consequences of the policy for children, especially in regard to maintaining a link with their heritage language and culture, and with its related sociolinguistic practices.

The first (un)intended consequence is regarding the policy's heightening of the existing discriminatory hiring policies and practices against non-Native English speakers. While Taiwan is culturally and linguistically diverse, English is not a language used on a daily basis. To create an authentic English learning environment and obtain 'qualified' English teachers, many school districts privilege the hiring of native English speakers to diversify the school community. In fact, foreign teachers have been framed as a key help in implementing the "Bilingual 2030" policy as it aims to have all public primary and secondary schools in Taiwan hire foreign English teachers or part-time foreign English Language Assistants by 2030 (National Development Council, 2018). It is thus not surprising that at the local level, the hiring flyers often include explicit statements that exclude nonnative English speakers. Ming-Yao, as a program director who is in charge of teacher hiring, reported a case of her being compelled to hire a "less qualified" foreign teacher over a "more qualified" domestic teacher (in her eyes) so that the school can be qualified for government funding allocated for schools that are in compliance with the policy requirements.

Taiwan's current bilingual policy and practices also inadvertently reinforced English hegemony and its related ideologies, at the expense of language variation (especially English variations), heritage language, and regional dialects. English proficiency is often used as the criteria for hiring bilingual teachers, instead of teachers' ability to foster students' love for learning English through creative and effective teaching. However, teachers who pass the English proficiency test may not be an effective teacher, or vice versa. Since the policy aims to push for subjects to be taught in English, it creates an impression that teachers' English proficiency has to be at a much higher level than before. Apparently, a narrow construct of English proficiency and teacher qualification has contributed to the shortage of bilingual teachers. A more flexible and multi-dimensional approach should be put in place to expand the pool of potential teachers. In fact, several classroom-based research projects have highlighted that due to the English proficiency of local Taiwanese teachers and students, it is a necessity for local teachers to adopt a translanguaging approach in which local languages are integrated into their teaching (Chen et al., 2020; Ke & Lin, 2017; Lin & Wu, 2022).

In addition to the shortage of bilingual teachers, students' readiness to receive bilingual instruction creates critical challenges in implementing bilingual education for subjects that are content-heavy and cognitively challenging, such as math, history, and science. During the transition period, many schools start English instruction in 'non-academic' subjects, such as arts, physical education (PE), or music, but ironically, these courses often are taught by teachers whose English is not their strong suit. This has prevented art or music teachers from delivering content in an effective way that students can enjoy and also put the most vulnerable students who are still developing their English proficiency in a particularly unfavorable position.

6 Discussion

Taiwan's colonial past and the constant threats from China have made the public believe in the need to find its own voice and space in any international platforms, and English is a means to connect Taiwan with the rest of the world. As a result, many teachers see it as an opportunity for Taiwan to be seen in the world, which is especially crucial for a small country that is ineligible for membership in many international organizations. As evident in Yao-Min and Po-Hui's teaching, their approach to English education is not just about bringing the world to Taiwan, but also about bringing Taiwan to the world.

However, the push for subjects to be taught entirely in English at all levels of education, including colleges, could negatively affect students' motivation and interest to learn English or other subjects taught in English. For example, the current reform, instead of alleviating the direct pressure of competition and democratizing the educational process and outcomes for minoritized students, has intensified the logic of competition more than ever. The national examinations remain to be a critically selective mechanism in the labor market and social mobility. In order to forge a "competitive advantage for young talents" (National Development Council, 2018, p. 3), school administrators, teachers, and parents have been under tremendous pressure as Taiwan's public schools have begun to implement bilingual education in response to the bilingual 2030 policy.

In a recent teacher survey that examined 88 local teachers' perspectives of the recent educational reform in Taiwan, Coudenys et al. (2022) identified three challenges to the implementation of the policy, including the impression of increased teacher responsibilities, the public's lack of understanding of the policy, and cultural challenges that still prioritizes academic success in high test exams over student-driven, inquiry-based learning approaches demanded by the reform. In a similar vein to Coudenys et al. (2022), we argue that the bilingual policy does little to lessen the grip of a test-driven culture and leaves little room for teachers and students to exercise their creativity and agency. In the end, the policy failed to challenge the power of English; on the contrary, it enforces the power of English by enacting nativism through its hiring and recruitment policy, and by elevating the role of English over the mother tongue education, in Taiwan's local cultures. In addition, despite the intent of the policy to address the rural-urban and socioeconomic disparity in English education, it works to intensify the gap. Children from rural areas and foreign workers from non-English speaking countries are especially vulnerable in bilingual classrooms. They are often under-resourced compared to students from urban areas to start with. They cannot afford to pay for after-school paid services or programs like other students. The current bilingual education policy takes little consideration of their home languages, and hence they are losing out on both fronts.

It should be noted that resistance from the bottom came in different forms. Resistance in the subtle form of contesting 'public transcripts' is usefully integrated into the everyday experience by making use of policy programs, prescribed roles, and language to resist the harm of neoliberalism and the logic of competition. The Ministry of Education earmarked NT$3.61 billion (US$124 million) for bilingual education in primary and secondary schools nationwide through promoting English-taught courses or English as a Medium of Instruction Courses (EMI) to enhance Taiwanese students' English proficiency and the overall international competitiveness of Taiwan's English education. However, part of the above-mentioned funding is made available for schools to apply for, and thus how each school can benefit from the funding relies heavily on how schools administrators and teachers are able to successfully navigate the system by creating place-based curriculum, integrating and mobilizing local and international resources while meeting the policy requirements for grants.

We acknowledge that both Ming-Yao and Po-Hui work in schools near/in big cities, and thus the opportunities that their schools are afforded are definitely different from schools in rural areas. However, their experiences also demonstrate that while bilingual education in Taiwan has been weaponized to serve the nexus of globalization, neoliberalism, and linguistic imperialism, local teachers find ways to develop innovative strategies to resist the policy mandates and foster student voices and agency in such a way to shield them from the potential harms of language weaponization.

7 Conclusion

Taiwan's Bilingual 2030 Plan, instead of moving towards a balanced bilingual education, has set its focus on accelerating the development of English learning. English proficiency was used as a weapon to serve a neoliberal agenda linked to the nation's goal for continued economic success in the global era. The neoliberal privileging of English as a global language consolidates linguistic imperialism at the expense of local languages. Our study shows that the neoliberal educational settings in Taiwan have exerted powerful influences on teacher education, teacher hiring policy, practices, and processes, curriculum redesign, assessment, and other school practices.

Through the weaponization framework, we reveal how the weaponization of education and language use can contribute to perpetuating the rural/urban divide, racial disparity, and, ultimately, socio-economic inequality. Our identities and positionalities as former English Language learners have made us more attuned to both oppressive and liberating effects of the power of English. To reduce harm, our study suggests a need to gain a more complete understanding of why the policy has the effects it does and, in particular, the dynamics within global English learning in the particular historical, social, and cultural contexts of Taiwan.

Hence our inquiry was driven by our deep desire to uncover and thus empower the voices and agency in the stakeholders' language use and practices. We found teacher practitioners were keenly aware of neoliberal language ideologies, and they have strategically leveraged English education to resist and navigate these powerful dynamics by glocalizing English education and diversifying curriculum and educational resources beyond the classroom walls. Our findings demonstrate teachers' and students' agency and creativity regarding the nuances and varieties of the English language in the context of the world's cultural and linguistic diversity. We conclude that their stories, by creating opportunities for student empowerment in their classroom environment, successfully challenged and rejected the oppressive and deficit framing of a neoliberal language education policy.

Appendix

Interview questions

1. 請跟我們分享一下你目前在學校的職稱和工作內容。
   Would you please share with us your job title at school and your responsibilities?
2. 這幾年台灣的英語教育有蠻大的變化,尤其是在108課綱和2030雙語國家政策下,英語課在國中小學更是與以前有很大的不同。可以跟我們分享一下你們在第一教學現場,這幾年所看到或是經歷的變化嗎?
   Over the past few years, English education has gone through dramatic changes, especially with the 108 Guidelines (Curriculum Guidelines of 12-Year Basic Education) and 2023 Bilingual Country policy. As a result, English classes in primary and secondary schools are very different from before. Can you share with us what you've seen at the teaching sites? What changes have you seen?
3. 推廣英語教育時,遇到最有成就感的時刻是何時?
   When you are in the field promoting English education, when did you have the biggest sense of accomplishment?
4. 面臨最大的困難是什麼?
   What are the biggest challenges that you have encountered?
5. 請跟我們分享一下,你們學校接下來的英語教育的短程和遠程目標是什麼?
   Please share with us the short term and long-term goals for the English education at your schools.
6. 請問你目前在台灣英語教學現場設計活動時,是否有時候會回想起你自己以前在台灣求學時候學英語的經驗呢? 如果有,可否跟我們分享一下你當時學習英語的經驗,以及現在擔任老師(或是行政),推廣英語教育的一些連結嗎?
   When you design an English lesson or activity for your students, would it remind you of your English learning experience as a student in the past? If so, can you share with us your English learning experience at that time and the connection to your current job as an English teacher or as a school administrator that promotes English education?

References

Al Hosni, Jokha Khalifa. 2015. Globalization and the linguistic imperialism of the English language. *Arab World English Journal (AWEJ)* 6(1). 298–308. https://dx.doi.org/10.24093/awej/vol6no1.23

Braun, Virginia & Victoria Clarke. 2006. Using thematic analysis in psychology. *Qualitative Research in Psychology* 3(2). 77–101.

Chang, Heewon. 2008. *Autoethnography as a Method*. Walnut Creek, CA: Left Coast.

Chang, Yu-jung. 2022. (Re)imagining Taiwan through "2030" bilingual nation": Language, identities, and ideologies. *Taiwan Journal of TESOL* 19(1). 121–146. https://doi.org/10.30397/TJTESOL.202204_19(1).0005

Ciprianová, Elena & Michal Vanco. 2010. English in the age of globalization: Changing ELT models, restructuring relationships. *The Journal of Linguistic and Intercultural Education* 3. 123–136. https://doi.org/10.29302/jolie.2010.3.8

Coudenys, Blansefloer, Gina Strohbach, Tammy Tang & Rachel Udabe. 2022. On the path toward lifelong learning: An early analysis of Taiwan's 12-year basic education reform. In Fernando M. Reimers, Uche Amaechi, Alysha Banerji & Margaret Wang (eds.), *Education to build back better: What can we learn from education reform in a post-pandemic world*, 75–98. Singapore: Springer.

Crystal, David. 2003. *English as a global language*. Cambridge, UK: Cambridge University Press.

Flores-Rodríguez, Daynalí. 2012. Language, power and resistance: Re-reading Fanon in atrans-Caribbean context. *The Black Scholar* 42(3–4). 27–35. https://doi.org/10.5816/blackscholar.42.3-4.0027

Hioe, Brian. 2022. Bilingual 2030 rebrand still criticized. *New Bloom*. https://newbloommag.net/2022/07/25/bilingual-2030-rebrand/

Huang, Teng. 2012. Agents' social imagination: The 'invisible' hand of neoliberalism in Taiwan's curriculum reform. *International Journal of Educational Development* 32(1). 39–45. https://doi.org/10.1016/j.ijedudev.2010.11.006

Lee, I-Chia. 2022. Union urges overhaul of the Bilingual 2030 Policy. *Taipei Times*. https://www.taipeitimes.com/News/taiwan/archives/2022/07/05/2003781171

Lin, Shumin & Jouyi Wu. 2022. Transforming identities and ideologies: Creating translanguaging space with overseas Chinese students in Taiwan. *Taiwan Journal of TESOL* 19(1). 87–120. https://doi.org/10.30397/TJTESOL.202204_19(1).0004

Ke, I-Chung & Shumin Lin. 2017. A translanguaging approach to TESOL in Taiwan. *English Teaching & Learning* 41(1). 33–61. https://doi.org/10.6330/ETL.2017.41.1.02

Kiyota, Akiko. 2022. Problematizing fluent speakers' unintentional exclusion of emergent bilinguals: A case study of an English-medium instruction classroom in Japan. *International Journal of Literacy, Culture, and Language Education* 2. 6–19. https://doi.org/10.14434/ijlcle.v2iMay.34385

Kosinski, Michal, Sandra C. Matz, Samuel D. Gosling, Vesselin Popov & David Stillwell. 2015. Facebook as a research tool for the social sciences: Opportunities, challenges, ethical considerations, and practical guidelines. *American Psychologist* 70(6). 543–556.

National Development Council. 2018. *Blueprint for developing Taiwan into a bilingual nation by 2030*. https://bilingual.ndc.gov.tw/sites/bl4/files/news_event_docs/blueprint_for_developing_taiwan_into_a_bilingual_nation_by_2030.pdf

National Development Council. 2021. *Bilingual 2030*. https://www.ndc.gov.tw/en/Content_List.aspx?n=BF21AB4041BB5255&upn=9633B537E92778BB

Pentón Herrera, Luis Javier & Kisha C. Bryan. 2022. Language weaponization in society and education: Introduction to the special issue. *International Journal of Literacy, Culture, and Language Education* 2. 1–5. https://doi.org/10.14434/ijlcle.v2iMay.34380

Phillipson, Robert. 1992. *Linguistic imperialism*. Oxford, UK: Oxford University Press.

Rutherford, Camille. 2010. Using online social media to support Preservice student engagement. *MERLOT: Journal of Online Learning and Teaching* 6(4). 703–711. http://jolt.merlot.org/vol6no4/rutherford_1210.pdf

VanLier, Leo. 1988. *The classroom and the language learner: Ethnography and second language classroom research*. Longman.

Wu, Ming-Hsuan. 2011. Language planning and policy in Taiwan: Past Present, and future. Language Problems and Language Planning, 35(1), 15–34

Kisha C. Bryan, Daphne Germain, Mama Raouf, Susan Githua, and Renee Figuera

Chapter 4
The price we pay: An autobiographical dialogue of linguistic violence in the African diaspora

Abstract: Representing different geographical areas and languages of the African diaspora, we engage in an autobiographical dialogue to examine the role(s) that racism, colonization, and standard language ideologies have played in their personal, social, and professional lives. We share the extremely high mental, economic, and sociocultural price that Black peoples who speak minority or local languages have had to pay. In reflecting on our personal, collective experiences in school and in society, we turn sociological eyes on our own lives and reflect on the ways that languages have been weaponized and have forced us to: 1) negotiate the teaching, learning, and/or use of our mother tongue(s) alongside the dominant languages in our particular contexts and 2) defend our (linguistic) identities. We conclude by suggesting a framework that promotes the resistance of harmful language practices (i.e., language weaponization) and policies through the concept of 'Ujima,' or work towards the common good to resolve problems that plague our linguistic communities.

Keywords: African diaspora, Black English, language weaponization, linguistic violence

1 Introduction

From Kenya to Benin to the United States to the islands of the Caribbean, the legacy of colonization and racism is evidenced in contemporary language policies and practices. Language weaponization is not only a tool, but a long-term result

---

Kisha C. Bryan, Susan Githua, Tennessee State University
Daphne Germain, Boston Public Schools
Mama Raouf, Eastern Connecticut State University
Renee Figuera, University of the West Indies

of colonization. In this chapter that is focused on the African diaspora,[1] we use the term *language weaponization* to describe the process in which words, discourse, and language in any form have been used/are being used to inflict harm on others (Bryan & Gerald, 2020; Pascale, 2019; Pentón Herrera & Bryan, 2022). In this definition, the term *harm* is of vital importance because it refers to how minoritized individuals, such as Black people, are affected by ideologies and practices that normalize historical inequities and injustices in their environments.

We, the authors, each identifying as Black or of African descent, have a vested interest in the practices and policies that have both marginalized us as minority language speakers and have lauded us as 'the exceptions'—highly credentialed, multilingual, and multicultural language education professionals and advocates. We recognize that while we may have reached the 'promised land' of academia and K-12 administration, many of our brothers and sisters in the African diaspora are suffering due to the vestiges of colonization and modern-day linguistic discrimination. As such, we thought it important to shed light on past and present linguistic violence in the African diaspora by sharing our thoughts on:

- the ways that specific language(s) have been weaponized in our specific contexts within the African diaspora;
- the ramifications of language weaponization and/or linguistic violence;
- viable solutions with regard to language weaponization; and
- implications for (language or social) policy and practice.

Thus, in this autobiographical narrative, we seek to answer the following research questions: What are the ways that language has been weaponized across the African diaspora, and what are the implications for language policy and practice?

2 Theoretical framework

This work is situated in our collective belief that across the African diaspora, there are four interconnected indicators of language weaponization. We have coined these terms the *4 L's*, and briefly describe them here.

---

[1] The worldwide collection of communities descended from native Africans or people from Africa, predominantly in the Americas (Ajayi, 1998). The term most commonly refers to the descendants of the black West and Central Africans who were enslaved and shipped to the Americas via the Atlantic slave trade between the 16th and 19th centuries, with their largest populations in Brazil, the United States, and Haiti (in that order) (Warren, 1985).

2.1 Linguistic imperialism

Linguistic imperialism (Austin, 2022; Canagarajah, 1999) is a side effect of colonization and slavery. During the colonial period, European languages such as English, French, Portuguese, and Spanish were imposed on African societies and used as the medium of instruction in schools. This has led to the marginalization of African languages and the promotion of European languages as the preferred languages of communication, education, and governance. Yakpo (2016) explored the nexus between language policies and ideologies in the West African context, where ideological factors have played a disproportionately large role in consolidating lingering colonist attitudes about the unfitness of Indigenous and local languages to serve as mediums of communication in high-prestige domains.

2.2 Language hierarchies

Language hierarchies (Johnson & Johnson, 2021; Lippi-Green, 2012; Von Esch et al., 2020) are ultimately the result of linguistic imperialism. European languages (and the 'lucky' local languages favored by colonizers) have been given higher status leading to the creation of language hierarchies. This results in the domination of European and 'standard' languages in many domains of life and in major institutions such as schools, businesses, the media, and governments. As a consequence, local languages have been relegated to lower status, and their use is restricted to informal settings. In 2019, the Jamaican Language Unit (JLU) at the University of the West Indies became one of the first Caribbean nations to address linguistic apartheid by submitting a petition to the Office of the Prime Minister demanding the government take the necessary steps toward recognizing patois (Jamaican) as an official language alongside English. That was but one attempt to shake up the linguistic hierarchy of that country.

2.3 Language policy neglect

Many governments have neglected the development and promotion of local languages in their language policies. This has resulted in the lack of resources and opportunities for the development and use of these languages, further perpetuating their marginalization (Bamgbose, 2000; Samuelson & Freedman, 2010). Chebanne and Monaka (2023), address the consequences of a delayed language in education policy for locals who have been victimized by the weaponization of English and Setswana. In a statement that demanded justice for the speakers of

Black English, a 2020 special committee of the Conference on College Composition and Communication wrote:

> As an organization that proclaims "to apply the power of language and literacy to actively pursue justice and equity for all students and educators who serve them," we cannot claim that Black Lives Matter in our field if Black Language does not matter! We cannot say Black Lives Matter if decades of research on Black Language has not led to widespread systemic change in curricula, pedagogical practices, disciplinary discourses, research, language policies, professional organizations, programs, and institutions within and beyond academia! We cannot say that Black Lives Matter if Black Language is not at the forefront of our work as language educators and researchers! (Baker-Bell et al., 2020, para. 5)

Language policy neglect always leads to limited access to education and economics for entire groups of people.

2.4 Limited access to education and economics

The use of European and 'standard' languages as the medium of instruction has limited access to education for many in the African diaspora who do not speak these languages proficiently (Barrett et al., 2022). DeGraff (2017) highlights Haiti as one of few nations in which there is one single language spoken by all citizens (i.e., Haitian Creole), while the school system, by and large, does not use that language as the main language of instruction and examination. Instead, the formal school system in Haiti has traditionally used French as a medium of instruction. Lack of access to education reinforces existing inequalities and perpetuates the cycle of poverty and the underdevelopment of entire communities resulting in a permanent underclass.

In this chapter, the 4 L's of language weaponization (linguistic imperialism, language hierarchies, language policy neglect, and limited access) are echoed throughout our life experiences. While we embrace the 4 L's as our primary theoretical framework, we simultaneously highlight the need to 'shout out' critical race theory (CRT) to provide justification for the value of the counter-narratives that we share in this chapter. Counter-storytelling is a central tenet of (CRT). It allows for the sharing of personal experiences that challenge and disrupt existing power structures with the intention of promoting advocacy, social justice, and change (Cooper & Bryan, 2020; Crenshaw, 1991; Delgado & Stefanic, 2001; Ladson-Billings, 1995; Solorzano & Yosso, 2001).

3 Methodology: An autobiographical dialogue among ourselves

Using an autobiographical dialogue as a methodological lens, we—Kisha, Daphne, Mama, Susan, and Renee—turn sociological eyes on our own lives as we have had to negotiate our racial and/or immigrant identities, our mother tongues, and the dominant languages that we have encountered in classrooms and boardrooms. Through (un)structured discussions, reflective writings, and informal feedback sessions, we realize that as children of the African diaspora, we each have had first-hand experiences about and desire to share the social, economic, and cultural price we and the peoples of our communities have paid. As such, the goal of this work is to provide a space for diverse voices to highlight historical and contemporary language weaponization within the African diaspora. In the narratives that follow, we, in our unique ways, share who we are, the linguistic landscape of our 'home(s),' and the linguistic price we (and our peoples) have had to pay.

4 Part I: Our (linguistic) identities and positionalities

In this section, we describe our identities and positionalities.

4.1 Kisha

I am a multidialectal linguaphile. I am of Gullah Geechee heritage. I am also a Black American who is a descendant of enslaved Africans. As such, I speak the language of the Gullah peoples, Black English, African American Vernacular English (AAVE), Ebonics, or whatever modern-day term is used to describe the variety of English spoken by Blacks in the U.S. I have also mastered standard English—the language of those who enslaved my ancestors. I now revel in Gullah Geechee/AAVE pride and promote linguistic self-love amongst groups whose languages are marginalized. Having learned several other varieties of English (AAVE, some Spanish, and a few words in Kiswahili, Gullah Geechee is still the language I think, dream, and cry in (Bryan, 2020).

I am first-generation *everything*. My family, God, and the spirits of the ancestors were at the University of Florida in 2012 when my doctorate in Teaching English to Speakers of Other Languages (TESOL) and Bilingual Education was conferred. Ten years later, I am a tenured associate professor and currently serve as an administrator in the College of Education at a medium size, public, Historically Black College or University (HBCU) in the mid-south. I have served as an English Language Specialist for the U.S. Department of State and currently serve on the TESOL International Association Board of Directors. My identities and experiences have dictated my professional dispositions as well as my teaching philosophies and methodologies.

In U.S. boardrooms and in international spaces, I readily provide a voice to those who often go unheard as I promote linguistic and social justice for the purposes of diversity, equity, inclusion, and access. In the context of my classroom, I parallel my experiences learning 'standard' English as a second dialect to that of emergent bilinguals learning English. When I teach applied linguistics, I use examples from Gullah. When I teach TESOL methods courses, I discuss methods of teaching students who speak minoritized varieties of English (i.e., AAVE, Gullah, Caribbean Englishes). I share the ways that racism and hegemonic linguistic ideologies operate as two sides of the same coin within the English language teaching profession (Rosa, 2019).

4.2 Daphne

My name is Daphne Germain. When it comes to the importance of names, my name (i.e., Daphne) means 'victorious' and 'fruitful.' As a Haitian-born, naturalized American citizen, my Greek, and Anglo-based name gives you an indication that I am not your usual 'cup of coffee.' In regards to my identity, I fully embrace and celebrate myself as a Haitian, Black-bilingual diaspora, a descendant of those who survived the middle passage and claimed their independence in 1804. I am a born-again Christian, 4th generation Pastor's kid, and an ordained minister. I am a mom, wife, sister, educator, community advocate, and one who has chosen to live fully in every space in which I exist without apology. I am a lover of humanity, language, and history.

In my experience being raised as a Black, bilingual immigrant in Boston and having worked in the educational, corporate, and religious sectors, the weaponization of language is something that I experience daily as a woman, parent, immigrant, and educational professional who does not recoil from the challenges of affirming my value in all spaces. That in of itself comes with many emotional strifes. As a black woman in the U.S., I affirm my identities even when I am not celebrated, nor my name is called when I have accomplished major feats. I support and promote work for inclusion and equity. I stand daily against the headwinds of bias because my light is needed for generations who may never know my name.

4.3 Mama

I am a native of Benin, a French-speaking country in West Africa. I speak five languages, two of which are my mother tongues: Fon and Yoruba. The other three languages are French, English, and Spanish. French is the official language in Benin, and I started learning it when I began my elementary school education at the age of six. English is the second most widely spoken foreign language in Benin after French. I started learning it when I entered secondary school at fourteen years of age. I decided to learn Spanish in my mid-thirties when I was contemplating applying for a job as a translator at the United Nations (UN). The reason why I am a college professor of English today and not a translator at the UN is that my command of the Spanish language was not good enough for me to pass the United Nations' recruitment exam for translators in 1992.

My identity as a writer and professor of English composition and literature and a writer has been determined not only by my introduction to English in secondary school and my love of the language but also, and more importantly, by my being a highly successful learner of it throughout my secondary school and college years; nor would I have made it through elementary or secondary school if I had not had a facility with the French language. The great paradox at the heart of my identity as a Beninese college professor of English teaching at an American university and as an award-winning writer both in French and in English, however, is that I am illiterate in both Fon and Yoruba, my mother tongues; and I can neither read nor write in my mother tongues through no fault of my own. The fault lies with Benin's colonial and post-colonial educational system, which has excluded the teaching of Beninese Indigenous languages from the curriculum and made the command of French, English, Spanish, and German the passport to gainful employment and professional advancement. I derive little consolation from my ability to tell stories professionally both in Fon and in Yoruba, for my mother, my aunt, and most of the storytellers of my childhood could do the same, though they could speak no word of French or English, let alone read or write in either language.

4.4 Susan

I am Kenyan. I am a black African woman of Kikuyu descent. I was born in central Kenya, and I speak three languages fluently: Kikuyu, Swahili, and English. Kikuyu is my first language, my mother tongue. This is the language everyone spoke when I was growing up. Throughout my primary school years, we spoke Kikuyu. At the lower primary level, the three languages (i.e. Kikuyu, Swahili, and English) were taught and used for instruction. However, this changed in upper primary and secondary school when Kikuyu was no longer taught. Swahili is my second language which I learned at school. Although both Swahili and English are taught in school at the same time, I learned Swahili before English, as is the case with most Kenyans. In high school, I learned to speak in English as it was a requirement. This stuck with me in college and even after, as English is my default language when I interact with my former high schoolmates even today. After undergraduate school, I worked in Eastern Kenya for nine years. The residents spoke Kikamba, and I learned basic Kikamba to help me navigate.

About 10 years ago, I moved to the United States. This move had a great impact on my and my family's spoken languages. My first-born daughter was five years old when we came to the U.S. and she could speak Swahili fluently. Swahili was her first language. According to our culture, my children are not considered to be from my tribe Kikuyu. They belong to their father's tribe. They are Ameru. Due to this reason, they did not learn Kikuyu. Over the years, although she understands Swahili, she speaks with a lot of difficulty. When young Kenyan children migrate to America, they forget Swahili because it is only spoken at home, and they spend most of their time at school. There is also pressure to perfect their spoken English to be able to communicate well with their peers. Disuse of Swahili lowers their proficiency in speaking and also impacts their identities as Kenyan.

4.5 Renee

I am the product of diverse national and cultural ethnicities within the Latin American and Caribbean region, so I see myself as an educator who has been molded by diversity. The primary ethnicities that have shaped my social consciousness include Afro-Caribbean, Venezuelan (Mestizo), Garifuna (Black Carib), Dominican, and St. Vincentian, nationalities from which French-Creole ethnicities have been derived. Since my ancestry stretches across part of the Caribbean archipelago, even to the African continent in Nigeria, I feel a sense of responsibility to be culturally authentic when speaking about the Caribbean and teaching and learning experiences in the Caribbean, or elsewhere where the Caribbean diaspora might be present. I speak an English-based Creole, English, and some French-Lexicon Creole because of my maternal grandparents, and have been exposed to Hindi because of my primary school experience. I learned French and Spanish at the age of 12 and pursued these as foreign languages at university, later becoming a teacher of modern languages and leveraging English, French, and Spanish, as European Languages for employment and professional activities, in local and international contexts.

I consider myself to be Creole-speaking but not necessarily Creole-predominant. I say this because my maternal grandparents were French-lexicon Creole speakers, and therefore, English-lexicon Creole would have been their next most comfortable language, after their home language. Because my parents were government officers, worked shifts, or were posted to work some distance from home, I spent many childhood days with my grandparents imbibing songs, stories, and proverbial wisdom. They did not speak French-lexicon Creole to us but around us. However, my mother insisted on English-only in the house, which really meant speaking in English when addressing her, as she did not censure my interaction with my sibling, except that we were within her earshot. I also went to a Hindu primary school, where Hindi was the ceremonial language, but the school prided itself otherwise on its academic reputation, good teaching, and the development of oratory skills in academic English. I have wondered if this is why I have always had strong oral skills in foreign languages, but would take a longer time to settle down to write or to compose academic papers.

5 Part II: The linguistic landscape of "home"

In this section, we describe the linguistic landscape of our homes. Home for each of us has a different meaning. Some of us are transnationals, while others were born and currently reside in the U.S.

5.1 Kisha

While I feel like I am a native of the world, I was born on St. Helena Island, South Carolina, U.S.A. St. Helena Island has a land area of about 64 square miles (170 km^2) and a population of 11,032 (U.S. Census, 2020). It is included as part of the Hilton Head Island-Beaufort County Micropolitan Area. The island is renowned for its rural Lowcountry character and being a major center of African-American Gullah Geechee culture and language. St. Helena Island is located in the Gullah Geechee Corridor (Figure 4.1). Gullah Geechee is a language of persistence, survival, and the link to the

Figure 4.1: Gullah Geechee Cultural Heritage Corridor Map.

African ancestry of the vast majority of Black people in the United States. In all of its beauty, its creation is shrouded in the country's ultimate sin—chattel slavery. Enslaved Africans from a variety of Central and West African ethnic groups developed this English-based creole that has helped preserve much of our linguistic and cultural heritage. Because of significant periods of relative isolation from whites, the language has remained one of the most beautiful indicators of Black life and culture on the Sea Islands. In the context of the U.S., Gullah stands in the shadows of African American Vernacular English (AAVE), commonly spoken and taught foreign languages (e.g., Spanish, French, Chinese, Arabic, etc.) and mainstream American English.

5.2 Daphne

There is much that has been written about the linguistic landscape of Haiti, as the first black republic of enslaved individuals who gained their independence. The

Haitian community is a polyglot community. In Haiti, the language of the people is Kreyol,[2] a French-based language influenced by various African tongues, Spanish, and English. It is a language born out of the resistance of enslaved people who, as early as the 1750s, began publishing texts and literature using Haitian Kreyol (Library of Congress, 2023). Today, students are formally taught French and Kreyol, but the journey to acknowledge the language of the masses in itself is another revolution against colonial and racist ideologies. Due to global economic opportunities, you will also find that many people in Haiti study English, Spanish and, in more privileged quarters, Chinese as they leverage language as a means to escape the continued instability that plagues the nation.

In the U.S. American diaspora, Kreyol was used in the 1980s as part of a formalized bilingual program to support immigrant students (Cerat, 2011). When my parents and I immigrated to Boston, the Boston Public Schools had already established a Haitian-based 2-year transitional bilingual program where our teachers spoke to us in Haitian Kreyol while we developed our language skills in English. Over time, many of these programs were phased out due to various political battles on English-only instructions for foreigners and anti-immigrant xenophobic biases played out within the public education institutions. Currently, Boston's Haitian-based programs are found in limited schools while the community has been able to leverage the political economic disposition for bilingual education to open and sustain the first in the nation Haitian dual language program.

5.3 Mama

Benin, a former French colony of about twelve million people, is a patchwork of linguistic communities comprising nearly fifty languages. The largest linguistic communities are the Fon (26%), the Yoruba (16%), the Bariba (14%), the Goun (10%), the Adja (8%), and the Aizo (7%). When Benin achieved independence in 1960 (it used to be called Dahomey then), the question of which of its Indigenous languages should be elevated to the status of official language and serve as the language of instruction, commerce, and diplomacy was a subject of lively and profoundly divisive debate. In the absence of any national consensus, French was adopted as a compromise solution. It is a matter of shame and great sadness to me that the vast majority of educated Beninese, especially the younger genera-

---

2 "Creole" and "Kreyol" are used interchangeably to refer to a group of languages that developed from a combination of different languages, usually as a result of colonialism or slavery. Creole, spelled with a "C" is often used to refer to English-based Creoles, where the version spelled with "K" usually refers to French-based Kreyols (DeGraff, 2007).

tions, speak French better than their mother tongues, and many make a point of ensuring that their children speak only French at home.

5.4 Susan

Kenya is a country located in East Africa, bordered by Tanzania to the south, Uganda to the west, South Sudan to the northwest, Ethiopia to the north, and Somalia to the east (see Figure 4.2). The country has two official languages: English and Swahili, with English being the language of government, education, and business.

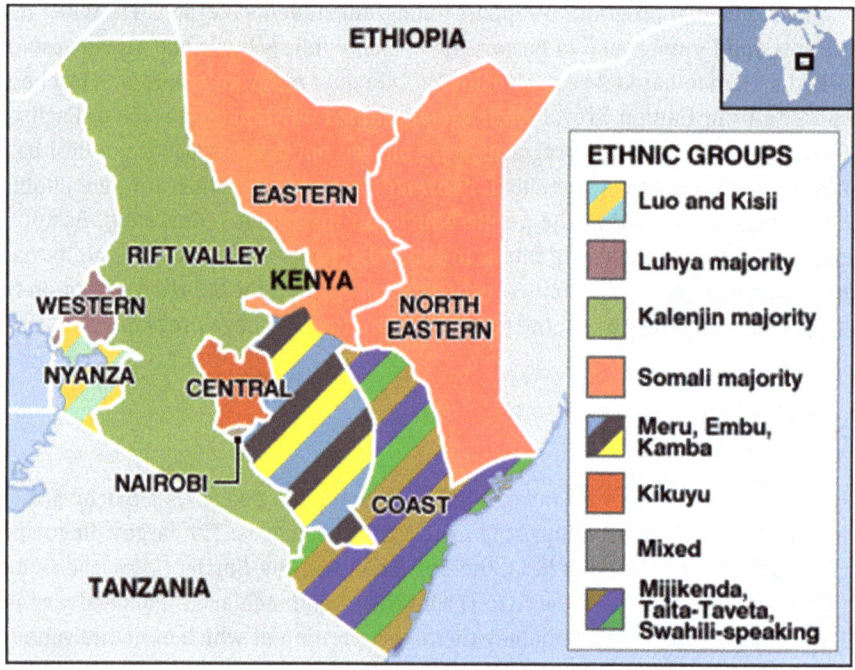

Figure 4.2: Kenyan Ethnic Distribution Map.
Source: Researchgate (Nathern S. A. Okilwa)

Kenya is a very linguistically diverse country, reflecting the country's multicultural heritage. In Kenya, one's geographical location or place of origin determines their ethnicity (tribe) and, in turn, their first language. However, there are more than 60 Indigenous languages spoken in Kenya, with Swahili and the Bantu language family being the most widely spoken. Both English and Swahili are taught as subjects in schools and used in news media, radio, and TV. Kenyans refer to their language as Kiswahili.

In Kenya, advertisements (e.g., billboards) are predominantly in English. Kenya is the regional business hub in East Africa. It also hosts the headquarters of global organizations such as the United Nations (UN), which may explain the use of English. The English language is widely spoken in urban Kenya (major towns and cities), and Sheng (slang) is often used as a marketing strategy to attract the youth. Advertisements targeting young people are now using Sheng (a mix of Swahili, Indigenous languages, and English). Outside of the capital city of Nairobi, some advertisements (very few compared to those in English) are in local languages.

5.5 Renee

The language of British colonizers, with its longest-standing influence, had the greatest prestige over the languages of the First Peoples, African languages of slaves and ex-slaves, the hybrid languages of their descendants, including French-lexicon and English-lexicon Creoles, and the languages of other diverse ethnic groups, who were designated indentured workers, and were speakers of Chinese, Arabic, Bhojpuri, among others. In Trinidad and Tobago, English is the official language, and it was effectively applied as a tool of colonization and control in the former colony of Trinidad. That was perhaps deemed 'unruly' because of Spanish aspirants to executive power, then, French-Creole members of influence, on invitation by the Spanish, and eventually, British colonizers in the 18th century. Hence, the English language served to neutralize a diverse linguistic landscape in Trinidad and Tobago through an anglicization policy in primary education beginning in 1851. London (2003) notes that all Indigenous languages effectively became defunct and that viable alternatives to English no longer existed. However, varieties of English-lexicon Creole and French-lexicon Creole, to a lesser extent, persisted in the community.

6 Part III: The (linguistic) price we've had to pay

In this section, the authors share their experiences with various forms of language weaponization and briefly discuss how it has impacted them and their families.

6.1 Kisha

It is traumatizing and extremely difficult to quantify the price that Black Americans have had to pay as a result of language weaponization. If we reflect back on the transatlantic slave trade, there were successful efforts to suppress African culture and prevent communication among enslaved Africans. Slave owners often imposed bans on the use of African languages and intentionally separated enslaved Africans who spoke the same language, making it difficult for them to organize resistance. After the emancipation proclamation, there were still laws that prohibited the descendants of slaves to receive a proper education. Jim Crow laws, preceded by the transatlantic slave trade, left millions of African Americans without a proper education and without definitive language and cultural histories beyond what can be documented in the geographical U.S. There is no amount of compensation or reparations that can remedy this loss.

The magnitude of this loss continues into the present. Gullah (and some would argue AAVE as well) was born out of the injustices of slavery. Yet, the language was described as lazy, uneducated, bastardized English. In his classic treatise, Africanisms in the Gullah Dialect, Lorenzo Dow Turner (1949) sought to dismantle beliefs that Gullah was a bastardized language with no linguistic value and demonstrated that it drew important linguistic features directly from the languages of West Africa. My metalinguistic awareness was developed early on. I figured out what was different about the Gullah language and culture, how to explain who we are, and how to counter people's beliefs about our identities and abilities based on the language(s) I speak. Most Gullah speakers agree that as soon as we open our mouths (even when speaking a more "standardized" variety), Black and whites alike hear the intonation of our speech and question our linguistic identities (and sometimes our ability to think).

I believe that it was during my high school years that I became fully aware of just how different (and beautiful) the Gullah language is. It was also during that time that I became fully aware of what W.E.B. DuBois termed double consciousness (DuBois, 1998). Dubois described it as

> a peculiar sensation . . . this sense of always looking at one's self through the eyes of others, of measuring one's soul by the tape of a world that looks on in amused contempt and pity. One feels his two-ness,—an American, a Negro [for me, a Gullah Geechee]; two souls, two thoughts, two unreconciled strivings; two warring ideals in one dark body, whose dogged strength alone keeps it from being torn asunder. (DuBois, 1897, para. 2)

I was a high-achieving student who had a broad social circle, but it became quite evident that students like me were not the standard bearers of language. I quickly realized that if I were to be successful, I had to be able to effectively use the language of the dominant group—the language of power, the language of oppression.

By the time I graduated from high school, language had really become a site of internal struggle. I embraced my Gullah identity; however, just the thought of going away to college put me on edge. I dreaded being in a context that valued a prescriptive standard and stigmatized varieties based on the extent to which they vary from that standard. While I was accepted at several predominantly white institutions within and outside the state, I decided to attend a small historically Black college in rural South Carolina, where I majored in English. The college was like being in Black language heaven. There were the Gullah/Geechees from Charleston, S.C., and other areas along the Gullah Geechee Corridor (see Figure 4.1), Black students from other states who spoke AAVE and varieties closer to the 'standard,' and international students from several countries in Africa. My goal back then was not to learn about the classics of English literature or to become a writer as it was with many of my peers. I simply wanted to speak English better. So, while I loved my home language, I had already internalized standard language ideologies (Lippi-Green, 2012) that placed 'standardized' English at the top of the hierarchy and Gullah at the very bottom (even below AAVE).

During my college years, I started to think back to the ways in which people in my community who could speak the 'standard' were selected to read the church announcements, take the lead in plays, or explain the views of the entire group. These were the people who seemed to have (linguistic) power in the community. While I did not realize it at the time, it was through watching these cultural/linguistic brokers that I saw the need to be bidialectal. I also thought about how entire communities unknowingly internalize and promote harmful linguistic ideologies. Because of my linguistic experiences, my senior thesis project was one of reconciliation, one that I thought would highlight the beauty of the Gullah language and its people, call out linguistic injustices, and set me on the path to (linguistic) self-love.

As I embarked on my language education journey in academia, my eyes are now open to the price that the newer generations of African Americans in the diaspora continue to pay (without their knowledge) when it comes to opportunities in language education. Black students are not provided equal opportunities to dual language education programs, nor are they provided opportunities for access to culturally and historically responsive education programming. Palmer (2010) suggested that dual language programs functions as white supremacy as "spaces in these programs are coveted by white community members, and the lottery system and other admissions processes operate in such a way as to make it very difficult for African-American children to gain entrance" (p. 98). Furthermore, an examination of dual language programs across the U.S., even in areas where there are large populations of immigrants from the African diaspora and African Americans, reveals that there are few programs that promote the learning of African languages.

6.2 Daphne

Internally within the community, though Kreyol is the language that connects the diaspora across continents and generations, there are still those indoctrinated within the French-based system who resist globalization and economic opportunity in promoting Kreyol as a viable international language. In the implementation of one of the first in the nation Haitian dual language programs, there was internal resistance in the community as the French versus Kreyol battle continued (Mathewson, 2017). The concern was which language would be more appealing to English or affluent families, who are the backbone of successful dual language programs. Comments were made by educators to the community about whether the Kreyol had enough educational material to support rigorous academic instruction as required in an English-based curriculum as a way to discourage the community from wanting this program. As the 1st cohort of students has taken the annual state exam, the work of a committed staff, community, and the capacity of a diverse student population has demonstrated that Kreyol is a viable language of instruction for all.

As a bilingual immigrant in the professional, educational setting, I have experienced intimidation, marginalization, and minimization by those who questioned my intellectual capacity because I am an immigrant. I have had colleagues attempt to publicly correct my grammar or word choice as a way to give themselves the upper hand in meetings because my command of the English language may not be as masterful as they perceive themselves to be. I have had colleagues reference my place of birth as a reason why they doubt my capacity to be a strategic thinker and partner in various projects. As a community advocate, I have observed language used to diminish access to rights, services, and support for parents so that they are not informed partners in the educational journey of their children. Further, I have observed decisions being made by those who identify as being privileged that are counter to the needs of parents' and families' desire and request for a bilingual instructional experience for their child.

6.3 Mama

When French was chosen as the official language in 1960, it was hailed as a happy compromise, a sweet antidote to the threat of inter-ethnic strife and bloodletting looming ever larger around the vexed question of which of the country's numerous languages should be declared the official language. On the evidence of the state of affairs in Benin over more than sixty years of independence, however, it stands to reason that what was once perceived as a 'happy compromise' was, in fact, a poisoned chalice that stunted the growth of Benin's Indigenous languages, prevented the emergence of authentic Indigenous literatures, fostered cultural alienation, and made a mockery of the country's independence.

More than 60 years after independence, Benin has yet to set up a fully-fledged center for the promotion of its Indigenous languages. Not a single university in the country boasts a department dedicated to the teaching of Indigenous languages or the promotion of research and writing in any of those languages. Nigeria, Benin's English-speaking next-door neighbor, has a flourishing Indigenous literature in Yoruba, Hausa, Ibo, and other languages. Writers like Daniel Fagunwa, author of The Forest of a Thousand Daemons, and Amos Tutuola, who wrote The Palm-Wine Drinkard, have helped make the Yoruba language and Yoruba works of literature a subject of study not only in Nigeria but also in the US, the UK, Canada, and other Western countries. Benin has yet to grow her Fungunwas and her Tutuolas, and one would search the Beninese literary or cultural landscape in vain for Benin's equivalents of The Forest of a Thousand Demons and The Palm-Wine Drinkard. Like a time bomb, the adoption of French as the official language in Benin has destroyed the country's ability to develop her native languages and stimulate the emergence of writers in those languages.

Perhaps the most brutalizing aspect of the weaponization of the French language in Benin is the notorious so-called signal commonly represented by a small turtle shell, a chicken bone—some sort of bogey calculated to strike terror into the heart of any schoolboy or schoolgirl caught speaking his/her mother tongue or any other so-called vernacular instead of French at school. Anyone who was handed the signal knew he/she was in for harsh corporal punishment and must do everything possible to pass it on to someone else before the teacher asked the much-dreaded question, "who has got the signal"?

That question resulted in the naming of all those through whose hands the signal had passed since the last time the same question had been asked. Everyone who had received the signal in that time period would endure severe corporal punishment in the form of caning, flogging, or birching, but whoever had got the signal last of all would be beaten the most severely. Whole generations of Beninese who entered elementary school in the run-up to independence or in the first ten to twenty years following independence were marked by personal experiences of receiving the signal at one time or another in the course of their schooling. Many harbor harrowing memories of punishments meted out to them simply because they were caught speaking their mother tongues at school. As a persistent recidivist with a penchant for speaking Fon and Yoruba in the precincts of the school, I was beaten by the teacher more often and more severely than most. To this day, I bear on the back of my right hand a scar to show for it.

The signal stands as a symbol of the weaponization of the French language against the Beninese people by the colonial power. In so far as Beninese schoolboys and schoolgirls were severely chastised for speaking any Indigenous languages at school; however, the signal also symbolizes the weaponization of Indigenous Beninese languages against the Beninese people as part of the French colonial power's plot to undermine the Beninese people's sense of identity and compromise the chances of Benin becoming a truly independent nation.

The ramifications of the weaponization of French in the Beninese context are multiform and multi-dimensional. The *signal*, for example, and the urge to get rid of it at all costs in order either to avoid punishment altogether or to avoid the kind of punishment reserved for whoever had the *signal* when the dreaded question was asked—who has got the *signal*?—made many victims turn traitor to friends and comrades or stoop to immoral practices. I, for one, had been tricked again and again into speaking Fon or Yoruba by boys and girls I trusted who were desperate to get the *signal* off their hands. And I remember with a great sense of shame how I was driven to steal money from my mother's piggy bank to pay or bribe whoever had handed me the *signal* so he or she could take it back and seek out another potential offender.

The *signal* also quelled in countless generations of Beninese schoolboys and schoolgirls the impulse to embrace and cherish their mother tongues. It also made them complicit in the ill-judged attempt to bring them to sound and behave like black replicas of French schoolboys and schoolgirls. And the brainwashing of entire generations of Beninese children resulted in much of Benin's educated population being illiterate in their own mother tongues and believing that the more they distanced themselves from their own mother tongues and cultures and the more they imitated the French, the more civilized they would be. The erroneous belief by many of my fellow Beninese that the more they imitate the French, the more they will resemble the French flies in the face of a warning, sounded long ago by one of Africa's greatest writers and thinkers, Seidou Badian—"Staying submerged under water won't turn the trunk of a tree into a crocodile." And this erroneous belief inevitably leads those who hold it to internalize racism, which makes the task of mental reeducation and decolonization all the more urgent.

Wordsworth got it absolutely right when he said that "the child is father of the man" (Wordsworth, 1807). The weaponization of the French language in the schooling of Beninese children has resulted in the cultural alienation of the majority of the educated elite of the country, who are unable to fully function in the Indigenous languages. And so long as the educated elite of the country remains culturally alienated, Benin will remain a backward country unable to leverage her cultural heritage and the knowledge and wisdom of the ancestors in breaking the shackles of economic, political, and intellectual dependence and pull her weight in the concert of nations.

6.4 Susan

Like in many countries around the world, and especially in multilingual societies, language has been used to discriminate against or marginalize certain groups of people. Language has been used as a weapon in various ways in the Kenyan context, often in the form of linguistic discrimination, marginalization, and even violence. During the colonial period, English was imposed as the official language in Kenya, which marginalized and oppressed the local languages and cultures. This policy favored the English-speaking elite and discriminated against those who spoke local languages.

Ethnic and tribal divisions have been a source of tension and violence in Kenya, and language has often been used as a means of exacerbating these divisions. For example, political leaders have been known to use derogatory language to refer to other tribes or languages, which can lead to violence and discrimination. The use of insulting language is prevalent among politicians. They use emotive language to polarize the country to meet their objectives. For example, Central Kenya politicians refer to people from certain regions as ihîî (derogatory for uncircumcised men), conveying the message that they are boys (not adult men). During the last elections in 2022, language was used to cast some politicians as dynasties and others as hustlers. Kenyans fell into either camp. Such labels cause divisiveness in the country. Among social media users, there is a common Swahili phrase, ogopa wanawake (fear women). The phrase is used to warn men against trusting women, and there are concerns that this and other similar phrases are causing weak-minded young men to act violently toward women, thus increasing the number of gender-based violence cases in Kenya.

The language used in schools and other educational institutions has also been a source of linguistic discrimination. In Kenya, English is the examination language and is used as the medium of instruction in schools, and students who do not speak English as their first language may be at a disadvantage. The emphasis is usually at the high school level because students are expected to have mastered English well enough to speak fluently. In fact, some schools have language policies, and students are expected to speak English Monday through Thursday and only speak Swahili on Fridays. This was the case in my high school. Those who did not observe the policy would be punished. They would be sent home, and upon returning to school, they were expected to buy and read English storybooks.

Furthermore, the media has also been a source of linguistic discrimination in Kenya. For example, English-language media outlets may not provide coverage or representation of local languages and cultures, which can contribute to the marginalization of these groups. However, there has been a rise in media houses or agencies that are tasked with creating advertising campaigns for different local languages. In some instances, these media houses have been blamed for fueling tribal hatred and violence.

Finally, language weaponization in Kenya has detrimental effects on the social class of citizens who have not had the opportunity (or desire) to become proficient in English. Kenya has a growing economy, and many companies operating in the country require employees to be proficient in English. As such, there is a strong correlation between English proficiency and economic advantage, as proficiency in English is often seen as a key factor in securing better-paying jobs and accessing higher education opportunities (Orwenjo, 2021; Wekesa, 2020). This leaves Kenyans who do not speak English at an economic and social disadvantage.

6.5 Renee

Misgivings about the literary and linguistic integrity of local writers, during the late 19th century, came about because many Trinidad and Tobago citizens spoke French-lexicon Creole in this period, and many early calypsos were also sung in French-lexicon Creole. Evidence of linguicism could be gleaned from the prefaces of novellas in Trinidad and Tobago, which were journalized in early 19th and 20th century newspapers. These early literary works not only indexed a self-conscious writing style among the colored, educated middle-class as a result, but motivated the demonstration of respectability and good-breeding, resulting from education, in their writing. The British also used the law to regulate the creation of newspapers as potential outlets of political and literary expression among non-white classes and non-British ethnicities. Roger Cave alluded to seventeen newspapers by non-whites which were significantly reduced by censorship. In this context, a newspaper publication was considered to be unlawful unless an affidavit was made and a bond of £200, plus two or more securities be entered into (Ordinance

No. 13 of 1853); moreover, they had to be published at intervals not exceeding 26 days. This attests to how the legislative apparatus was invoked to regulate language, journalism, cultural ideology, and the cultural uptake of literature from local colored authors and writers.

The impact of linguicism was also felt within the civil service as writing exams in English became an institutionalized part of becoming a white-collar professional under the British administration of the civil service, preceding Trinidad and Tobago's independence in 1962. Civil service examinations still remain an entrenched rite of passage for those aspiring to executive posts in centralized government, to this day, especially for officers in the foreign service, and Permanent Secretaries who preside over the financial disbursements of various government ministries. Any attitudes of interrogation or regimentation that persist towards language choice, today, would come from middle-class aloofness that denies the reality that medium English-lexicon Creole varieties co-occur alongside a standard Trinidadian English variety in most community spaces. In tandem, with this attitude of linguicism has emerged a trickster-wordsmith-orator in the orature of Trinidad and Tobago, and in the carnivalesque arts of Midnight Robbers, Pierrot Grenades, and Brer (Brother) Anansi-s, that have been subverting vestiges of colonial education by perfecting speech-making, creative orthography, mnemonics, and counternarration as a trait of our linguaculture. Anecdotes and stories about West Indian alter-egos with superior intelligence could also be found among Johnny Bobo in Anguilla; Ozzie Moore in Barbados; Sensible Bill and Stupidy Bill and Balgobin Stories in Guyana, and Bobo Johnny in St. Kitts and Nevis, although these may be less known among contemporary youth.

On the other hand, there is a greater acceptance of code-mixing, which is part of the modern Trinbagonian communication style, without conscious acknowledgment of separateness between medium varieties of the English-lexicon Creole and Standard English. Parliamentarians would insist that English is the language of debate and representation of politics, yet many use Creole varieties for pragmatic purposes of emphasis (Alexis & Singh, 2014). No university-educated Trinbagonian, of any ethnicity, would claim monolectal English as their linguistic identity. In addition, educated citizens have become masters of accommodating to communication contexts where English or English-lexicon Creole may be required predominantly, in academic and community spaces, even while the society has grown more accepting of mixed codes.

Within the school system, English-as-a-mother-tongue pedagogies still persist, as a carry-over from the colonial period, although the ineffectiveness of this method of instruction has been correlated to declining proficiency in Caribbean English examinations (London, 2003). Monolectal attitudes to English Language instruction greatly impact students in rural and coastal areas of Trinidad, where there may be a lack of localized expertise in language education pedagogies, despite a culturally prolific environment of the arts, orature, and sports (Foote, 2007). Foote (2007) remarks on the range of skills/talents in the school-age population, oriented towards creative arts, sports, science, literary fields, and modern studies, in a one-sided system that does not actively cultivate these talents, but still panders to examinations and written competence. Moreover, anglicization by education has relegated English to a subject that does not necessarily require professionalization, in order to be taught within the school system. Indeed, the expectations of mother- tongue pedagogies still persist to debar or admit school age students, with no clear-cut governmental policy on language education, save for the recommendation of linguists (Robertson 2010).

7 Part IV: Concluding discussion: Seeking linguistic justice

Our stories are evidence of the ways that language is weaponized in global contexts, including the African diaspora. With the use of Black Englishes, Gullah, and (Haitian) Kreyol in the U.S. context, to the minority languages of Benin and Kenya, we see that linguistic imperialism, colonization, and slavery undeniably result in language weaponization. When language hierarchies are formed and reinforced by governments and other systems, language policies favor the local majority and colonial foreign languages such as English and French. This places the speakers of minoritized languages in a precarious situation. As with the case in Benin, the *signal* was a physical mark of linguistic inferiority that was used in schools to force (and physically cause harm to) children to ignore their mother tongues and use French at all times. In Haiti and the U.S., the journey to acknowledge Kreyol is a site of continuous struggle and revolution against colonial and racist ideologies. A so-called 'standard' English continues to plague Black Americans who speak Black English varieties like Gullah and AAVE. Finally, in Kenya, a lack of proficiency in English results in economic disadvantages and fewer social and professional opportunities.

In our discussions about what can be done to stem the tide of language weaponization, we continued to come back to ujima—the importance of individuals working together for the common good of the community. The term *ujima* comes from the Swahili language and is associated with the idea of participatory democracy, where all members of a community have a voice in the decision-making process. Furthermore, it emphasizes the importance of mutual support and collaboration as individuals come together to address common challenges. For us, ujima is a collective call for citizens, leaders, policymakers, and stakeholders across the African diaspora to seek and demand linguistic justice. We believe that the battle to undo the damage that has been done begins with the decolonization of the mind, an approach the great Kenyan novelist Ngugi Wa Thiong'o advocated in his book entitled *Decolonizing the Mind* (Wa Thiong'o, 2018).

Mama suggests that for anyone committed to changing the current position of Benin for the better, it is obvious that the inferiority complex most educated Beninese feel consciously or unconsciously regarding France and the French strikes at the very root of their sense of belonging and their cultural identity. He can think of no better antidote to that inferiority complex than the decolonization of the minds of those afflicted by it. As part of the mental decolonization of the Beninese people, they must be taught, to paraphrase Chinua Achebe in his essay entitled *The Novelist as a Teacher* (1975), that their ancestors' lives were not a long night of savagery out of which the white man, acting on God's behalf, dragged them; that Africans had a highly developed culture with customs and traditions which gave them a sense of belonging and served them as a moral compass on their journey through history. Victory is inconceivable without the creation throughout the country of centers, institutes, and university departments dedicated to research in Benin's cultural heritage and the teaching and promotion of Benin's native languages, Indigenous literatures, and folktale traditions.

Kisha and **Susan**, in collaboration with **Renee**, suggest that there can be no reconciliation without acknowledgment of inequities and injustices that result from historical acts of language weaponization. To move forward, there must be grassroots attempts to undo what colonization and white supremacist thought have done to language education policies, practices, and programming. Black people around the world have a right to their language(s), and Black linguistic justice should be at the forefront of school and language education reform in African diasporic contexts. They stand in solidarity with language and literacy experts who suggest that African diasporic literacy situated in schools have the possibility of "challenging and critiquing social and equity issues while building the racial and ethnic uplifting of people who are often on the margins in society" (Boutte et al., 2017, p. 68).

Daphne suggests that in our time, we have the capacity to own our narrative as a community. What worked in the establishment of the Haitian dual language program in Boston that promotes Kreyol was a resistance to be defined within the structures of the hegemony. While the data did not indicate that there would be large numbers of students nor was the Haitian-American community 100% aligned with Kreyol as the language of instruction, the community continued to press on. Entrenched language ideologies were an internal community matter. In spite of the challenges, leaders in the community still demanded that the school district collaborate to establish a way forward, as the Haitian-American community resolved their internal debate. Daphne suggests that ujima can be put into practice by doing the following: (1) Always refuse to be silenced—continue to speak up, even when others interrupt rudely to correct your language use; (2) continue to show up in spaces others do not expect, even when you are refused access to the table, builds your own; and (3) Know your "why" for the fight. It is great to have allies and co-conspirators, but many times, it is your integrity in the fight that will make the difference. Dare to shine your light and be the change.

References

Achebe, Chinua. 1975. *Morning yet on creation day: Essays*. Albany, NY: Anchor Press.
Austin, Tasha. 2022. Linguistic imperialism: Countering anti Black racism in world language teacher preparation. *Journal for Multicultural Education* 16(3). 246–258. https://doi.org/10.1108/JME-12-2021-0234
Baker-Bell, April. 2020. *Linguistic justice: Black language, literacy, identity, and pedagogy*. New York, NY: Routledge.
Baker-Bell, April, Bonnie J. Williams-Farrier, Davena Jackson, Lamar Johnson, Carmen Kynard & Teaira McMurtry. 2020. *This ain't another statement! This is a demand for Black linguistic justice!* Conference on College Composition and Communication. https://cccc.ncte.org/cccc/demand-for-black-linguistic-justice
Bamgboṣe, Ayọ. 2000. *Language and exclusion: The consequences of language policies in Africa*. Hamburg, Germany: LIT Verlag Münster.
Barrett, Rusty, Jennifer Cramer & Kevin B. McGowan. 2022. *English with an accent: Language, ideology, and discrimination in the United States* (3rd ed.). New York, NY: Taylor & Francis.
Boutte, Gloria, George L. Johnson, Kamania Wynter-Hoyte & U. E. Uyoata. 2017. Using African diaspora literacy to heal and restore the souls of young black children. *International Critical Childhood Policy Studies Journal* 6(1). 66–79.
Bryan, Kisha. 2020. On being Gullah Geechee: A story of identity reconciliation and linguistic self-love. Mosaic Newsletter. NYTESOL Summer 2020.
Bryan, Kisha C. & J. P. B. Gerald. 2020. The Weaponization of English. *Language Magazine*, 1–8. https://www.languagemagazine.com/2020/08/17/the-weaponization-of-english/
Bryan, Kisha, Mary Romney-Schaab & Ayanna Cooper. 2022. The Illusion of inclusion: Blackness in ELT. *The CATESOL Journal* 33(1). 1–13.
Canagarajah, A. Suresh. 1999. *Resisting linguistic imperialism in English teaching*. Oxford, UK: Oxford University Press.
Cerat, Marie Lily. 2011. Myths and realities: A history of Haitian Creole language programs in New York City. *Journal of Haitian Studies* 17(2). 73–91.
Cooper, Ayanna & Kisha C. Bryan. 2020. Reading, writing, and race: Sharing the narratives of Black TESOL professionals. In Kristen Lindahl & Bedrettin Yazan (eds.) *In-service language teacher identities, pedagogies, and practices*, 190–201. New York, NY: Routledge.

Crenshaw, Kimberlé W. 1998. Race, reform, and retrenchment: Transformation and legitimation in antidiscrimination law. *Harvard Law Review* 101(7). 1331–1387. https://scholarship.law.columbia.edu/faculty_scholarship/2866

Daise, Ron. 2014. *Gullah Geechee—The me I tried to flee*. TEDEx Charleston.

DeGraff, Michel. 2007. Kreyòl Ayisyen, or Haitian Creole (Creole French). *Comparative Creole Syntax: Parallel Outlines* 18. 101–126.

Delgado, Richard & Jean Stefancic. 2001. *Critical race theory: An introduction*. New York, NY: New York University Press.

Du Bois, William E. B. 1897. *The conservation of races*. Washington D.C.: American Negro Academy.

Dubois, William E. B. 1998. Double consciousness. In Nicholas Mirzoeff (ed.), *Visual culture reader*, 124–125. New York, NY: Routledge.

Foote, R. 2007. Education for development: The case for a skills-based approach. In *Proceedings of the 2007 Biennial Cross-Campus conference in Education, 23–26 April*, 441–446. School of Education Faculty of Humanities and Education. The University of the West Indies St. Augustine, Trinidad and Tobago.

Johnson, David C. & Eric J. Johnson. 2021. *The language gap: Normalizing deficit ideologies*. New York, NY: Routledge.

Ladson-Billings, Gloria. 1998. Just what is critical race theory and what's it doing in a nice field like education? *International Journal of Qualitative Studies in Education* 11(1), 7–24. https://doi.org/10.1080/095183998236863

Library of Congress. 2023. *Freedom in the Black Diaspora: A Resource Guide for Ayiti Reimagined*. https://guides.loc.gov/haiti-reimagined/haitian-creole#:~:text=Scholars%20consider%20the%20poem%20Lisette,Creole%2C%20dating%20to%20approximately%201757.

Lippi-Green, Rosina. 2012. *English with an accent. Language, ideology, and discrimination in the United States*. New York, NY: Routledge.

London, Norrel A. 2003. Ideology and politics in English-language education in Trinidad and Tobago: The colonial experience and a postcolonial critique. *Comparative Education Review* 47(3). 287–320. https://www.jstor.org/stable/10.1086/378249

Mathewson, Tara G. 2020. How discrimination nearly stalled a dual language school in Boston. *The Atlantic*. https://www.theatlantic.com/education/archive/2017/04/how-discrimination-nearly-prevented-a-dual-language-program-in-boston/522174/

Norton, Bonny. 2013. *Identity and language learning: Extending the conversation*. Bristol, UK: Multilingual Matters.

Orwenjo, Daniel O. 2021. Beyond English: Multilingualism and education in Kenya. *Africa Education Review* 18(3–4). 1–30. https://doi.org/10.1080/18146627.2022.2147559

O'Rourke, Brigid. 2020. Bringing a dying language back to life. *Language Magazine*. https://www.languagemagazine.com/2020/07/02/bringing-a-dying-language-back-to-life/

Pascale, Celine-Marie. 2019. The weaponization of language: Discourses of rising right-wing authoritarianism. *Current Sociology Review* 67(6). 898–917. https://doi.org/10.1177/0011392119869963

Pentón Herrera, Luis Javier & Kisha C. Bryan. 2022. Language weaponization in society and education: Introduction to the special issue. *International Journal of Literacy, Culture, and Language Education* 2. 1–5. https://doi.org/10.14434/ijlcle.v2iMay.34380

Robertson, Ian E. 2010. *Language and language education policy: Seamless education project unit*. Ministry of Education. Government of the Republic of Trinidad and Tobago. https://sta.uwi.edu/rdifund/projects/ttel/documents/ROBERTSON_Language_Languag_Education_Policy.pdf

Rosa, Jonathan. 2019. *Looking like a language, sounding like a race*. Oxford, UK: Oxford University Press.

Samuelson, Beth L. & Sara W. Freedman. 2010. Language policy, multilingual education, and power in Rwanda. *Language Policy* 9. 191–215. https://doi.org/10.1007/s10993-010-9170-7

Singh, Kavita A. 2014. *Translative carnivalism: Performance and language in the Caribbean text*. Cornell University dissertation.

Solorzano, Daniel G. & Tara J. Yosso. 2001. From racial stereotyping and deficit discourse toward a critical race theory in teacher education. *Multicultural Education* 9(1). 2–8.

U.S. Census. 2020. Population on St. Helena Island, S.C. https://www.census.gov/programs-surveys/acs/data.html

Von Esch, Kerry S., Suhanthie Motha & Ryuko Kubota. 2020. Race and language teaching. *Language Teaching* 53(4). 391–421. https://doi.org/10.1017/S0261444820000269

Wa Thiong'o, Ngugi. 2018. Decolonizing the mind: State of the art. *Présence Africaine* 1(197). 97–102.

Wekesa, Nyongesa B. 2020. A historical development of language in education and language testing in Kenya. *International Journal of Current Research* 12(9). 14010–14016. https://doi.org/10.24941/ijcr.39659.09.2020

Wordsworth, William. 1807. *My heart leaps up. Poems in two volumes*. London, UK: Longman.

Yakpo, Kofi. 2016. "The only language we speak really well": the English creoles of Equatorial Guinea and West Africa at the intersection of language ideologies and language policies. *International Journal of the Sociology of Language* 239. 211–233.

Xinyue Zuo and Denise Ives

Chapter 5
"That's easy": An analysis of speech acts in an instance of cross-cultural miscommunication

Abstract: "That's easy" is commonly used to suggest that something is unchallenging and straightforward. However, due to the open and implicit nature of language use, the uptake of the expression varies. In the incident described, the language use triggered a conflict between a lecturer and two international students, as well as between the lecturer and the department coordinator. This chapter focuses on unintended exclusion resulting from the weaponization of language in higher education. Through a pragmatic perspective, we examine the speech acts of the instructor's utterance "that's easy," different possibilities for students' meaning-making, and the issue of microaggressions. We also offer a discussion identity, discourse, and power, which also play a role in communication and understanding. As different implications could be packed into a seemingly simple, neutral sentence, we must cultivate an awareness of our language practices so that our words will not unintentionally inflict harm—in the form of emotional and physical damage, exclusion, and deterioration of relationships. Finally, recommendations for minimizing miscommunication and avoiding microaggression are provided.

Keywords: cross-cultural communication, miscommunication, microaggression, international students, higher education, speech acts

1 Introduction and background

It happened during my (the first author's) second year in a Ph.D. program in Teacher Education and Curriculum Studies at a university in the Northeast of the US. One day, somewhere around the middle of the semester, while browsing aimlessly through a biweekly newsletter from the graduate school, a notice about an open discussion session titled "Lessons Learned as International Instructors" attracted my attention. It said that this would be a great opportunity to start a conversation with other international faculty, postdoctoral fellows, and graduate

Xinyue Zuo, Denise Ives, University of Massachusetts Amherst

https://doi.org/10.1515/9783110799521-005

students, as well as anyone teaching international students. "Hmmm. I am an international graduate student, and I hope to work at a university as an international staff or faculty member," I mumbled to myself, "This sounds interesting, plus it offers pizza for lunch. I am in!"

The event brought me to a meeting room at noon on a Thursday in the Graduate School Hall, where there was a small gathering of roughly ten individuals seated around a conference table, including two event hosts. As an icebreaker, we introduced ourselves to one another and explained why we were attending the event. Among us were eminent university professors, novice lecturers, and graduate students, coming from a variety of racial and ethnic backgrounds. When asked what led us here, one international professor described with a heavy heart that, as a non-native English-speaking teacher, he felt less confident and lacked classroom authority compared to other colleagues who speak English as their first language, and students held lower expectations of him. Then, another professor expressed concerns over the situation that fewer and fewer international students were registering for intercultural and international communication courses, which focused on the geopolitical, technological, and cultural relations among peoples, societies, nations, and communities. One international student highlighted an issue relating to the social integration of international students. He described, with disappointment, that contrary to his expectations, some international students mingled exclusively with peers from their home country and collaborated only with these classmates on laboratory-based group projects, unwilling to communicate with those with different linguistic and cultural backgrounds. Additionally, one student participant complained that the content of certain courses was not inclusive, as professors constantly made references to American pop culture, assuming all students had familiarity with it.

When it came to the turn of a native English-speaking lecturer named Aria (pseudonym), she recounted, quite emotionally, an incident that occurred recently in her entry-level Spanish class—two of her international students filed a complaint against her to the program coordinator, claiming they were offended by her frequent use of the expression "that's easy" in the class. The coordinator took the issue seriously and conducted some classroom observations. After several visits, the coordinator assured her that her teaching style and techniques were fine. During the seminar with us, she explained that her frequent use of expressions like "that's easy" and "you can do it" was merely intended to encourage learners to practice speaking the language (i.e., Spanish) and volunteer for teacher-led activities. Aria lamented repeatedly that the coordinator's immediate move to initiate evaluation took a toll on her spontaneity and freedom as a lecturer.

As she continued to defend herself, a native English-speaking professor interjected that there had been miscommunication between her and the students and that we, as teachers, should be cautious about what we say in class. Aria concurred but added that she had lost her sense of spontaneity as a result of being obliged to care for all the students, which was completely impossible, and emphasized that the trust between herself and the department had disappeared. Then, a professor of Japanese origin shared his viewpoint, adding that if he were one of Aria's students, he would approach the instructor first and then seek assistance from the department if the issue remained unsolved. Aria agreed once again, stressing the need for trust both between students and teachers, and between teachers and the department. She closed by thanking everyone for giving her the chance to talk about this.

The episode of miscommunication depicted in the vignette is by no means unusual. On today's increasingly diverse college and university campuses, it might occur in any classroom on a regular basis. Students, particularly those from 'minoritized' groups, which may not be minorities numerically but continue to be systematically oppressed and excluded (Crandall & Garcia, 2016), are highly likely to experience instances of racism, sexism, and linguistic discrimination from various school members (e.g., professors, peers, and staff) (Boysen, 2012), though some instances are unintentional (Bourke, 2010). Words are powerful. They can be wielded in ways that unite and include, as well as divide and harm (McConnell-Ginet, 2020). Thus, the role of communication in teaching and learning and the significance of language-in-use, or discourse, can not be overestimated.

Over the past four decades, extensive research has been conducted on intercultural and cross-cultural communication (Huang et al., 2012; Tran & Pham, 2016). Terms such as *misunderstanding* and *miscommunication* are frequently used to describe communication breakdowns in which interlocutors fail to make sense of the intentions underlying another's utterances and, therefore, lack a shared understanding (Liu, 2015). While cultural differences have often been regarded as the leading cause, misunderstandings could also be linguistic in origin and associated with power dynamics (Piller, 2012), assumptions and stereotypes (Halvorson, 2015), and thus give rise to social exclusion and marginalization (Kiyota, 2022).

Centering around a cross-cultural miscommunication incident, this chapter focuses on language practices and unintended exclusion in multilingual and multicultural higher education settings, a topic that may be of interest to instructors, international students, school administrators, sociolinguists, and discourse analysts. It is not intended as a chapter on language per se, yet it does involve some of the principles and mechanisms that underlie language use in order to analyze the causes of miscommunication, as well as the effects, including the emotional pain that language may inflict on nondominant ethnolinguistic groups. The goal of this chapter is to investigate how language use may lead to conflicts, highlighting the interpretive nature of discourse, for the purpose of raising higher education practitioners' awareness of pragmatic competence and microaggression, and identifying feasible solutions to minimize communication conflicts. Through a pragmatic perspective, this chapter examines the speech acts of the instructor's utterance "that's easy" and the students' interpretations and responses, alongside the interrelations between language, identity, and power.

2 Language, interpretation, and meaning

2.1 Ambiguity in language

People tend to think of language as a transparent and neutral medium for the transfer of information. Nonetheless, even when employed literally, language can convey multiple meanings and arouse distinct emotional experiences. Broadly speaking, there are two ways to describe the meanings of an expression: denotation and connotation, which coexist to deliver messages. Denotation is the conceptual or formal meaning, the 'dictionary definition,' whereas connotation refers to the 'real world' associations, namely, the psychological, cultural, personal, and/or emotional signals conveyed (Quiroga-Clare, 2003). Given that language is a symbolic system that is situated and embedded in the environment, words, phrases, or statements are often open to multiple interpretations, and ambiguity is frequently present (Quiroga-Clare, 2003).

In this chapter, we acknowledge the complexity of language itself and do not see it as a problem to be fixed. Adopting a pragmatic perspective, we argue that the interpretation of utterances frequently involves searching for meaning beyond the literal and requires consideration of many factors, including the relative distance between interlocutors, the identities of the interlocutors, the situation (both cultural and physical), the goal of interaction, and the like (Yule, 1996). In this light, the variations and nuances of meaning may evoke disparate interpretations and impede participation and relationship-building among interlocutors (Quiroga-Clare, 2003). Moreover, a lack of shared expectations may result in a mismatch between the message's reception and the speaker's intention, thereby rendering co-constructed exclusion and marginalization (Kiyota, 2022).

2.2 The cooperative principle and implicatures

Linguistic exchanges are regulated by rational and cooperative endeavors (Grice, 1975). The cooperative principle (CP) underlies speakers' pragmatic behavior and elucidates what it means to cooperate in a conversation (Cruse, 2000). To achieve effective communication, interlocutors are expected to observe the following guideline: "Make your conversational contribution such as is required, at the stage at which it occurs, by the accepted purpose or direction of the talk exchange in which you are engaged" (Grice, 1975, p. 45). Speakers employ this framework to express their meanings, including those that are not explicitly said. Successful communication also requires listeners to demonstrate some level of cooperation (although they do not always) and recognize the speaker's intention even if speakers use implicit language (Davies, 2000). The CP serves as an especially useful tool for understanding how people get their meaning across, and how effective conversational communication is achieved.

As the CP illustrates, speakers frequently imply things when engaging in linguistic practices (Grice, 1975), assuming that these stuffed yet implicit signals are known or inferable by listeners (Gee, 2010). Implicatures point to such communicative intention (Bach, 2006). Davis (2019) explains, "to work out an implicature is to infer it in a specific way" (Gricean Theory section) by drawing on interacting sources, such as the semantic meaning of the utterance, the identities and references that may be involved, the CP and its maxims, the context and other features of the utterance, and the background knowledge available to or assumed by interlocutors. Nonetheless, the ambiguity and multiplicity of meaning grant the possibility of the emergence of a "resistant listener" with alternative, or even opposite, interpretations (Gee, 2010, p. 18), as inferring speakers' implicit meaning is not a straightforward task.

2.3 Speech act theory

People use language not merely to transfer information but also to perform particular types of actions, such as explanations, compliments, promises, and requests (Green, 2021). The actions performed via utterances are referred to as speech acts. Speech act theory explains the functional dimensions of language (Bachman, 1990). It highlights that in interpreting utterances, non-linguistic aspects of communication and social institutions within which speech acts are produced should be emphasized (Searle, 1969). This is especially important in the context of cross-cultural interaction, during which linguistic and cultural norms,

as well as values and assumptions, play a role (Cheng, 2012). According to Austin (1975), there are three levels of speech acts:
- Locutionary forces—referential value
- Illocutionary forces—performative function
- Perlocutionary forces—perceived impact

To illustrate, let's examine the utterance "The teachers are coming here," adapted from *the Stanford Encyclopedia of Philosophy* "Ambiguity" entry by Sennet (2021). The locutionary act presents the fact that the teachers will arrive at the speaker's location soon. The illocutionary act intended by the speaker, depending on the circumstances, could be: voicing a complaint about the hearers (i.e., classmates) being noisy and disobedient; or suggesting that classmates relax and not be overly worried; or expressing delight in seeing teachers after a long break, and such. Accordingly, the perlocutionary act could be manifested in classmates' contrite behavior and subsequent behavioral change; or classmates' confidence that everything can be taken care of; or classmates dashing out of the classroom and greeting the teacher's return. As such, the same utterance can convey different illocutionary and perlocutionary forces under different situations.

Searle (1976) emphasized the importance of the social institution within which speech acts are produced and further identified five categories of illocutionary acts:
- Representatives: stating the facts (assertion, claim, report, conclusion)
- Directives: getting the listeners to act (suggestion, request, order, command)
- Expressives: expressing speakers' feelings (apology, complaint, thank, congratulate, welcome)
- Commissives: speakers committing themselves to act (promise, threat, refusal, offer)
- Declaratives: altering the situation of affairs (decree, declaration, christening, marrying)

In the utterance "The teachers are coming here," at least three distinct types of speech acts could be carried out, namely, the representative (statements), the expressive (relief or welcome), and the directive (warning). Specifically, this utterance could be employed to communicate that the teachers are on their way; to show relief that the teachers are finally arriving as a student is hurt in the playground; to urge peers to behave well. These three illocutionary acts, among others, represent the multiple, possible hidden needs that speakers may seek to fulfill in their language use. Nonetheless, in real-life scenarios, a lack of mutual understanding could give rise to a false consensus, leading individuals to believe that their words will be reliably interpreted in a singular manner (i.e., one that aligns perfectly with their own), meaning that the audience will actively listen throughout the conversation, pick up the exact same signal, deduce the identical illocutionary force from it, and act upon it following the cooperative principle. However, deciphering the speaker's more significant meaning can be demanding for any hearers, especially for those who are less familiar with the speaker as well as the context. Uncertainties and communication breakdowns naturally occur when the elements that influence mutual understandings are hampered.

2.4 Analysis

Returning to our story, in which a lecturer's words and intended meaning were allegedly misinterpreted by two international students, relying on Author 1's recollection of Aria's retelling of the incident, we adopt an interpretive approach using speech act theory to trace the potential causes of the misunderstanding inherent in the conversation, discuss the discourse ambiguities, and most importantly, demonstrate how such ambiguity could unintentionally inflict harm.

2.4.1 Speech acts of "that's easy"

Locutionary act
To determine the source of the conflict between the instructor and the two students in her class, we start with the locutionary act, that is, the literal meaning of the utterance. As the word "that" is an indexical, its meaning can only be inferred from the context. With situated knowledge, we know "that" refers to a specific classroom speaking activity. The word "easy" is a polysemy (a word with multiple meanings) and its major denotative meanings include: uncomplicated, compliant, casual, calm, and comfortable. Given that it is used to characterize an activity, the meaning *uncomplicated* fits well. Hence, the locutionary act of this declarative sentence can be thought of as an act of stating. That is, the speaker, Aria, is putting forward the proposition that the task is unchallenging. In other words, the instructor is indicating that the difficulty level of accomplishing the task is low.

While the statement is well-formed syntactically, it is conceptually incomplete. It does not indicate that the task is easy in comparison to what and for whom, thus something must be done to fill in the gap so as to deliver a complete and definitive argument (Bach, 1994). For instance, the speaker, Aria, could have made her message explicit and courteous by adding, "I have heard you do this successfully before" or "this activity is just like the one we just did." She could have even sought clarification from the learners to ensure her direction was clear. In so doing, the misunderstanding and unnecessary harm escalated by a breakdown in communication might have been avoided, instead of letting the listener fill in the gaps based on what was said and the context in which it was said (Gee, 2010).

Illocutionary act
As mentioned, speakers can also use language to perform illocutionary acts. With "that's easy," Aria is not only making the assertion, but perhaps she is also encouraging her students to participate in the speaking activity by ensuring them the task is not demanding; or requesting students to take up their responsibility and practice the language; or cautioning them not to make any mistakes; or motivating students to push their limits with an assignment that is above average learners' competence; or criticizing and expressing her discontent with their performance. Or perhaps Aria is merely being odiously ironic, showing a feeling of patronizing superiority because of her expertise. Accordingly, the illocutionary acts of "That's easy" could be categorized as follows:
- That (the task) is easy. (representative act)
- That's easy. That won't be mentally challenging. (commissive act)
- That's easy. You all should actively practice. (directive act)
- That's easy, and I am reminding you to read carefully. (commissive act)
- If you use more of your willpower, that's easy. (directive act)
- That's easy. Why can't you even read it? (expressive act)

Again, due to illocutionary act that Aria plans to undertake not being explicitly delivered, and both parties failing to seek clarification, the intended meaning behind the words did not match with the perception of the two international students. Consequently, the disconnect in understanding persisted.

Perlocutionary act
In analyzing perlocutionary acts, the focus is placed on the effects of the utterance on the receiver. By declaring, "that's easy," Aria may effectively boost some learners' confidence and inspire them to participate in the speaking activity. She may also succeed in persuading some unmotivated learners to take on both their individual and, more importantly, collective responsibilities as a part of a shared learning experience to be responsible for each other's process in language learning. Additionally, following Aria's cautionary note, some students may approach the task with greater care and accurately read out aloud one sentence at a time. Nonetheless, it is also likely that some learners might be discouraged after self-assessment, realizing that they lag hugely behind.

As the perlocutionary act is practically contingent on every aspect of interaction, such as the speaker's voice and tone, the content and context of the utterance, the hearer's state of mind, and the physical environment of the interaction (Davis, 1979), its effects on learners are oftentimes independent of the speaker's intentions, thoughts, and beliefs. Thus, we highlight the distinction between "the act of attempting or purporting" and "the act of successfully achieving or consummating," as well as intended and unintended consequences (Austin, 1975, p. 61) in our interpretation of the exchanges.

2.4.2 Student (mis)interpretation

To understand how the miscommunication occurs, it is indispensable to examine how students take in and respond to Aria's utterance. Here, we do not intend to make a priori assumptions about shared inferencing. Rather, we aim to trace the causes of the miscommunication and reveal the hypothesis formation process by which the listeners assessed the meanings the speaker intended to deliver (Gumperz & Cook-Gumperz, 2012).

As Aria's intention in saying "that's easy, that's easy" is not explicitly conveyed, and no effort to clarify the intention is made, paths of interpretation are opened up, and the onus of interpretation resides in the students. Some may follow this inference logic: (a) based on the conventions of languages, the teacher is putting stress on *easy* and using repetition; (b) it can be determined that by applying such rhetorical devices, the teacher is offering certain cues; and (c) this way of expressing is often used when a speaker wants to make a point that a certain task is not at all demanding. Then, by applying the maxim of relevance, they infer that it's highly probable that the instructor is boosting their confidence and indicating that they should feel safe to try it out.

Nevertheless, this interpretation may not be the only truth. Some students, drawing the conclusion that the task requires minimal effort, may belittle the efforts Aria has put into designing the curriculum and choose to be non-supportive and non-responsive. Yet, some may be fully aware of the value of learning and practicing but lack the skills in meaningful participation. Still some, not being ready to approach the speaking exercise, may feel offended by Aria's making the stakes of the exercise incredibly high. Then, they may debate whether to overtly verbalize their concerns towards the instructor, and there might be good reasons for not doing that, such as not disrupting the peace and harmony of the class, having to maintain participation records, or feeling insecure by speaking up. They may also think over whether to behave in a manner that preserves Aria's face, for instance, by letting go of the uneasiness or having a side conversation with her afterwards. Alternatively, some learners may decide not to keep silent and file a complaint to the coordinator after class, as the two international students in this case did.

According to Austin (1975), speakers' failure to elicit the desired perlocutionary acts may occur under two conditions. First, miscommunication happens when the speaker fails to perform the right things to bring about the desired act, for example, not being deliberate about the signals that they sent and not clarifying the meaning. Second, despite the speaker's best efforts, the message doesn't get through for reasons such as the listeners not hearing well, lack of attention (Austin, 1975), or purposeful refusal (Gee, 2010). For instance, when students are inattentive, they may not follow the instructor's directions. On top of that, if they perceive the instructor to be unhelpful and uncaring, they may refuse to complete assigned tasks.

Stereotypes, assumptions, and microaggression
It is noteworthy from the previous analysis that some learners interpreted Aria's repeated utterance of "that's easy" negatively–as microaggressive, believing the underlying message was "you are so unintelligent for not being able to accurately perform this simple task." Microaggressions are "brief, everyday exchanges that send denigrating messages to certain individuals because of their group membership (e.g., race, gender, culture, religion, social class, sexual orientation, etc)" (Sue, 2010, p. xvi). Studies show that experiences of microaggressions can be associated with themes such as classroom ascription of being less abled, pathologizing culture and communication styles, and institutional negligence (Sue et al., 2007). However, we often remain oblivious to the existence of microaggressions or may dismiss them as being important due to the fact that such stereotypes and assumptions are so ingrained in our ways of being as to be below the level of our awareness (Sue et al., 2007).

As introduced previously, the expressive illocutionary act of "that's easy" might convey the instructor's dissatisfaction with the students' lack of engagement, carrying a negative implicature that the students are not smart enough to read aloud basic sentences, and/or they are not trying hard enough. Those who are diffident about their Spanish, regardless of their actual level of mastery, may interpret this as a denigration of their intelligence or qualification. For students from minoritized backgrounds, such as international students, the utterance may further imply that their "values and communication styles . . . are abnormal" and that "assimilat[ion] to dominant culture" is the only way to get accepted and welcomed in class (Sue et al., 2007, pp. 277–278). Thus, they may feel alienated and marginalized with their language skills, attitudes, and even intelligence being questioned and their classroom behaviors being unfavored.

Besides, the ingrained and unconscious bias further complicates the inspection of this instance of miscommunication. Specifically, some students (including the two international students) may feel unequally treated, humiliated, and excluded by Aria's words, while Aria, the instructor, may be annoyed at students' indifference in the classroom and later confused at being complained about. Additionally, the distinctions between saying and implicating also have an impact on how we evaluate the exchanges. Since the scenario is largely grounded in Aria's post facto discussions of her communication intention, it is hard for us to determine whether she intentionally committed microaggression or not. Nevertheless, the harmful impact and the experiential reality have already been made.

Language has the power to shape people, their beliefs, motivation, and behaviors, as well as the initiation and maintenance of relationships. The pragmatic ambiguity in linguistic practices opens up chances for differing interpretations and almost inevitably brings about misunderstandings (Blum-Kulka & Weizman, 1988).

3 Identity, discourse, and power

Gee (2010) stated that "we use language to get recognized as taking on a certain identity or role" (p. 112). Communication is not merely the exchange of information via language, it is also "the act of sociality" (Huang et al., 2012, p. 37), which entails interlocutors' assuming an 'appropriate' identity and establishing and maintaining social relationships with other people, groups, and institutions (Gee, 2010). From the post-modern orientation, identity is viewed as a social construct (Burr, 2015), constituting "multiple, often contradictory self-representations" (Gregg, 1995, p. 617), rather than a fixed and unified feature assigned to individuals. In line with people's perceptions of themselves and others, different identities may be invoked and performed in different social contexts. For instance, we perform differently when interacting with someone as a professional colleague than when relating to them as a friend; identities are thus dynamic and contextualized (Gee, 2010).

In addition, power, language, and identity are intricately interwoven. Foucault (1990) argued from the interpretive standpoint that "power is everywhere" and that "discourse transmits and produces power" (Foucault, 1990, p. 101). Hence, language is neither neutral (Freire, 2018) nor innocent (Pentón Herrera, 2022), and linguistic practices are "purposeful," shaping and being shaped by social institutions and power relationships (Barton & Hamilton, 2000, p. 7). Just as Barkhuizen (2016) noted, "Who we are (our identities) is inextricably linked to the languages we know and use" and "it is in discursive interactions between people and between people and institutions (i.e., language as a social practice) that relations of power become evident and the negotiation of identities takes place" (Barkhuizen, 2016, p. 2). As such, language mirrors the identities we assume and our ways of doing and being, as well as certain power dynamics and social realities. This notion has profound implications for research on minority/minoritized group positioning.

3.1 Analysis

With the evolution of the incident, Aria's social identities varied, as did her use of language. In the analysis presented below, we seek to understand how interactional goals are negotiated, how identity and power are played out in the discourse interactions involved, and most importantly, how language is being used to 'weaponize' US higher education discourse against a more pluralistic, dynamic, and inclusive conception of school culture.

3.1.1 Identities as a seminar attendee

Aria participated in the open discussion session as an attendee. Since all the attendees were either international students, scholars, or educators of international students, they more or less had shared experiences in cross-cultural communication, especially with regard to the struggles and challenges. As a result, when narrating the incident to the event audience, Aria viewed the audience as her allies. She kept grumbling about being hurt and distrusted by the department while giving little attention to alternative solutions proposed by some fellow attendees. Her choice of words like "hurt," "distrust," and "loss of spontaneity and freedom" made the students' complaints appear unreasonable or less important while making her emotional grouch more legitimate and worthy of attention. Her strenuous defense conveyed the messages that her students' accusations were untenable and that they were being too sensitive, negating the possibility that her utterance might have already conveyed denigrating meaning and inflicted emotional injury. In addition, her repeated emphasis on her agency as a teacher with "spontaneity and freedom" suggested that she saw accommodations in cross-cultural communication as losses of self. Evidently, her narrative mainly served to vent discontent and seek solace, rather than resolve the conflicts.

3.1.2 Identities as a department-employed lecturer

Aria was a female Anglo-American in her thirties, holding a lecturer position at a public university. Due to the institutional hierarchy and the administrative relationship, Aria was the less-privileged individual in her interaction with the program coordinator, who was a senior leadership team member. Besides, students' complaints and grievances, a form of evaluation in practice, put Aria in an even more unfavorable situation, posing a threat to her teaching position, as student evaluation of teaching has a significant impact on university decision-making regarding, for instance, faculty promotions and auditing practices, which could also potentially affect admission and university ranking (Goos & Salomons, 2017). Thus, despite Aria's disappointment with the coordinator's move to audit, which implicated advocacy for the learners and protection for the standing of the university, and her insecurity of being treated with suspicion, she had no choice but to accept the fact in the hope of retaining her position. "I felt relieved after getting the endorsement," she revealed in her narration, indicating the strain and anxiety she underwent.

3.1.3 Identities as a lecturer in the classroom

In the Spanish 101 class, Aria assumed the role of an instructor who was entitled to power in various formats for serving as the manager of the class by default (Bourdieu & Wacquant, 1992). On one hand, she cultivated learners' Spanish language skills by exerting expert authority. On the other hand, she compelled learners to participate in instructional activities by enacting the privilege endowed by coercive authority. Yet, she might be insufficient in demonstrating attractive authority (i.e., rapport with learners and winning their trust) or reward authority (i.e., positive reinforcement such as awards, praise, and grades). She acted and interacted in ways that did not show sufficient empathy toward learners. Halvorson (2015) comments that when people are in a position of power, they tend to overlook the unique needs and specialties of the individuals. In so doing, Aria failed to create an inclusive space, demonstrating care for every student. Under such circumstances, Aria's utterance, "that's easy," may exclude and marginalize some learners, and thereby could be viewed as a microaggression. To openly take a stand against it, the two international students took on an active role in the "judgment process" to promote diversity, equity, and inclusion in the organizational structure of higher education (Bloxham & Boyd, 2007).

4 Discussion

In studying miscommunication, it is crucial to note that "effects may not reflect intentions" (Tannen, 2012, p. 153), especially in the context of cross-cultural communication, where diversity is the underlying theme, and communicative practices entail not only encoding and decoding messages but also negotiating shared or unshared background assumptions (Gumperz & Cook-Gumperz, 2012). Analysis reveals that ambiguity in the instructor's language accompanied by the microaggressive message, the hierarchy of power in higher education, and the lack of rapport may affect the interpretation of interlocutors' words and behaviors and lead to unintended exclusion and relationship degradation.

First and foremost, to conclude that cultural mismatch is the only key variable in cross-cultural misunderstandings is untenable. As mentioned, certain misunderstandings could be linguistic issues in nature, as interlocutors may have varying levels of language proficiency, especially with respect to the contextualization cues of the dominant language (Piller, 2012). The ambiguity of language usage could make the nuanced meanings hard to pin down. In addition, social variables (e.g., divergent perspectives towards teaching and learning, power dynamics in organizations, and prior communicative experiences) shall all be factored into the failure of getting the meaning across. It is thus essential not to over-generalize while examining miscommunications.

Though not all miscommunication involves microaggressions, there are occasions in which "perceptions of subtle racial discrimination that do not necessarily involve negative treatment may account for the 'sting' of racial microaggressions, influencing the emotional well-being of racial minorities" (Wang et al., 2011, p. 1666). In our story, microaggressions could be regarded as a contributory factor to the tension, even though there is no verbal evidence on the surface level. As noted earlier, microaggressions are usually unintentionally committed and hard to pin down, throughout Aria's recounting, she remained defensive and negated any implicit discrimination in her utterances, as if unaware that "racial and ethnic stereotypes, disciplinary communication patterns, and students' interactions with each other, affect the way students' discourse in the classroom is interpreted" and that instructors' potential biased assumptions (i.e., labeling some learners as less able or slow) is a strong version of exclusion that could inflict genuine harm on students (Godley, 2012, p. 464). Admittedly, the miscommunication and tension were co-constructed in this context (Kiyota, 2022), which will be elucidated further in the subsequent sections.

To minimize future occurrences of miscommunication or microaggression, we put forward the following suggestions. First and foremost, avoid imprecise language, and formulate messages with the audience in mind (Krauss & Chiu,

1998). It is critical to keep in mind that as language is open for interpretation, the diverse backgrounds and experiences that interlocutors bring into conversations shape their meaning-making and uptake. Therefore, clearly and explicitly communicating the objective of the message could be the most effective and efficient strategy for preventing miscommunication.

Besides, feedback exchange and meaning negotiation are instrumental in promoting mutual understanding. As Krauss and Chiu (1998) articulated, "feedback, and the knowledge of its availability, transforms the communication situation by permitting speakers to modify tentatively formulated assumptions about what listeners know as the interaction proceeds" (p. 11). When speakers constantly seek the audience's feedback, they become cognizant of listeners' understanding, thereby being capable of steering the conversation toward the intended outcome, as opposed to relying heavily on the audience's ability to make meaning (Krauss & Chiu, 1998). Similarly, the audience's responses not only demonstrate listenership, but also aid in the procession of the conversation. In our instance, if the instructor had rephrased her statements, had inquired about the students' disinterest, or had invited students to ask questions, or if the students had approached her outside of the classroom and initiated a dialogue about her instructional and linguistic practices, the miscommunication might have been settled in a peaceful way, without the escalation.

Furthermore, it is essential to foster educators' and students' pragmatic and sociolinguistic competence. Pragmatic competence refers to the capability to use language effectively and appropriately in given situations (Thomas, 1983). Developing international students' pragmatic competence will help them manage conversations in terms of relevance, politeness, and effectiveness (House, 1996) while raising educators' pragmatic awareness will enable them to recognize indicators of miscommunication and be responsive to students' needs and expectations. Additionally, sociolinguistic competence concerns the ability to apply the "knowledge of the sociocultural rules of language and discourse" (Brown, 2000, p. 247). It empowers one to communicate using socially appropriate linguistic practices and properly interpret contextualized meanings. Developing instructors' and students' sociolinguistic skills could assist them in integrating into multicultural classrooms, and universities should create an inclusive space for the exchange of diverse narratives to foster reciprocal cross-cultural learning.

Last but not least, on globalized campuses, strengthening everyone's awareness of microaggressions and offering relevant guidance would help reframe the academic environment. Strategies for dealing with microaggressions recommended by the Center for Teaching and Learning at the University of Washington are: 1) examining our own biases and assumptions in communication and reflecting on whether they may be harmful to those who receive them; 2) differentiating intent and impact;

3) establishing ground rules and norms for discussion; 4) responding to microaggression incidences; 5) following up as needed and identifying additional sources of support; and 6) affirming the diversity within minoritized communities (Addressing Microaggressions in the Classroom, 2019).

5 Conclusion

Surrounding an incident recounted by a lecturer at a university in the northeast US, this chapter focuses on miscommunication in one instance of cross-cultural communication in higher education. Through a pragmatic perspective, it examines speech acts related to the instructor's utterance "that's easy" and students' interpretation, uptake, and responses, as well as linguistic microaggressions related to the underlying message that "you are so unintelligent." It also discusses identity, discourse, and power, all of which play a role in cross-cultural communication.

It highlights the criticality of language-in-use in cross-cultural communication in multicultural classrooms, and argues for the need to (1) acknowledge language as a non-neutral medium that is subject to various interpretations; (2) reflect on linguistic practices, looking for signs of ambiguity and assessing unconscious biases; (3) reframe cross-cultural interactions by evaluating institutional structure and associated conditions that may inhibit communication; and (4) provide venues for facilitating communicative language competence and cross-cultural learning.

Through in-depth analysis of a seemingly straightforward expression, this chapter contributes to our understanding of the nature of language and its possible impact, indicating that unnoticed and unnegotiated divergences in meaning encoding and decoding can lead to miscommunication and even microaggressions. It also offers recommendations for construction of a more welcoming and inclusive educational environment, stressing individuals developing a greater awareness of how they are using language and attentiveness to others' linguistic practices.

References

Addressing microaggressions in the classroom. 2019. *Center for Teaching and Learning*.
   https://teaching.washington.edu/topics/inclusive-teaching/addressing-microaggressions-in-the-classroom/
Austin, John L. 1975. *How to do things with words* (2nd ed.). Boston, MA: Harvard University Press.

Bach, Kent. 1994. Conversational implicature. *Mind and Language* 9(2). 124–162. https://doi.org/10.1111/j.1468-0017.1994.tb00220.x

Bach, Kent. 2006. The top 10 misconceptions about implicature. In Betty J. Birner & Gregory Ward (eds.), *Drawing the boundaries of meaning: Neo-Gricean studies in pragmatics and semantics in honor of Laurence R. Horn*, 21–30. The Netherlands: John Benjamins Publishing Company. https://doi.org/10.1075/slcs.80.03bac

Bachman, Lyle F. 1990. *Fundamental considerations in language testing*. Oxford, UK: Oxford University Press.

Barkhuizen, Gary. 2016. Narrative approaches to exploring language, identity and power in language teacher education. *RELC Journal* 47(1). 25–42. https://doi.org/10.1177/0033688216631222

Barton, David & Hamilton, Mary. 2000. Literacy practices. In David Barton, Mary Hamilton, Roz Ivanic (eds.), *Situated literacies: Reading and writing in context*, 7–15. New York, NY: Routledge.

Bloxham, Sue & Pete Boyd. 2007. *Developing effective assessment in higher education: A practical guide*. New York, NY: McGraw-Hill Education.

Blum-Kulka, Shoshana & Elda Weizman. 1988. The inevitability of misunderstandings: discourse ambiguities. *Text—Interdisciplinary Journal for the Study of Discourse* 8(3). 219–242. https://doi.org/10.1515/text.1.1988.8.3.219

Bourdieu, Pierre & Loïc J. D. Wacquant. 1992. *An invitation to reflexive sociology*. Chicago, IL: University of Chicago Press.

Bourke, Brian. 2010. Experiences of black students in multiple cultural spaces at a predominantly white institution. *Journal of Diversity in Higher Education* 3(2). 126–135. https://doi.org/10.1037/a0019025

Boysen, Guy A. 2012. Teacher and student perceptions of microaggressions in college classrooms. *College Teaching* 60(3). 122–129. https://doi.org/10.1080/87567555.2012.654831

Brown, H. Douglas. 2000. *Principles of language learning and teaching*. New York: Longman.

Burr, Vivien. 2015. *Social constructionism*. New York, NY: Routledge.

Cheng, Winnie. 2012. Speech acts, facework and politeness: Relationship-building across cultures. In Jane Jackson (ed.), *The Routledge handbook of language and intercultural communication*, 164–179. New York, NY: Routledge. https://doi.org/10.4324/9780203805640.ch9

Crandall, Jennifer & Gina A. Garcia. 2016. "Am I overreacting?" Understanding and combating microaggressions. *Higher Education Today*. https://www.higheredtoday.org/2016/07/27/understanding-and-combatting-microaggressions-in-postsecondary-education/

Cruse, D. Alan. 2000. *Meaning in language: An introduction to semantics and pragmatics*. Oxford, UK: Oxford University Press.

Davies, Bethan. 2000. Grice's cooperative principle: Getting the meaning across. *Leeds Working Papers in Linguistics and Phonetics* 8(1). 1–26.

Davis, Steven. 1979. Speech acts, performance and competence. *Journal of Pragmatics* 3(5). 497–505. https://doi.org/10.1016/0378-2166(79)90025-0

Davis, Wayne. 2019. Implicature. In Edward N. Zalta (ed.), *The Stanford encyclopedia of philosophy* (Fall 2021). Metaphysics Research Lab, Stanford University. https://plato.stanford.edu/entries/implicature/

Foucault, Michel. 1990. *The history of sexuality: An introduction, volume 1*. New York: Vintage Books.

Freire, Paulo. 2018. *Pedagogy of the oppressed: 50th anniversary edition*. New York, NY: Bloomsbury Publishing.

Gee, James P. 2010. *How to do discourse analysis: A toolkit*. New York, NY: Routledge.

Godley, Amanda J. 2012. Intercultural discourse and communication in education. In Christina Bratt Paulston, Scott F. Kiesling & Elizabeth S. Rangel (eds.), *The Handbook of intercultural discourse* and communication, 449–481. Malden, MA: John Wiley & Sons. https://doi.org/10.1002/9781118247273.ch22

Goos, Maarten & Anna Salomons. 2017. Measuring teaching quality in higher education: assessing selection bias in course evaluations. *Research in Higher Education* 58(4). 341–364. https://doi.org/10.1007/s11162-016-9429-8

Green, Mitchell. 2021. Speech acts. In Edward N. Zalta (ed.), *The Stanford Encyclopedia of Philosophy* (Fall 2021). Metaphysics Research Lab, Stanford University. https://plato.stanford.edu/archives/fall2021/entries/speech-acts/

Gregg, Gary S. 1995. Multiple identities and the integration of personality. *Journal of Personality* 63(3). 617–641. https://doi.org/10.1111/j.1467-6494.1995.tb00508.x

Grice, H. P. 1975. Logic and conversation. In Peter Cole & Jerry L. Morgan (eds.), *Speech acts*, 41–58. Leiden: Brill/Sense. https://doi.org/10.1163/9789004368811_003

Gumperz, John J. & Jenny Cook-Gumperz. 2012. Interactional sociolinguistics: Perspectives on intercultural communication. In Christina Bratt Paulston, Scott F. Kiesling, Elizabeth S. Rangel (eds.), *The Handbook of Intercultural Discourse and Communication*, 63–76. Malden, MA: John Wiley & Sons.

Halvorson, Heidi. G. 2015. *No one understands you and what to do about it*. Boston, MA: Harvard Business Review Press.

House, Juliane. 1996. Developing pragmatic fluency in English as a foreign language: Routines and metapragmatic awareness. *Studies in Second Language Acquisition* 18(2). 225–252. https://doi.org/10.1017/S0272263100014893

Huang, Jinyan, Erin Dotterweich & Ashleigh Bowers. 2012. Intercultural miscommunication: Impact on ESOL students and implications for ESOL teachers. *Journal of Instructional Psychology* 39(1). 36–40.

Kiyota, Akiko. 2022. View of problematizing fluent speakers' unintentional exclusion of emergent bilinguals. *International Journal of Literacy, Culture, and Language Education 2*. 6–19. https://doi.org/10.14434/ijlcle.v2imay.34385

Krauss, Robert M. & Chi-Yue Chiu. 1998. Language and social behavior. In Daniel Todd Gilbert, Susan T. Fiske & Gardner Lindzey (eds.), *The Handbook of social psychology*, 41–88. New York, NY: McGraw-Hill.

Liu, Min-Sun. 2015. Intercultural verbal communication styles. In Janet M. Bennett (ed.), *The SAGE encyclopedia of intercultural competence*, 530–535. Thousand Oaks, CA: SAGE Publications. https://doi.org/10.4135/9781483346267.n173

McConnell-Ginet, Sally. 2020. *Words matter: Meaning and power*. Cambridge, UK: Cambridge University Press.

Pentón Herrera, Luis Javier. 2022. Is the language you teach racist?: Reflections and considerations for English and Spanish (teacher) educators. *International Journal of Literacy, Culture, and Language Education* 2. 58–70. https://doi.org/10.14434/ijlcle.v2imay.34390

Piller, Ingrid. (2012). Intercultural communication: An overview. In Christina Bratt Paulston, Scott F. Kiesling & Elizabeth S. Rangel (eds.), *The Handbook of intercultural discourse and communication*, 3–18. Malden, MA: John Wiley & Sons. https://doi.org/10.1002/9781118247273.ch1

Quiroga-Clare, Cecilia. 2003. Language ambiguity: A curse and a blessing. *Translation Journal* 7(1). 57–61.

Searle, John R. 1969. *Speech acts: An essay in the philosophy of language*. Cambridge, UK: Cambridge University Press.

Searle, John R. 1976. A classification of illocutionary acts. *Language in Society* 5(1). 1–23. https://doi.org/10.1017/S0047404500006837

Sennet, Adam. 2021. Ambiguity. In Edward N. Zalta (ed.), *The Stanford encyclopedia of philosophy* (Fall 2021). Metaphysics Research Lab, Stanford University. https://plato.stanford.edu/archives/fall2021/entries/ambiguity/

Sue, Derald Wing. 2010. *Microaggressions in everyday life: Race, gender, and sexual orientation*. Malden, MA: John Wiley & Sons.

Sue, Derald Wing, Christina M. Capodilupo, Gina C. Torino, Jennifer M. Bucceri, Aisha M. B. Holder, Kevin L. Nadal & Marta Esquilin. 2007. Racial microaggressions in everyday life: Implications for clinical practice. *The American Psychologist* 62(4). 271–286. https://doi.org/10.1037/0003-066X.62.4.271

Tannen, Deborah. 2012. Turn-taking and intercultural discourse and communication. In Christina Bratt Paulston, Scott F. Kiesling & Elizabeth S. Rangel (eds.), *The Handbook of intercultural discourse and communication*, 135–157. Malden, MA: John Wiley & Sons. https://doi.org/10.1002/9781118247273.ch8

Thomas, Jenny. 1983. Cross-cultural pragmatic failure. *Applied Linguistics* 4(2). 91–112. https://doi.org/10.1093/applin/4.2.91

Tran, Ly Thi & Lien Pham. 2016. International students in transnational mobility: intercultural connectedness with domestic and international peers, institutions and the wider community. *Compare: A Journal of Comparative and International Education* 46(4). 560–581. https://doi.org/10.1080/03057925.2015.1057479

Wang, Jennifer, Janxin Leu & Yuichi Shoda. 2011. When the seemingly innocuous "stings": racial microaggressions and their emotional consequences. *Personality & Social Psychology Bulletin* 37(12). 1666–1678. https://doi.org/10.1177/0146167211416130

Yule, George. 1996. *Pragmatics*. Oxford, UK: Oxford University Press.

Gabriel T. Acevedo Velázquez
Chapter 6
A critical look at 'Pato' y 'Maricón': Puerto Rican Gay teachers' interventions with homophobic language

Abstract: In this chapter, the author employs critical discourse analysis (CDA) alongside a narrative frame to interrogate how interventions against homophobic slurs in Puerto Rico are thought of and/or understood by gay teachers. Data was collected from three Puerto Rican teachers who identify as gay. An analysis of the data revealed two broad themes that characterized how these teachers thought of and engaged with the *pato/maricón* rhetoric: 1) talking or hesitating about homophobic language and 2) drawing upon personal Puerto Rican queer culture references and/or experiences to communicate with students. In addition to the themes, counterexamples that directly tie into the participants' understanding of the two main themes are provided. The findings highlight the benefits of these teachers' having the lenses and experiences to understand and make sense of homophobic slurs as well as implement interventions that may prevent the harmful and weaponized way language may be utilized.

Keywords: Homophobic language, Puerto Rico, Language weaponization, Critical Discourse Analysis

1 Introduction

> Lo ideal sería que yo jamás en mi vida,
> mientras este dando clases, tenga que intervenir
> con un estudiante por decirle pato a otro – Carlos, June 2022.

In discourse about homophobia, much of the attention focuses on cultural groups and societal practices enacted that either enable such discourse or the aftermath of how to deal with such issues. This is even more prevalent in communities in which intersectional identities are crucial to the construction of such conversations. Employing critical discourse analysis (CDA) alongside a narrative frame (Fairclough, 2013), I interrogate how interventions against homophobic slurs in Puerto Rico are

---

Gabriel T. Acevedo Velázquez, Arizona State University

https://doi.org/10.1515/9783110799521-006

thought of and/or understood by gay teachers. The educational system in Puerto Rico has a feeble track record when dealing with queer and homophobic issues in schools. Though the educational system on the island does not directly tackle or have ordinances in place for such behaviors, I argue that teachers', especially gay teachers', conceptualizations of homophobic instances become part of the more extensive educational narrative as well as part of their self-understandings.

This qualitative case study is guided by the following research question: *How do gay teachers in Puerto Rico utilize discourse to reveal their understandings and interventions concerning homophobic slurs?* Utilizing CDA and narrative tools of systematic self-reflection, I interpret transcripts of conversations between myself and three gay Puerto Rican teachers about their thoughts and actions against the use of homophobic slurs in Puerto Rican classrooms. My analysis focused on discourse indicating participants' understanding of their relationship with homophobic slurs and their expressed interventions or lack thereof. I offer conclusions with the hope that not only queer Latinx teachers find it insightful, but educators and non-educators can reflect upon their relationship with homophobia and the process behind intervening in such instances in classroom spaces and beyond.

2 Understanding queer experiences in Puerto Rico

In order to contextualize the findings of this study, it is necessary to understand queer experiences in Puerto Rican schools. As of early 2023, the Puerto Rico Department of Education does not have specific guidelines to deal with queer youth and/or incidents in schools. Because of Puerto Rico's colonial status with the United States, the island follows the protocols established by the U.S. Department of Education. In fact, in 2015, Senate Bill 184 seeking to ban conversion therapy was voted down by the New Progressive Party (PNP), the Popular Democratic Party (PPD), and Joanne Rodriguez Vevé from Proyecto Dignidad Party (PDP). Despite social advances in the last decade, queer identities have been attacked by political structures around the country, including Puerto Rico.

A body of research shows how schools can be hostile and dangerous towards queer students and teachers at all levels (Espelage & Swearer, 2008; Ferfolja, 2007; Jackson, 2006; Kosciw et al., 2010). Studies also show that verbal harassment is the most common form of harassment for students who identify as queer (GLSEN, 2017; Kosciw et al., 2010). The most recent study on queer experiences in Puerto Rican schools was done by the Gay, Lesbian & Straight Education Network (GLSEN) in 2017. To say the results of the survey were alarming would be an understatement. School environments are hostile for a distressing number of queer students in Puerto Rico. Over two-thirds of students surveyed (69%) felt unsafe at school, and (63%) of students felt the schools were unable to protect them. The overwhelming majority of students, 96.2%, routinely heard anti-queer language (i.e., *pato* or *maricón*), and almost all queer students surveyed, 99.5%, heard some sort of homophobic remark. Lastly, 78.8% of students heard homophobic remarks come from school officials.

2.1 Making sense of *Pato* and *Maricón*, the Puerto Rican Gay Slurs

Homophobic verbal harassment has been shown to have mental and educational consequences for queer students (Guerin, 2005; Kosciw et al., 2010; Swearer et al., 2008). Burn et al. (2005) argue that verbal homophobic harassment is utilized to intimidate someone, whether or not they identify as LGBTQ+. The ubiquitous nature of homophobic language continuously used in Puerto Rico situates educators in precarious situations when intervening. For decades the use of the word fag(got) in public discourse has caused ideological struggles in and outside the queer community. A derogatory term weaponized to harm queer people, it has also been reappropriated by the queer community as a testament to power and resilience.

In Puerto Rico the slur equivalent of *fag* is "pato" or "maricón." Being referred to as pato or maricón is quite a traumatic and disconcerting moment as both terms have become weaponized against queer people on the island to produce harm. Pentón Herrera & Bryan (2022) refer to the notion of harm as "how minoritized individuals, as well as their cultures and languages, are affected by ideologies and practices that normalize inequity and injustice" (p. 3). La Fountain-Stokes (1999) looks at how *pato* and *maricón* have evolved into a source of fear for queer Puerto Ricans and a slur. Henderson (2003) refers to a slur as a word used to refer to a member or members of a group in an offensive manner. This definition, however, suggests that slurs are static or stable, yet slurs become weaponized for an ideological struggle within and against a specific targeted group.

Sociohistorical contexts are of the utmost importance in understanding the notions behind slurs as they fuel the marginalization, in this case, of the sexual identity of their target (2003). In this case, Puerto Rican ideas of machismo and queerness shape the homophobic understanding of these slurs. Machismo and queer ideologies are constructions that create and divide the relationship between genders and cultural spaces, in this case, rhetoric (Ramírez, 1999). Views of masculinity and queerness become an important area of scrutiny, for they are deemed as domestic creations of body and space that not only confine to binary constructions but shows how they are produced. Such ideas become problematic when being presented in specific geographical spaces and contexts, in this case, Puerto Rico. It is essential to understand how both machismo and queerness are perceived in Puerto Rico. Within the last decade, heteronormative assumptions (Warner, 1991) have been challenged by queer geographical and cultural analysis. Knopp (2007) defines this phenomenon as "a self-conscious intellectual movement . . . highlighting the fluid nature of sexual subjectivities, and it reimagines geographical dimensions of these accordingly." Current queer geographies contribute significantly to the reconceptualization of "queer geographical imaginations" (p. 22).

Binnie (2007) argues that queer sensibilities are often theorized and analyzed through academic, professional, white, and Western lenses. She adds that the marginalization of politics has accompanied such homonormativity and "the visibility of affluent white gay men . . . and highlighted the exclusion of race, class, gender, and disability in queer communities" (p. 34). While trying to understand queer Latino spaces, it is essential to contend with the idea that queer is not a term that can be effectively transferred or translated into Spanish (Rodríguez, 2003). Therefore, it allows for the construction of geographical and contextual discourse. This is seen in Puerto Rico as maricón or pato and used to refer to gay people, particularly gay males (Ramírez, 1999). When the term pato o maricón is used, it is seen as a loaded word. Utilizing such rhetoric demonstrates an understanding of identity that a particular person adheres to but is weaponized against that person.

3 Methodology

3.1 Understanding Critical Discourse Analysis (CDA)

This study utilizes tools of Critical Discourse Analysis (CDA) as its primary framework, both theoretically and methodologically. CDA is a method that combines critical social theories with discourse analysis perspectives to interpret significant relationships between discourse, texts, social contexts, social levels, and institutions (Fairclough, 2013, Wodak & Meyer, 2016). Rogers et al. (2005) conceptualized CDA as a way in which language as a cultural tool "mediates relationships of power and privilege in social interactions, institutions, and bodies of knowledge" (p. 367). Using CDA, researchers and analysts are driven by complex and crucial social issues, including language weaponization. They also seek to acknowledge language's effects on reproducing social inequalities and uphold social power (van Dijk, 1993).

CDA goes beyond other approaches to discourse analysis by seeking to interpret language in use and analyze, describe, and explain the role and significance of representations embedded in discourse. For a CDA analysis to be meaningful, a working definition of discourse should be presented. For this study, I define discourse as the language and language experiences framing one's understanding.

Discourse and language are essential to a CDA framework. Discourse is a central component of CDA as a method and theory. Discourse and the study of discourse have been defined from the perspectives of critical linguistics, cultural and media studies, and social semiotics (Rogers, 2011). Discourse reflects a social practice of language (Fairclough, 2003; Rogers, 2011) that is ideologically and historically confined (Fairclough & Wodak, 1997). As a social practice, discourse constructs meaning related to systems of belief and knowledge (ideational), social relationships between people (relational), and social identities (identity) (Fairclough, 1992). Gee (2000) emphasizes power relations between actors and validates the way discourse provides knowledge over others. Language, in CDA, is assumed to never be neutral, given its power relationship. Power is a commodity that can be given, received, transferred, or taken away (Bloome et al., 2005). Language also reflects meaning linked to societal, cultural, and political practices (Fairclough & Wodak, 1997). Fairclough (2013) argues that "power is won, held, and lost in social struggles" (p. 98). Therefore, language both contributes to and provides social struggle, given its power relationship, which can be used for social good and misused as social control by one group over another, which then allows for patterns of intervention in institutional, political, or societal problems (Gee, 2000).

Selecting CDA as the primary framework was guided by the anti-queer nature of Puerto Rico's educational and cultural system and queer individuals' role in anti-homophobic movements on the island. Very few studies have been conducted in which a CDA approach is applied to the analysis of heteronormative and homophobic discourse in Puerto Rican or Latinx contexts, and even fewer studies have been conducted looking at educational and queer spaces. This study seeks to locate itself at the intersection of CDA and Queer/Latinx educational spaces, showing the interconnected relationship between language and homophobic discourses.

3.2 Understanding narratives

In addition to CDA, this study draws insights from a series of stories participants shared about their experiences in Puerto Rican classrooms when engaging with situations of homophobic rhetoric in schools. Some questions were more open-ended; for instance, participants were asked, "What is an incident that you clearly remember . . . what did you do? How did the school handle the situation?" or "What do you wish would have been done in order to rectify such situation?" Other questions more directly addressed their identities within the context of any situation, including, "As a gay man, how did hearing students call each other *'pato'* affect you?" and "Did you have any self-reflection on the way you engaged with any homophobic situation in schools?" The shared stories and experiences showcase pictures of the events that occurred and illustrate the participants' understanding of how they see themselves and their perceptions and reactions when confronting homophobic instances as gay teachers (Olsen, 2008). Alongside Rhetorical Listening and CDA, I utilize Clandenin and Connelly's (2000) narrative conception as a complementary conceptual lens for comparing and making sense of my participant's stories.

Narration allows for the examination of individuals' life experiences told through stories (Clandenin & Connelly, 2000), and it is often used in studies centered on educational experiences (Chase, 2005). It allows the researcher to engage with and prioritize an in-depth understanding of the complexities of a participant as they reflect on their experiences while: creating a researcher-participant relationship that allows a learning process for both; valuing language as a representation of complex experiences; and a variety of valid ways of knowing (Pinnegar & Daynes, 2007). Utilizing a critical narrative inquiry allowed me to capture the emotions of what was described and discussed through narrative storytelling as I collected and re-storied the participant's narratives to understand their unique experiences (Sparkes et al., 2013). Although a critical stance is not necessarily attached to narrative inquiry, a critical narrative inquiry allows me to understand my participant's stories, experiences, and actions in a manner that can be layered alongside rhetorical listening and CDA. By utilizing a narrative inquiry model, I engaged with the participants' experiences in a way that allowed me to examine and bring them to life critically.

3.3 Where did the stories come from?

The data was collected via in-depth interviews and a focus group interview. Between 2018 and 2020, over 30 interviews were conducted with eight gay teachers in Puerto Rico. In June 2022, follow-up interviews were done with three participants. Their data transcripts were selected for this study. Since gayness, homophobia, and teaching are collective *and* individual experiences, interviews allowed individuals to express and explore their engagement with those mentioned above. Furthermore, due to the sensitive nature of the topic under study, one-on-one interviews and the focus group interview between the researcher and participants allowed for more vulnerable and open conversations about the issue. This method also allowed participants to share their personal experiences and insights on the phenomenon under study.

Individual in-depth interviews are a fundamental tool in narrative inquiry and were selected as the primary method for data collection in this study. In-depth interviews can capture a participant's perspective of an experience (Creswell, 2007; Denzin & Lincoln, 2018). One of the main advantages of doing interviews is how useful for discovery and gaining insight into the subject, as well as the capability to entirely focus on, analyze and describe a research topic (Collis & Hussey, 2003; Shuy, 2002). Interviewing allowed participants to recount narratives through which a sense of their experiences was shared. Interviewing allowed an interest, alongside narrative inquiry and CDA, in understanding the experiences of the participants and their interaction with homophobia. Table 6.1 includes the specific demographics of the participants as it relates to this study. The names are pseudonyms.

Table 6.1: Participants.

Name	Age	Institution Type	Years Teaching	Subject Taught	Social Identities	# of interviews
Adai	33	Public, non-denominational, Spanish-oriented Institution	10	Mathematics (Secondary)	Puerto Rican, Gay, middle class, bilingual, working-class	3 individual interviews, 1 focus group, 2 follow-ups (member checks)
Carlos	32	Public, non-denominational, Bilingual Institution	10	ESL, Literature, Public Speaking (High School)	Puerto Rican, Gay, middle class, bilingual	3 individual interviews, 1 focus group, 2 follow-ups (member checks)
Theo	29	Public, non-denominational, Spanish-oriented institution	5	Math, Science, History, Spanish (Elementary)	Puerto Rican, Gay, middle class, bilingual	3 individual interviews, 1 focus group, 2 follow-ups (member checks)

4 This is what I found!

The analysis revealed two broad themes that characterized how the participants thought of and engaged with the *pato/maricón* rhetoric: 1) talking or hesitating about homophobic language and 2) drawing upon personal Puerto Rican queer culture references and/or experiences to communicate with students. After presenting the two main themes, I present counterexamples that directly tie into the participants' understanding of the two main themes. These counterexamples relate to *pato/maricón* on the participants' permissive attitudes. I illustrate the two representative themes by presenting excerpts of the participants' interviews as I draw upon their experiences and stories.

4.1 Prevarication, talking or not about homophobic language: "Not in my classroom, outside maybe."

In many instances across the interviews, participants either directly engaged in conversations about the language used (i.e., pato or maricón) or hesitated before having such conversations. In some instances, participants decided not to address the situation or send students to higher-ups (i.e., social workers or the principal) to avoid engaging with the situation in the classroom. When prevaricating, participants often pointed out they would pause or false start as they were thinking about how to address homophobic incidents in schools. For instance, Theo explained that although he knew students calling each other pato or maricón is wrong, he would carefully consider how to address the situation as well as how to speak to students; he added, "When I was [pause] as an openly gay kid I would constantly [pause] be called pato, but as a gay teacher [pause] there are different mechanics to calling that out." Theo begins his statement with "When I was" but does not finish the sentence by saying "in school." Instead, he paused before identifying himself as a gay kid. By engaging in this discourse, Theo adequately placed himself at the center of queer-based terminology, "gay kid," rather than making a direct correlation to the context of school, which would directly tie into his identity as a teacher who engages with relatable queer experiences.

In another example of prevarication, Adai discussed the struggles he encounters when engaging with students about not using homophobic language, especially as a gay man himself. He paused before stating, "I find it funny that [pause] because in the back of my mind, I am always thinking that my students are thinking that I will be coming at them from a personal rather than a teacher angle [pause] um, [pause, excitement] what's the balance." In this statement, Adai made word choices that balanced out his thoughts and possible blame for the reaction he might get from students. Adai used the phrase "I find it funny" to start by describing his thoughts on starting an intervention with students rather than a more direct or severe alternative. Additionally, he used the pronoun "I" three times in that statement, further centering himself not only as the teacher but as an active participant in the intervention discourse that will occur. He also utilizes the phrase "... I am always thinking that my students are thinking that I..." to achieve a similar sense of prevarication that allows a shift of blame if the intervention on homophobic slurs does not go as intended.

Each of these discourse choices served to walk into homophobic interventions with a more comfortable and guarded mindset that prepares, in this case, Adai, for different scenarios. In fact, at the end of his statement, in an excited and laughing manner, he says, "What's the balance," which shows an awareness of his discourse choices and possible outcomes of homophobic interventions. In a follow-up meeting to discuss my analysis and transcriptions, Adai further reflected by sharing, "I can see what you are saying, and yes, I definitely think of possible scenarios which might shift blame if what I expect to happen does not. It is my way of keeping some sort of control over the situation."

In addition, there were instances in that participants directly jumped to mitigate the situation, albeit with reservations. One example of such a moment comes from Carlos's assertion that he does not allow homophobic rhetoric in his classroom. He added, "Listen, I'm gay and open about it, I went through hell as a gay teenager in schools, and I don't want to see that happen to anyone. But I just don't pass judgment; I ask about the situation first and then act." Carlos's inclusion of "but" tells us to his position of trying to engage with a similar mindset in any homophobic situation even though he begins by asserting that such situations are harmful when he says, "I went through hell." When asked about this assertion, he lingered on it but mentioned another situation in which he acted quickly and decisively. He shares, "While heading to my classroom, once I heard a student say to another, "A la verdad que tú eres bien pato," (you truly are very faggot) I immediately jumped in to mitigate the situation. I never allowed the student to explain himself as it is unacceptable to utilize homophobic language." In contrast to his previous story, Carlos's decisive nature shows the distinction between everyday occurrences as an educator. Carlos presented no pause or hesitation in that conversation, and his tone always remained assertive, and no act of prevarication was present this time.

Meanwhile, Theo and Adai shared how they directly approached students about not using pato/maricón towards others students. Interestingly enough, both these instances were about situations outside of their classrooms. When asked about this, Adai shared, "Well [pause] to be honest, I teach 50-minute classes, so I rather send them to the principal or talk about the situation later if it happens in my class." Theo added, "Yeah, like Adai, [pause] if it is in my classroom, I rather deal with it later. I know it's a great moment to have a class discussion about it, but if I were to stop and do that for every bad word, I would never be able to teach anything." I understood both of them to interpret these experiences as contextual, meaning we can handle it if it does not affect my class. This interpretation was endorsed through the transcript member-checking process and a brief phone call with both of them. Though not paired with facial expressions as we were on the phone, when endorsing the transcript and analysis, Theo said, "I had never thought about it [pause]. I just wanted to get through the novel we were reading." Adai jumps in and shares, " . . . yeah [pause] now I feel a little bit bad because I know it's wrong, but I have to work." Both pauses allowed their experiences and the handling of such experiences to sink in and serve as self-assessments of the balancing act of teaching and the mitigation of homophobic classroom instances.

4.2 Puerto Rican queer culture and experiences: "We all know what it means."

Throughout the interviews, I felt the participants drew upon our shared Puerto Rican queer knowledge and experiences without directly stating them. There was an unspoken adherence or confirmation that some ideas and experiences did not require further explanation when shared between them. A clear pattern in the data was the way the participants relied on context, including the relationship between the aggressor and the victim, to indicate that this type of language contributed to maintaining, solidifying, or disrupting social interactions and relationships. Warwick and Aggleton (2013) differentiate how homophobic language is used as a slur or how it is used acceptably between agreeing people.

When asked, Theo made the connection on some instances when openly out queer students utilized what could be perceived as homophobic words about each other without malintent behind it. He shares that with all homophobic words, it is different when using them as an attack or as a term of endearment between queer people there is this acceptance that if gay men in PR call each other "pato" (faggot) o "patito" (little faggot), it is an acceptable form of communication that does not become homophobic. If you are with your friends or someone you get along with, then you start utilizing these words with each other without feeling judged or slandered.

This explanation contextualizes commonality factors between queer people that come into play when interpreting or making sense of language that may come off as homophobic in other instances. Discourse, out of shared experiences, like the example provided above, could be viewed as homophobic, but the same discourse can be viewed as communicative and even positive between parties that share a commonality.

Furthermore, Adai discussed how the queer community in Puerto Rico has retaken pato and maricón as monikers of power for them, "When I'm with my friends, we call each other *patito* or use *maricón* with each other." After sharing that, Theo says, "I do the same thing in any context with my friends or when I see other gays around," Carlos jumps in as well and shares, "I do that as well with friends." In Puerto Rican queer culture, it is common to use pato or maricón as monikers within your queer circles. Neither of them explained this idea further. Instead, it is confirmed as something that just is, allowing them to visually cue and affirm their experiences as they share cultural capital.

Carlos made similar discourse moves in talking about his experiences as a teacher through the Puerto Rican queer cultural lens. He is operationalizing language from the notion that I, as a Puerto Rican gay teacher, would understand the references and relate to his experiences through our shared commonality. While explaining how he has engaged with how others have perceived his gayness, Carlos inserted an aside (indicated by speaking fluidity and tone changes) to help contextualize his surroundings. He shared that since he was younger and now as an adult, he doesn't police his gayness as much as you would think, even though there is an expectation to do that in educational spaces. I have always been the gay guy, right? You always have to act or are expected to act a certain way, do you know what I mean?

Carlos engages with me utilizing rhetoric as "right?" and "You know what I mean?" Even though he may not have been seeking a verbal response to either inquiry, each rhetorical gesture indicated a conjecture that I would understand and related to his social experiences as a gay man in a predominantly heteronormative space. Carlos assumed I would relate and understand his description within a larger, more significant point: that even though there is an expectation of self-policing queerness in educational spaces, these expectations did not directly come into play in his experiences as a gay student or teacher.

Theo also connected ideas of gayness and Puerto Ricanness in unspoken rhetorical nuances he assumed I would understand. In response to an inquiry about whether more conversations around queerness in school would impact homophobic rhetoric in schools, he shared.

It is a tough call because kids are in school for only a certain amount of time. So many other factors go into talking to them about queerness. If these conversations occur, it would hopefully click for some that slurs like pato and maricón should not be used, especially in schools. I've had conversations in my classroom about it, and it has clicked for some students.

Theo used the wording "click" a couple of times to express his desire for these conversations to occur that show his preference for engagement with homophobic slurs. Generally, utilizing such a phrase between two Latinx gay men in response to an inquiry about queerness indicates a specific reference to queer identity. Theo clarifies that his comments concern people identifying as "straight." It is clear he anticipated a follow-up as he quickly adds the following: "In reference to talking about those topics and how it can click for some, I clearly mean people who identify as straight, you know?" Adding this clarification, Theo likely thought I would draw a different conclusion based on his phrasing. Theo makes one final indication: "I've had conversations in my classroom about it, and it has clicked for some students." His positive experiences in the classroom and engaging with such topics serve as Implications that those interventions will always work though he does not provide additional layers of specificity about their experiences, especially when in regards to outside his classroom.

In such situations, the presumptive language I shared contexts communicates more information that might be suggested, even if considered homophobic. In a one-off comment, Carlos explained how homophobic language (i.e., pato and maricón) demonstrate membership in a social group, "From what I say in my circle of friends and what I have even heard gay students say ... those words in no way mean anything bad as long as it goes from their mouths to their counterparts' ears." Social contexts and interactions played a part in shaping the meaning of homophobic language to the point that it could be socially beneficial to specific groups within a determined chosen community. These cultural experiences employ a relationship and a show of membership to a group that facilitates the development of cultural relationships and understandings that have positive outcomes.

4.3 Permissive attitudes: "It's not about me."

In rare instances, participants utilized direct terminology that explicitly references homophobic language when talking about their own identities. In all the interviews and follow-up member-checking procedures, only four times were the terms pato/maricón referenced in direct connection to the participant's identities and experiences. Theo mentioned his experience with homophobic language as a teenager and even as an adult. He explained how he was called pato many times while in school and has been called maricón as an adult just walking down the street. Adai shared similar instances, specifically focusing on his school experiences and how they stay with you, "It is weird because every time I hear it in the school I work at, it just triggers me to some degree." Neither Theo nor Adai wanted to discuss their experiences in follow-up inquiries. Adai replied, "I'll talk about it, sure, but not today [laughs]."

Carlos shared a story about the difficulties of knowing when students and colleagues are talking about you and how when those instances occur, he is transported to the kid who was bullied and called "pato." He attributes feelings of insecurities to everlasting shame and feeling helpless as a teenager when bullied and called homophobic slurs. He provided two examples of his experiences to make his point. First, he shared his interaction with homophobic language as a kid that clearly, "scared me to the point it still lingers." Second, he talks about how it affects his adult life, specifically his teaching identity, " . . . as a gay teacher who was called all those things, it sucks reliving it a few times a week." All three participants provide nuanced engagements with homophobic language. In phrases like "triggers me" and "scared me," they confirm the everlasting impact that homophobic languages like *pato* and *maricón* have on their identities.

These experiences become characteristically permissive as they have come to accept and tolerate such language usage, as some interventions are not done promptly. Permissive attitudes towards homophobic language directly tie into intervening attitudes (Troop-Gordon & Ladd, 2015) as, through previous experiences, the normalization of certain acts occurs through specific actions. By seeing all three participants barely acknowledge or want to answer follow-up inquiries about their relationships with homophobic language, you can argue that there is a personal detachment from confronting such experiences' effects on them. From these counterexamples, I suspect that queer teachers who hold less permissive attitudes towards the use of *pato* and *maricón* will more likely act quicker and intervene timely when homophobic behavior occurs around them.

5 Let's discuss this!

The guiding question for this chapter centered on how gay teachers in Puerto Rico utilize discourse to reveal their understandings and interventions concerning homophobic slurs and what that reveals about their perceptions of such language. I explicitly acknowledge that the experiences presented here do not reflect all gay men in Puerto Rico or all gay men who work in pedagogical contexts. Many illustrations are presented in this chapter that shows the active engagement or lack thereof with homophobic language, how queer cultural contexts affect language usage and relationships, and how permissive attitudes often come into play when referencing or not the participants' identities.

The perspective of participants in this study addresses homophobic language in several ways, including prejudice and in terms of endearments in specific contexts. The participants' perspectives present the notion that homophobic language is utilized by individuals who seek to attack or harm gay identities. These assumptions and experiences present a picture of the interactions gay teachers have with homophobic languages utilized in schools. The complexity of homophobic language usage and its functions bring implications for educators and schools. By some participants picking and choosing when and how to engage with such language, there is a lack of pattern that brings awareness in framing homophobic language as negative and how intervening in those usage instances may potentially lead to a conversation around the eradication of language usage in ways that are harmful and weaponized. The question then becomes: How can gay teachers ultimately be prompted to intervene in homophobic instances?

As a Puerto Rican gay teacher, I could notice and relate to the patterns and experiences the participants were sharing. By sharing not only the same cultural background but the same queer identity, I was able to pinpoint hesitations and silences in our conversations that allowed me to press the issue further. Additionally, the participants felt comfortable being more direct or making shared assumptions of ideas, not necessarily speaking out loud because of our shared commonality. However, such commonalities are insufficient to effectively listen and pick up on rhetorical experiences. Critical self-reflection (Reyes & Zermeño, 2018; Rios et al., 2003) begins with thinking about oneself, one's worldviews, and how they fit into power structures that organize society. I used this strategy to listen for words not directly spoken or messages from my participants I might have otherwise missed. As part of this process, our biases are examined and what they mean, adopt the viewpoint of others in accepting such viewpoints, and use reflection to push one to take action. Because it begins with the practitioner, in this case, the participants, critical self-reflections provide a framework for thinking about numerous interactions with diverse individuals.

A hegemonically dominant communicative form (mainly heteronormative) must be acknowledged to accomplish this task effectively. Identifying the contours of the relationships between cultural background, sexuality, and queerness identity markers with specific participant groups will help determine how the three affect and, in turn, impact each other. It is essential to consider this since these Puerto Rican gay men's commentary might not explicitly link these three concepts together. Many works that simultaneously examine sexual orientation, cultural background, and queerness do so intending to conduct critical analysis that will highlight unequal institutional dynamics (Acker, 2006; Gillborn, 2015). Educational researchers who wish to engage in discourse studies with culturally different groups must tune their interpretation tools to grasp meanings that could otherwise be overlooked or dismissed as irrelevant. In order to combat the pervasive consequences of living in an unfair society, which extends to their professional educational contexts, these modes of communicating and relating to one another include avoiding direct discussion of specific subjects like their LGBT identities.

6 Final thoughts

To conclude, I take a break from the conventional conclusion section and give the final word to Carlos, who encapsulates the purpose of this work. When making sense of and explaining his interview and transcriptions in a follow-up conversation, Carlos started picking up on behavioral patterns he had not before made sense of. Carlos noted how many of his actions or inactions sometimes go against his professed notions of being a gay political educator in Puerto Rico. He explained:

> Since you sent me the files of our interviews and I went over them, I have been a bit hard on myself. I have been very proud of being gay for almost 20 years now, and to see my hesitation in acting up when homophobic situations are happening is kind of shocking. All the feelings that have been noticing my inactions are the same feelings that came up when I was bullied or called in schools or the streets. I didn't have the support I wish I had, and now that I am in that position of power to help queer students, I see myself not doing it entirely as jarring. Having the opportunity to work with you in the last few years has given me a better sense and viewpoint of how having a sense of connection and understanding to queer experiences and homophobic instances can be an asset to putting a stop to it. It is a fresh take that my gay self is and can be an asset to queer students and, hopefully, an asset to putting a stop to the derogatory disgusting language people still use today.

Carlos's comment is a realization and an internal plea for himself and others around him to be present and act in situations they feel and know are wrong. Having such lenses and experiences to understand and make sense of homophobic slurs allows Carlos and other educators to facilitate such interventions about the harmful and weaponized way language may be utilized.

References

Acker, Joan. 2006. Inequality regimes: Gender, class, and race in organizations. *Gender and Society* 20(4). 441–464. https://doi.org/10.1177/0891243206289499

Binnie, Jon. 2007. Sexuality, the erotic and geography: Epistemology, methodology and pedagogy. In Jason Lim & Kath Browne (eds.), *Geographies of sexualities: Theory, practices and politics*, 29–38. New York, NY: Routledge.

Bloome, David, Stephanie Power Carter, Beth Morton Christian, Sheila Otto & Nora Shuart-Faris. 2005. *Discourse analysis and the study of classroom language and literacy events*. New York, NY: Routledge.

Burn, Shawn M., Kelly Kadlec & Ryan Rexer. 2005. Effects of subtle heterosexism on gays, lesbians, and bisexuals. *Journal of Homosexuality* 49(2). 23–38. https://doi.org/10.1300/J082v49n02_02

Chase, Susan E. 2005. Narrative inquiry: Multiple lenses, approaches, voices. In Norman K. Denzin & Yvonna S. Lincoln (Eds.), *The Sage handbook of qualitative research*, 651–679. Thousand Oaks, CA: Sage.

Clandinin, D. Jean & F. Michael Connelly. 2000. *Narrative inquiry: Experience and story in qualitative research*. San Francisco, CA: Jossey-Bass.

Collis, Jill & Roger Hussey. 2003. *Business research: A practical guide for undergraduate and postgraduate students*(2nd ed.). Hampshire, UK: Palgrave Macmillan.

Creswell, John W. 2007. *Qualitative inquiry and research design: Choosing among five approaches* (3rd ed.). Thousand Oaks, CA: Sage.

Denzin, Norman & Yvonna Lincoln (eds.). 2018. *The Sage handbook of qualitative research* (5th ed.). Thousand Oaks, CA: Sage.

Espelage, Dorothy L. & Susan M. Swearer. 2008. Addressing research gaps in the intersection between homophobia and bullying. *School Psychology Review* 37(2). 155–159.

Fairclough, Norman. 1992. *Discourse and social change*. Berkeley, CA: Blackwell.

Fairclough, Norman &Ruth Wodak. 1997. Critical discourse analysis. In Teun van Dijk (ed.), *Discourse studies: A multidisciplinary introduction* (Vol. 2), 258–284. Thousand Oaks, CA: Sage.

Fairclough, Norman. 2003. *Analysing discourse*. New York, NY: Routledge.

Fairclough, Norman. 2013. Critical discourse analysis and critical policy studies. *Critical Policy Studies* 7(2). 177–197. https://doi.org/10.1080/19460171.2013.798239

Ferfolja, Tania. 2007. Teacher negotiations of sexual subjectivities. *Gender and Education* 19(5). 569–586. https://doi.org/10.1080/09540250701535584

Fountain-Stokes, Lawrence M. 1999. *Culture, representation, and the Puerto Rican queer diaspora*. Columbia University dissertation.

Gee, James P. 2000. Identity as analytic lens for research in education. *Review of Research in Education* 25(1). 99–125. https://doi.org/10.3102/0091732X025001099

Gay, Lesbian, andStraight Education Network. 2017. *Snapshot school climate in Puerto Rico–Glsen*. (n.d.). Gay, Lesbian and Straight Education Network.

Gillborn, David. 2015. Intersectionality, critical race theory, and the primacy of racism: Race, class, gender, and disability in education. *Qualitative Inquiry* 21(3). 277–287. https://doi.org/10.1177/1077800414557827

Guerin, Bernard. 2005. Combating everyday racial discrimination without assuming racists or racism: New intervention ideas from a contextual analysis. *Behavior and Social Issues*14(1). 46–71. https://doi.org/10.5210/bsi.v14i1.120

Henderson, Anita. 2003. What's in a slur? *American Speech* 78(1). 52–74. https://doi.org/10.1215/00031283-78-1-52

Jackson, Janna M. 2006. Removing the masks: Considerations by gay and lesbian teachers when negotiating the closet door. *Journal of Poverty* 10(2). 27–52. https://doi.org/10.1300/J134v10n02_03

Kosciw, Joseph G., Emily A. Greytak, Elizabeth M. Diaz & Mark J. Bartkiewicz. 2010. *The 2009 National School Climate Survey: The experiences of lesbian, gay, bisexual and transgender youth in our nation's schools*. Gay, Lesbian and Straight Education Network.

Olsen, Brad. 2008. How "reasons for entry into the profession" illuminate teacher identity development. *Teacher Education Quarterly* 35(3). 23–40.

Knopp, Larry. 2007. On the relationship between queer and feminist geographies. *Professional Geographer* 59(1). 47–55. https://doi.org/10.1111/j.1467-9272.2007.00590.x

Pentón Herrera, Luis Javier & Kisha C. Bryan. 2022. Language weaponization in society and education: Introduction to the special issue. *International Journal of Literacy, Culture, and Language Education* 2. 1–5. https://doi.org/10.14434/ijlcle.v2iMay.34380

Pinnegar, Stefinee &J. Gary Daynes. 2007. Locating narrative inquiry historically. In D. Jean Clandinin (ed.), *Handbook of narrative inquiry: Mapping a methodology*, 3–34. Thousand Oaks, CA: Sage Publications.

Ramírez, Rafael L. 1999. *What it means to be a man: Reflections on Puerto Rican masculinity*. New Brunswick, NJ: Rutgers University Press.

Reyes, G. T. & Bernadette Pilar Zermeño. 2018. Of course she will learn: A cultural pedagogy in bilingual transitional kindergarten with newcomer students. *Multicultural Education* 25(3–4). 18–22.

Rios, Francisco, Allen Trent & Lillian Vega Castañeda. 2003. Social perspective taking: Advancing empathy and advocating justice. *Equity & Excellence in Education* 36(1). 5–14. https://doi.org/10.1080/10665680303506

Rodríguez, Juana María. 2003. *Queer Latinidad: Identity practices, discursive spaces*. New York: New York University Press.

Rogers, Rebecca. 2011. Tracking educational trajectories and life pathways: The longitudinal nexuses of critical discourse analysis and ethnography. *Critical Discourse Studies* 8(4). 239–252.

Rogers, Rebecca, Elizabeth Malancharuvil-Berkes, Melissa Mosley, Diane Hui & Glynis O'Garro Joseph. 2005. A critical review of critical discourse analysis. *Review of Research in Education* 75(3). 365–416. https://doi.org/10.3102/00346543075003365

Senate Bill 184. 2015. https://www.govinfo.gov/link/bills/114/sres/184?link-type=pdf

Swearer, Susan M., Rhonda K. Turner, Jami E. Givens & William S. Pollack. 2008. "You're so gay!": Do different forms of bullying matter for adolescent males? *School Psychology Review* 37(2). 160–173.

Shuy, Roger W. 2002. In-person versus telephone interviewing. In Jaber F. Gubrium & James A. Holstein(eds.), *Handbook of interview research: Context and method*, 537–555. Thousand Oaks, CA: Sage.

Smith, Brett, Andrew C Sparkes, Cassandra Phoenix & Joanna Kirkby. 2013. Qualitative research in physical therapy: A critical discussion on mixed-method research. *Physical Therapy Reviews* 17(6). 374–81. https://doi.org/10.1179/1743288X12Y.0000000030

Troop-Gordon, Wendy & Gary W. Ladd. 2015. Teachers' victimization-related beliefs and strategies: Associations with students' aggressive behavior and peer victimization. *Journal of Abnormal Child Psychology* 43. 45–60. https://doi.org/10.1007/s10802-013-9840-y

van Dijk, Teun. 1993. Principles of critical discourse analysis. *Discourse & Society* 4(2). 249–283. https://doi.org/10.1177/0957926593004002006

Warner, Michael. 1991. *Introduction: Fear of a queer planet*. Durham, NC: Duke University Press.

Warwick, Ian & Peter Aggleton. 2013. Bullying, 'cussing' and 'mucking about': Complexities in tackling homophobia in three secondary schools in South London, UK. *Sex Education*14(2). 159–173. https://doi.org/10.1080/14681811.2013.854204

Wodak, Ruth & Michael Meyer. 2016. *Methods of critical discourse studies* (3rd ed.). Thousand Oaks, CA: Sage Publications.

Anderson Chebanne and Kemmonye Monaka

Chapter 7
The weaponization of Setswana: Implications for marginalized languages in Botswana

Abstract: Botswana, a Southern Africa country of about 3 million inhabitants is multilingual with more than 25 ethnic communities most of whom speak various languages. However, this multilingualism is overlooked as only English and Setswana are recognized. English is privileged as it is the language of record in all services of the state. In education, the adverse impact of this restrictive language use is that from the primary school level, all learners from various ethnic and linguistic groups are required to use these two languages from the first day of school. Regrettable consequences of this are that ethnic groups whose languages are marginalized quickly get assimilated, leading to acute language and ethnic endangerment. This chapter takes the view that the actions of the state (i.e., the elevation of English and Setswana above Indigenous languages) are a form of weaponization as they are undemocratic, oppressive, and violate the language and cultural rights of a sizable portion of the population.

Keywords: Botswana, multilingualism, oppressed languages, language use practice, language policy

1 Introduction

1.1 The beginnings of the misconstruction of a monolithic Tswana society

Botswana has for a long time been presented in official discourses as the land of Batswana, who speak the Setswana language (Monaka & Chebanne, 2019). Botswana is a landlocked country in southern Africa, sharing borders with South Africa, Namibia, Zambia, Zimbabwe, and Mozambique. Notwithstanding the fact that it is inhabited by more than 25 different ethnic groups of people, including people of Tswana extraction, these varied groups are nonetheless called Batswana. Furthermore, of

---

Anderson Chebanne, Kemmonye Monaka, University of Botswana

the many Indigenous languages spoken by these different groups of people, only Setswana was promoted by the colonial administration, missionaries, and subsequently by post-independence administration as the language of inter-ethnic communication, among other things. As a result, the country is known as Botswana, the land of Batswana people who speak Setswana language. The term 'Tswana' is often used to denote attributes related to people of Tswana extraction.

The point that this chapter wishes to reiterate and push forward is that Botswana is a multilingual and multicultural country. As outlined in Chebanne (2022), languages within the borders of the country are distributed across five broad groups: (1) *Sotho-Tswana*, which consists of Setswana (a de facto Botswana national language and the only one used in education, inter-ethnic communication, and state records), Shekgalagari, Shebirwa, Silozi, and Chetswapong, (2) *Shona-Nyai* which comprises iKalanga, Nambya, isiNdebele, and Shona, (3) *Herero-Kavango* which includes Otjiherero, Shiyeyi, Kwangale, Chiikuhane (Sesubiya), Thimbukushu, and Rumanyo, (4) *San* which comprises !Xóõ, Ju|'haonsi, ǂHuan, and Sasi, and finally (5) *Khoe* which includes G‖ana, G|ui, Naro, Shua, Danisana/ Danisani, Cua, Goro, Tshwa, Cire-cire, Ts'ixa, Khwedam (A‖nikhwe, Bugakhwe, |Anda and Khwe), and some already extinct languages (Deti, Haise, Cara, and Caite) (see also Andersson & Janson, 1997; Smeija, 2003).

The Khoe and San languages are the most speckled and wide-ranging, presenting diverse cultures (Güldemann & Vossen, 2000). Embedded within this multiplicity of Khoe and San languages is the critical question of vitality, demography, and development. Khoe and San languages are the most endangered since they are fast losing ground to the most powerful languages they come in contact with, as well as other enabling environments; they are losing their vitality in important social language domains. The fact that they are also spoken by demographically minute[1] speech communities, and are restricted to family speech domains (Chebanne, 2010) facilitates the loss greatly. Furthermore, the majority of them are less researched and not properly documented. Literacy in them becomes an almost insurmountable uphill battle (Batibo, 2015 a,b). Languages that are not used in the education system are also disadvantaged in that the young speakers adopt languages they meet in school, relegating the mother tongue to the position of weakness (Batibo, 2015b, 1998; Monaka & Chebanne, 2021). These internal dynamics make Khoe and San languages readily absorbed by or assimilated into demographically and other-

---

[1] Estimate demographics made over two decades ago indicated that the Khoe and the San people are numerically the fewest in Botswana. The most numerous group is the Nama at 12 000 and the least numerous are the ǂHuan, and Sasi estimated at 250 each (Batibo & Chebanne, 2020).

wise advantaged languages: the Sotho-Tswana, Shona-Nyai, and Herero-Kavango languages (Chebanne, 2015a; Batibo, 2015a, b).

The minimalist view that Botswana is a monolithic land of Batswana people who speak the Setswana language has entrenched the position of a monolingual state in which Setswana is the only indigenous language (Chebanne, 2015a, b; Chebanne, 2002a, b; Nyati-Ramahobo, 1997). This misconstruction stems from two official considerations: (i) during the colonial period, most of the government activities were centered in the southern part of the country, which was and is still predominantly Setswana-speaking. The colonial government, therefore, was more directly involved with Setswana chiefs, and governed as if no other ethnic group existed or had chiefs. The assumption was that since all non-Setswana ethnic groups in the south were already subjects of ethnic Setswana chiefs, they were not, territorially, meriting recognition or self-governance (Bennett, 2002). The northern, northwestern, and western parts of the country, which were and still are multilingual, were incorporated into the protectorate much later, after the establishment of Tswana hegemony (Ramsay, 1998; Bennett, 2002). The perpetuation of the status quo appears to give credence to the view that Botswana is a country of Batswana people only, who speak the Setswana language only. This view circulates freely without paying attention to the ethnic composition of the country.

Since then, the issue of ethnic languages and cultures is hardly ever given any serious consideration in socio-political and (some) academic discourses on Botswana and its economic development. The fact is that *there are* diverse ethnic groups who are citizens of the country and who speak mother-tongue languages that are *not* Setswana, and Botswana is a multilingual and multicultural country (Jotia & Jankie, 2017; Smeija, 2003). The ecology of Botswana languages presented by Andersson and Janson (1997) was not a new revelation. This linguistic and ethnic ecology of the country had been noted during the colonial era by Schapera (1954) and Dornan (1917) but was overlooked by the colonial government as the British indirect rule favored bigger and more organized chieftainship rules (Bennett, 2002). At independence, the perpetuation of the colonial language practice was predicated on the idea that independence meant freedom for all those who had the right to territory and could freely vote, and language and culture did not feature in any legal document as a right (Batibo, 2015a; Chebanne, 2010; Chebanne, 2020).

1.2 The predominance and weaponization of Setswana

Linguistic choices that were upheld by the missionaries, the colonial government, and the post-independence administration meant that Setswana was and has been weaponized by being elevated from among the more than 25 indigenous languages and given prominence as the only national language and language of literacy in the nation. With full knowledge and awareness of the linguistic diversities of the Southern African territory, missionaries opted to limit their Bible translations to Setswana only (Moffat, 1842; Livingstone, 2006; Wookey, 1913). In the 1800s, Setswana was propelled across southern Africa by Bible translation work, and the subsequent spreading of missionary work across the region further solidified the position of the language as a main language in the region. Ancillary projects in translation, such as the building of missionary schools and the development of literacy materials, focused on and adopted Setswana because of its expansion across the land. This rather significant missionary work afforded Setswana a demographically large-scale communication tool. It was widely spoken or understood from the Lesotho mountains to the Okavango Delta and Zambezi River (Livingstone, 2006). Setswana was, therefore, the only indigenous language taught, read, and written to indigenous masses, most of who spoke other languages. It thus became the language spoken by the majority of people in Botswana as a first, second, and third language. Monaka and Chebanne (2021, p. 76) state that "over the years, it has been argued that [Setswana] facilitates unity and contributes significantly towards the building of one nation, that it is the pride of "Batswana," a cultural symbol by which the various ethnic groups identify themselves," averring further that "this has given an impression of linguistic homogeneity in the country."

The domination and consequent suppression of other languages that have persisted for close to six decades since independence have added to the spread of Setswana as a lingua franca in the country (Monaka & Chebanne, 2019). The resultant detriment of other languages (and cultures) includes large-scale abandonment of mother-tongue languages, adoption of the lingua-franca/national language, as well as the acquisition of Setswana by younger generations as mother-tongue. From all appearances, the use of the Setswana language in the country was designed as a weapon to subjugate other indigenous languages, to make them irrelevant and even invisible in the public and social communication domains, and to assimilate their speakers into Tswana culture.

2 Architects of the oppression and weaponization of languages in Botswana

The Tribal Land Act 2, as encapsulated in the Botswana Constitution of 1976, which apportions land according to the different tribes resident in the country, does so based on territorial considerations enacted during the establishment of the British Bechuanaland Protectorate. According to this Act, only eight Tswana subgroups were registered as having tribal reserves in which symbolic autonomism was practiced (Bennett, 2002). The Khoe, San, the Sotho-Tswana, Shona-Nyai, and Herero-Kavango found themselves subsumed under the Tswana subgroups by whose name the tribal reserves were called. They were administratively taken to form a single entity with those Tswana subgroups that 'had' land. Since all and only the Tswana subgroups were recognized to be the ones who 'had' land, it covertly followed that these other ethnic groups falling under them by virtue of the land they 'controlled' had to adopt linguistic and cultural identities of the Setswana speaking group (Bennett, 2002; Nyati-Ramahobo, 2002).

In official post-independence discourses, some of the non-Setswana speaking groups would be and are now referred to by the name of the Setswana speaking subgroups under which they are subsumed, with some of these communities having been subjugated by the Tswana before and during the colonial period (Nyati-Ramahobo, 2002). For instance, the Hambukushu, Wayeyi, ovaHerero, and others in the northern region of Botswana called Ngamiland are referred to as Batawana, a Tswana-speaking subgroup that historically dominated and ruled these ethnic communities, with the domination continuing to present day. Vossen (1988a & b) reported that Batawana constitutes only 15% of the regional population of Ngamiland, with Nyati-Ramahobo (2000) and Westphal (1962) putting it even lower at 1% and 5%, respectively. The Bakalanga in the Central District of Botswana are referred to as Bangwato, a Setswana-speaking ethnic group who rule over them. Ethnic leaders from these non-Setswana groups are called and renumerated as sub-chiefs and are subordinate(s) to any of the Tswana paramount chiefs (Nyati-Ramahobo, 2002). This strategy of favoring the Setswana language regardless of the low number of speakers regionally is a weaponizing of Setswana into swallowing others, and ideologically marginalizing and minoritizing other indigenous languages and groups. The intention is to make the non-Tswana invisible (Nyati-Saleshando, 2010; Chebanne, 2010; Nyati-Ramahobo, 2002).

Pre-colonial, colonial, and post-colonial handling of Botswana's situation was and is a methodical and deliberate strategy to subdue non-Setswana-speaking communities (Bennett, 2002). Bennett argues that within the Setswana sociopolitical order, the exact status of non-Tswana ethnic groups occupies the status of serfs for the Khoe and the San, and subaltern for the other Bantu groups. In this social order, all the non-Setswana speaking groups did not and do not qualify to be members of a ward in a *morafe* (tribe), and their membership and rights were and are not recognized within Setswana tribes. Discussing the question of ethnic identity and nationhood in Botswana, Nyati-Ramahobo (2002) presents figures of existing ethnic communities and languages, yet the country operates on the model of one national language, Setswana, and a foreign language, English. All other ethnic languages are disregarded. She argues that since independence,

" . . . the Government of Botswana has worked tirelessly to achieve the ideal goal of a homogenous nation state in which ethnic identities would disappear or would lose significance" (p. 17).

When the subjugated linguistic and ethnic communities argue against this situation and agitate for an all-inclusive dispensation, they are quickly branded fomenters of tribalism (cf. Bennett, 2002; Nyati-Ramahobo, 2002). In Botswana, the question of which rights are important and fundamental has always been controverted by the government (Saugestad, 2001). The government is adamant that social and economic protection of citizens from deprivation of basic necessities and elementary rights is what is paramount, and not the upholding of social, cultural, and linguistic values and identities (Saugestad, 2001). At independence, the new leaders of Botswana adopted policies that promoted "a common national identity" as an approach to building a united nation (Mulimbi & Dryden-Petersen 2018, p. 152). This nation-building required that all groups of people within the borders of the country who are citizens be identified as Batswana (Hays, 2011), and this is a vision that the various leaders of the country have tenaciously held onto over the years, even to this very moment. Legally, therefore, Botswana envisions that within its boundaries, there are no indigenous people or minorities that may be qualified as separate from Setswana tribal groups.

Within this social-ideological perspective, it is difficult for marginalized communities to make progress in a positive and liberating direction. It is even a cultural question since other language groups would wish to make developmental choices on the basis of their civilizational values, as Saugestad (2001, p. 64) eloquently argues:

> The options, in Botswana as elsewhere, should not be a choice between remaining with an old lifestyle or assimilating into the dominant society's culture. Indigenous people want to participate in development on their own terms, not to reject development. A living culture's chance to survive and develop itself depends on its ability and opportunity to control the introduction of technologies and other modern elements, not to turn them down. To achieve this, values codified by the minority must be recognized as complementary to the codification of the majority culture. In other words, minority culture should be accepted as 'different from but equal in value.'

Botswana, as an independent and sovereign country that, for all intents and purposes, desires to uphold democratic ideals and values, seems not to be aware of how damaging the current socio-political policies are to the existence and identity of other ethnic and linguistic groups. A mono-ethnic appeal to develop a national entity is not something that an African country should adopt for nation-building. The idea of resolving ethnic diversity by creating homogeneous tribal entities where the recognized *merafe* (tribes) are empowered to rule and decide the fate of other surrogate ethnic communities is not only unfair but is just not right (Saugestad, 2001). The consequences of this restrictive language use practice are, for all intents and purposes, ethnocidal, and yet the government defends its position by merely appealing to modernism and mono-developmental models (Chebanne, 2020).

3 Current language and education practices

The Education Policy of Botswana is documented in the White Papers of the 1977 and 1993 National Commissions on Education (NEC), which translated into the Revised National Policy on Education (RNPE) of 1994, and the various Curriculum Blueprints issued from the submissions of these Commissions. The social and pedagogical consequences of Botswana's education policy are documented and critically analyzed by Nyati-Ramahobo (1991, 1997), and central to this policy is the idea of mono-ethnicity and monoculturalism. In fact, since independence in 1966, education practice and policy formulations thereof in curriculum development and teacher training processes (cf. Education for Kagisano, 1977; RNPE, 1994) have underscored this agenda. Thus the de facto monolithic, ethno-linguistic state policy on education has been used as a weapon to relegate into oblivion anything to do with marginalized languages and their expression of the cultures embedded within them in any domain of learning. Effectively, the country has upheld a megalomaniac, hegemonic, and supremacist view in matters of language and culture in formulating the philosophy of education and access. This has happened even as the world is replete with alternative experiences of educational policies that favor the mother tongue in the formative years of education.

Again, since independence in 1966, policy documents such as the National Development Plans (NDP) have been unambiguous on the issue of creating enlarged school access, importantly on the question of equality in access and the guarantee of ten years of basic education for all (cf. RNPE, 1994; National Development Plan Eight (NDP 8, 1997). Thus, education in Botswana has been characterized by the "education for all" (cf. Education for Kagisano, 1977) type of mass education where the state, by all means bearable, financially speaking, went on to provide free education at all levels of school. This approach has created a belief that there is equality in education, and arguments for it have been provided (Chebanne & Moumakwa, 2017). This socio-political strategy is a weapon that has, for a long time, determined the framework and the scope of educational processes (Nyati-Saleshando, 2010; Dipholo, 2010).

Education took and has remained center-stage in national development; even from the first National Development Plan (1967), it was viewed largely as an engine of development, and impressive services and amenities in the provision thereof have been evidenced by the sustained budget allocation. In the echelons of African development, this achievement has been spectacular and convincing. But if one is right to rejoice about this state of things, the flipside is inequity (Chebanne & Moumakwa, 2017). For, the great means put at the disposal of education do not guarantee the equitable and quality nature of the system (McCarthy, 1999). What needs to be underlined is that the educational landscape of Botswana is characterized by a mismatch between the national ideals of democracy and the minority aspirations of self-identity. And these utopian ideals are never in touch with the objective outcomes of the educational processes (Chebanne, 2015 a & b; Chebanne & Kewagamang, 2020; Nyari-Saleshando, 2010).

4 Marginalization of languages in education as a weapon

The foregoing sections clearly demonstrate an insidious and surreptitious agenda to create a linguistic homogeneity to support the political ambitions of an illusionary homogenous nation. This perspective is flawed, for a minimum of information demonstrates that no matter how nations are composed or envisioned to become or evolve into, complete or absolute homogeneity can never be attained. Even as Botswana would have itself considered homogenous with a mono-cultural, mono-ethnic dispensation, there is diversity in terms of social class and status, socio-economic access, languages, and political situations, among others, and all these need specific developmental responses (Chebanne, 2020; Dipholo, 2010). The issue of ethnic differences is exacerbated by a political perspective that was carefully crafted to avoid or conceal linguistic diversity, which was evidently viewed as an inconvenience that would negatively impact the system. With respect to the San in Botswana, Good (1999), quoted in Cassidy et al. (2001, p. 73), writes:

> Indigenous languages should be integrated into school curriculum, and respected and developed within national formal education. Incorporating San culture, languages and history in school teaching is an essential step towards according recognition to San national affairs, and more importantly, towards providing an education system that is better suited to the special needs of some San learners. Quality education is vital if San are to be better equipped to lift them out of poverty and powerlessness.

Mother-tongue education is the one important way to ensure that every learner finds less traumatizing learning experiences in education. When one is seized with defining the objectives, outlines, and conditions of success of an education policy, the issues of equality, equity, and quality are ever-present, and equity is primordial. This is so because education is critical in the development of an individual (Nyati-Ramahobo, 1997). Educational values are not exoteric but come from within the positive learning experiences of the citizen—when education responds to aspirations, when it re-confirms cultural values, and when it empowers the communities to be self-reliant and not depend on the state. Education is not just opening the admissions ajar for all to come in, as equals, but providing an equitable learning environment that every learner would find welcoming and relevant in life, and the importance of this cannot be overstated. Therefore, the most effective weapon for the exclusion of other languages is education.

It should be mentioned that, for the sake of cross-border consideration by the colonial masters, Nama, Silozi, isiNdebele, and iKalanga did feature in a casual way in literacy in the first year of primary schools in regions where they were dominant. This, however, was discontinued after independence (Chebanne, 2022; Nyati-Saleshando, 2011; Chebanne & Nyati-Ramahobo, 2003), and only Setswana and English were made the languages of education. The excruciating consequence of this is that there are still children who come to school without any knowledge of the two school languages, and research has demonstrated that they are traumatized. School is not a friendly environment for their learning (Chebanne, 2022), and how they are expected to learn and be educated becomes a real-life challenge (Chebanne & Moumakwa, 2017; Chebanne & Monaka, 2005). When the current long-term vision of the country, Vision 2036, is examined at the end of its tenure, it would be imperative to ask and state where these children will be, and to state what contribution to the development of the country they will make or will have made. The point underscored here is that their own languages play a pivotal role in this contribution since they have a role in extricating their speakers from illiteracy and development impediments. Such is realizable only with equitable and equal opportunities in education and social advancement. These issues of multiculturalism have been topical and debated for decades, but it is regrettable that there is still no headway almost six decades after independence (Chebanne, 2022; Chebanne & Kewagamang, 2020).

As mentioned earlier, post-colonial discourses on Botswana languages now present a linguistic and cultural homogeneity that rejects the heterogeneity of ethnic and language communities (Chebanne, 2022; Nyati-Ramahobo, 1999). Nonetheless, the perennialization of language rights debates has resulted in the Government (seemingly) conceding and proposing an inclusive language-in-education policy (Chebanne, 2022), but it does not look like this will materialize as post-estimations are hinting at a budget that is insufficient to support the initiative. An inclusive language-in-education policy would be a significant development stride presenting an opportune time for Botswana to take marginalized languages on board. This is the only other way that its democracy can be enhanced: when its citizens are accorded all rights to enjoy their lives and education in their languages and cultures (Nyati-Saleshando, 2010; Chebanne, 2010). As we have argued, the greatest impact of a positive language policy or language practice is in education. When children learn in their mother tongues, when teachers are trained to accommodate other languages, and when the curriculum provides for the mother-tongue medium of instruction, then there is the democratization of education. The language deficiencies that characterize children from other language communities cannot be remedied by pedagogical strategies which do not put the mother tongue in that equation (Kamwendo et al., 2009; Nyati-Ramahobo, 2004).

Education should not be part of weaponization; it should be used as a means and principle of equitable and harmonious experiences in life. Any predisposition, antipathy, and ethnic differences in the society and place of learning that make learning traumatic bring disquiet in the social environment (Batibo, 2015a, c; Chebanne, 2002; Nyati-Ramahobo, 2000). The lack of languages of the other social strata in education cannot be justifiably detached from the value-base of a society and its development (Motshabi & Saugstad, 2004). Neglecting the positive aspect of culture in education can decimate value in the education system in the sense of worthless outcomes that are reflected in society (Lauder, 1999). In the current socio-educational setup, it is reasonable to argue that at the end of their education, these learners would be and are certificated rather than educated. In this regard, there is no way we can objectively talk about quality assurance when the whole presentation is not equitable. Education cannot be viewed solely as the successful provision of amenities but as the success of a humane system that looks into the totality of concerns and needs of all citizens in their ethno-linguistic diversity (Batibo, 2015, a, b, c; Motshabi & Saugestad, 2004; Nyati-Ramahobo, 2004).

In the 1980s, nationwide community advocacy joined debates by scholars and researchers, seeking the revitalization of languages, cultural identity, and pushing for inclusion in education (Nyati-Saleshando, 2011). There was a resurgence of organizations like the Society for the Promotion of iKalanga Language (SPIL), Lentswe la Batswapong (the Voice of the Batswapong), RETENG: The multicultural coalition of Botswana (n.d.), Chelwa ya Shekgalagari (Shekgalagari Seed), and many other, which agitated for the rights of marginalized groups, including language rights. These debates gained impetus in 1993 after the publication of the report of the National Commission on Education (Botswana Government, 1993), which recommended a third language in schools. During the consultations, various ethnic groups in the country advocated for the inclusion of their languages in the school system. What became remarkable, however, is that the third language recommendation by the Revised National Policy on Education (RNPE) of 1994 was reserved for a foreign language, French, and this in the face of research and debates that pushed for mother-tongue education in schools (Nyati-Ramahobo, 1999, 2004, 2011). The available research and ongoing debates had argued fervently that the minimalistic approach of the Botswana education system regarding the language issue was neither ideal nor equitable for learners (Chebanne & Moumakwa, 2017). They laid bare the negative impact of the monolithic pedagogical practices and, indeed, how the one-sided cultural content of the curriculum presented a serious bias for learners at the elementary (K-12) level (Dipholo, 2010; Mooko, 2009). It is still not clear at this point in time what the reasons for avoiding local languages were, and whether or how soon an inclusive national languages-in-education could be used to resolve the learning difficulties that children from other local language communities are facing.

5 Consequences of a delayed inclusive language-in-education policy

The tragic consequences of delayed implementation of policies to manage multilingualism and multiculturalism in Botswana have been regretted by many local researchers (Bagwasi, 2016; Batibo, 1015 a, b, c; Chebanne, 2015a; Nyati-Saleshando, 2010). The recent momentum of language debates has resulted in the ruling Botswana Democratic Party's promises to introduce local languages in education in their 2019 election manifesto (Botswana Democratic Party, 2019). This electioneering promise was followed up in the State of the Nation Address of in 2020 (Office of the President, State of the Nation Address, 2020), which saw the then Ministry of Basic Education (now Ministry of Education and Skills Development) embarking on a national consultation on the development of an inclusive language in education policy (Botswana Daily News, 2021; Chebanne, 2022). However, researchers are skeptical that much of what is presented by the government as a response to debates on multiculturalism and multilingualism is a ploy, if not a delay tactic, to still pursue homogeneity at cultural and language levels (Nyati-Saleshando, 2010; Chebanne, 2020).

It can be hard not to regard the delay of implementation as a critical indication that the socio-political and education system of the country has always been envisioned as establishing and endorsing Setswana hegemony, ethnically and linguistically (Nyati-Ramahobo, 1999; Mazonde, 2002). Potential indicators of delay are the deliberate association and misconstruing of languages in education debates with debates against the architects of the Constitution, especially Sections 77, 78, and 79. What is astounding, further, is that though Sections 77, 78, and 79 were ultimately rescinded after a referendum that was as acrimonious as it was considered controversial and unsatisfactory; this did not in any way provide an opportunity for ethnic languages to be introduced in schools (Chebanne & Moumakwa,

2017). This notwithstanding, the unwillingness of the political system and the unflinching ideology of dominance and hegemony by the established majority Setswana ethnic groups have never silenced the voice of the oppressed who speak other languages and practice other cultures.

Temperatures were raised when the Khoe and the San put a spirited agitation against the government of Botswana for the recognition of their ancestral territories where they had, from time immemorial, freely exercised and enjoyed their language and culture. Nyati-Saleshando (2010) argued that even though the landmark High Court Judgment in 2006 gave the Khoe and the San communities the right to their ancient lands, it only served to make evident unwillingness on the part of the Government to recognize the cultures of other groups within the current constitutional framework (Batibo, 2018a). These rights are fundamental human rights, and if the social policies of Botswana lack them, then the concerned groups will ever feel that the Government is using such policies to deny them their language and culture development and enjoyment (Chebanne, 2021; Chebanne, 2020).

6 Supporting the revitalization of other languages

The lack of supportive language policies (Batibo, 2015 a & b; Kamwendo et al., 2009; Nyati-Ramahobo, 1991, 1997; Nyati-Saleshando, 2010) and legal guarantees for the preservation of linguistic and cultural identities in this country have aggravated and precipitated an unprecedented case of mass language death. This situation should be changed by ensuring that all indigenous Botswana languages are assisted in revitalizing to maintain vibrant and functional cultures. There must therefore be a definite, deliberate, and significant intervention clearly thought out and spelled out, designed, and executed by the state and other stakeholders sooner rather than later (Chebanne, 2002). This intervention is fundamental, as it is the only way that the country can fully respect and sustain its indigenous languages, which are the fabric of its authentic cultures, and this question appeals to the deep conscience of a nation that has within its midst minority people and their language. Chebanne (2002) also argues that change is desirable and inevitable and that things cannot and must not be left to their own fate, especially if Botswana is convinced of its democratic values and human rights (Chebanne, 2020). The development of an equitable and democratic language policy is the first step in that direction. Other steps include research in ethnology and in linguistics of minority language communities, teaching, or education as an instrument of empowering minority communities to preserve their cultures and languages, and effective community participation in the management of cultural affairs and linguistic resources (Chebanne, 2010; Nyati-Saleshando, 2010).

The exclusion of other languages in education does not bode well for these languages, and the argument underscored here is that such a policy perspective is a deliberate weapon to overlook other languages. What is worrisome is that this seems not to bother law and policymakers in the country (Chebanne, 2020, 2002; Nyati-Ramahobo, 2002). When the nation affirms in its vision, Vision 2016 Botswana Government, 1917), that it wants to be equitable, democratic, prosperous, educated, and informed, and that no one will be disadvantaged in the education system because of a mother tongue that is different from the one that is used in schools, no voice asked how and by what means. And when Vision 2016 expired, no one asked why its aspirations were never achieved. The country is now in the Vision 2036 (Botswana Government, 2016) dispensation, the nation's long-term vision which has promised, through its second pillar, *Human and Social Development*, that Botswana will be a moral, tolerant, and inclusive society that provides opportunities for all. However, as alluded to earlier, it is already hinting at an insufficient budget to realize an inclusive language policy in schools. When the Education and Training Sector Strategy Plan (ETSSP) was developed in 2012, it proposed that mother tongue education should be introduced at elementary levels of education (Botswana Government, 2015). ETSSP seemed to respond to the argument that learners who spoke other indigenous languages other than Setswana were hampered in learning because of language hurdles (Chebanne & Moumakwa, 2017; Bagwasi, 2016; Nyati-Saleshando, 2010). The timelines for the plan were a five-year period between 2015 and 2020. However, by the end of 2020, only Setswana was the indigenous language used in schools; no other language had been introduced or experimented with, and the country was right back where it always was, with only Setswana as the language of literacy and government (Chebanne, 2022 a & b).

Taking into account postmodernist viewpoints regarding democratization and social equity that seem to be recurring in major socio-political debates—language rights as human rights, democracy, development, equality, and self-identity—of these days (Jotia and Jankie, 2015; Kamwendo et al., 2009; Nyati-Ramahobo, 2002, Okoth-Okombo, 1999), it is not wise to think that the status quo will have better outcomes at any age. Negligence and injustice in the area of linguistic rights cannot beget justice and equality in the end (Chebanne, 2002). Chebanne (2021) has argued that social policies on ethnic and language issues are discriminatory as they lack social justice and inclusion. These are the sort of practices that demonstrate that the exclusion of other languages in development is a weapon used to entrench hegemony, assimilation, and subsequently, language endangerment and death occur (Chebanne, 2020; 2010).

Ethno-cultural barriers in education and other domains develop into negative stereotypes, and teachers develop a dislike for the children they feel are displaying inappropriate behavior through "unwarranted linguistic expression" (Chebanne & Nthapelelang, 2000, p. 82). The children, in turn, detect a sense of rejection, and the classroom becomes an unpleasant place for them. The students are likely to develop low self-esteem, underperform, and even drop out of school. School dropout rate is one of the indicators of an inequitable education (Chebanne, 2015 a&b; Motshadi & Saugestad, 2004), and the quality of life of dropouts and that of their society are almost always negatively impacted.

7 A way forward

The current situation, as previously discussed, is not tenable in a country whose hackneyed chant is democracy and progress (Jotia and Jankie, 2013; Dipholo, 2010). It would be in order to conclude by spelling out two directions in the context of Vision 2016, which emphasizes social equitability and tolerance. The article submits that it is crucial that deliberate government actions in the form of constitutional provisions be made in Botswana to ensure that autochthonous people and their languages, and the other marginalized languages, will endure for future generations. The intervention and what they will require are very difficult and problematic matters (Chebanne, 2003, 2002), as indeed, Indigenous minority language speakers and their communities have been part of a historical and developmental process. They themselves, as people, have not died, but they see something that is part of them, and part of their history and culture disappear and die, and in its place, they have been assimilated (Chebanne, 2020; 2010; Nyati-Ramahobo, 2002) benefiting the Tswana groups. Possible interventions could include:

a) A comprehensive and inclusive policy on indigenous languages and their inclusion in education and functionality in their social spaces (Batibo, 2015a; Chebanne & Kewagamang, 2020; Chebanne & Molosiwa, 1997; Nyati-Ramahobo, 1997). This has been amply demonstrated in many forums where issues of minority people and their languages arose (Mazonde, 2002; UN (CERD) Multiculturalism Conference, Gaborone, 2002).

b) The support of languages for cultural expression through performing arts (Jotia and Jankie, 2015; M'bokolo, 1995) and multilingual education. This is necessary to the extent that cultural expression cannot be reduced to reading about old monuments and past cultures, or just performing traditional dances. In regard to indigenous languages, dramatic and performing arts form one of the crucibles in which diverse literary traditions and customs coexist-

ing in the national space can melt together in the most spontaneous and convincing fashion (Chebanne, 2010).
c) The definition and protection of ethnicity, cultural plurality and peculiarity should integrate language, legal/constitutional, and territorial rights/rural administration rights (Chebanne, 2021; Mazonde, 2002; UNESCO 31st Session Universal Declaration on Cultural Diversity, 2001).
d) Removal of clauses that allow marginalized ethnic or linguistic groups to be subsumed under other groups. This has permitted hegemony and domination of different languages and cultural groups (Nyati-Saleshando, 2011, 2004; Chebanne, 2010; Chebanne, 2020; Batibom, 1998).

Essentially, these are matters that are subsumed in the draft UN Declaration on the Rights of Indigenous Peoples (UN, 2001). As may be observed, this culture-infused ethnic definition of rights to education, articulated on linguistic consideration, and designed to reinforce national unity, may contribute to the consolidation of democracy and social harmony (Batibo, 2015a & b; M'bokolo, 1995). These values must be inculcated, maintained, and valorized through the national and ethnic construct. It behooves institutions and state agencies (schools and media), as well as independent associations and cultural organizations, to practice this ethnic definition. However, in regard to educational processes and the accessibility to cultural knowledge, only Setswana has the means and privileges that accrue to it from the Education Policies and several mentions in the Constitution (Batibo, 2015a; Chebanne, 2020; Chebanne & Molosiwa, 1997).

The argument made here is that if Botswana wants to seriously talk about ethnic and linguistic issues permeating all social domains, the identity and value of ethnic development and democracy, it needs to understand the elements that constitute and operationalize language and culture rights. In the context of this discussion, these elements must be explicit in the Constitution and in cultural policies. The fact is, throughout their history, Botswana's ethnic and linguistic communities have developed linguistic and cultural knowledge and technologies that make them culturally viable, and their languages provide the most vivid and practical way of communicating their vision of the world and the understanding of their existence.

8 Conclusion

This chapter has taken the view that in Botswana, the current language in use practice is designed to be a weapon to diminish other languages, many of which are experiencing a decline and others almost moribund. There is no equity, and the equality of citizens spoken about is not predicated on natural and national justice when it comes to the provision of services, and importantly in the education of young children who still speak these languages. This weaponization of one indigenous language, Setswana, against the other (over 25) indigenous languages impacts other social policies that affect service delivery to these other language communities. For any person in a speech community to thrive in their ethnic, cultural, and linguistic context, they must have the human right to express themselves freely in their own language and to enjoy their own culture (M'bokolo, 1995). This is the quality of life that Nyati-Ramahobo (1999, 2004) argued for decades. This can happen only when state policies view language as a resource and not a problem. Failure to plan for languages in Botswana clearly leaves one to believe that languages are viewed as a problem, and the only weapon to eliminate the problem then becomes the strict language use practice that makes only Setswana the only recognized Indigenous languages.

References

Andersson, Lars-Gunnar & Tore Janson. 1997. *Languages in Botswana: Language ecology in Southern Africa*. Botswana: Longman Botswana.

Bagwasi, Mompoloki Mmangaka. 2016. A critique of Botswana's language policy from a translanguaging perspective. *Current Issues in Language Planning* 18(2). 199–214. http://dx.doi.org/10.1080/14664208.2016.1246840

Batibo, Herman M. 2015a. An ideal language policy for an inclusive and sustainable development in Africa. In Peter Sköld, Moa Sandström & Maitseo Bolaane (eds.), *Under the same sun:Parallel issues and mutual challenges for San and Sami peoples and research*, 71–78. Vaartoe: Center for Sami Research (CeSam).

Batibo, Herman M. 2015b. Patterns of identity loss in trans-cultural contact situations between Bantu and Khoesan groups in western Botswana. *Studies in Literature and Language* 11(1). 1–6.

Batibo, Herman M. 2015c. Ten commandments for Setswana to be a resourceful vehicle of development in Botswana. *Marang: Journal of Language and Literature* 26, 41–54.

Batibo, Herman M. & Anderson Chebanne. 2020. Sasi language of Botswana: Marginalisation, endangerment and observed death. In Emmanuel Chabata & Philip Mpofu (eds.), *Language revitalisation: A matter of survival for marginalised communities and cultures*, 21–36. Zimbabwe: University of Zimbabwe Press.

Batibo, Herman M. 1998. The state of the Khoesan languages of Botswana. In Matthias Brenzinger (ed.), *The endangered languages in Africa*, 1–18. Germany: Rüdiger Köppe.

Bennett, Bruce. 2002. Some historical background on minorities in Botswana. In Isaac Ncube Mazonde (ed.), *Minorities in the millennium: Perspectives from Botswana*, 5–16. Botswana: Lightbooks/Lentswe la Lesedi.

Botswana Daily News. 2022. *Mother tongue learning in 2021/22 fiscal year*. http://www.dailynews.gov.bw/news-details.php?nid=55053

Botswana Democratic Party. 2019. *2019 election manifesto: Advancing together towards a more inclusive economy*. Botswana Democratic Party.
Botswana Government. 1997. *National development plan 8*. Government Printers.
Botswana Government. 1977. *National commission on education. Education for Kagisano Vol. 1 & 2*. Government Printers.
Botswana Government. 1967. *National development plan 1*. Government Printers.
Botswana Government. 1977. *Vision 2016: Long term vision for Botswana*. Government Printers.
Botswana. Government. 2015. *Education and training sector strategic plan (ETSSP 2015-2020)*. Government Printers.
Botswana. Government. 2016. *Vision 2036: Achieving prosperity for all*. Lentswe La Lesedi.
Botswana Government. 2020. The state of the nation address. Office of the President, Gaborone, Botswana.
Botswana Government. 1965. *Botswana constitution*. Government Printers.
Botswana Government. 1993. *Report of the national commission on education*. Government Printers.
Botswana Government. 1994. *Revised national policy on education*. Government Printers.
Botswana Government. 1998. *Vision 2016: Report on the long-term vision for Botswana. Presidential commission on the long-term vision*. Government Printers.
Brenzinger, Matthias (ed.). 1992. *Language death: Factual and theoretical explorations with special reference to East Africa*. Berlin: De Gruyter Mouton.
Cassidy, Lin, Kenneth Good, Isaac Ncube Mazonde & Roberta Rivers (eds.). 2001. *Regional assessment of the status of the San in Southern Africa: An Assessment of the status of the San in Botswana. Report Series No. 3 of 5*. Legal Assistance Centre (LAC).
Chebanne, Anderson. 2020. The internal colonisation of the San peoples of Botswana. *Marang: Journal of Language and Literature* 32. 16–38.
Chebanne, Anderson. 2015a. Negative multicultural consequences of Botswana restrictive language policy in education: Mourning the loss of Khoisan languages. In Agreement Latihi Jotia & Dudu Jankie (eds.), *Multicultural education discourses: Breaking barriers of exclusion in selected African contexts*, 5–24. Namibia: Zebra Publishing.
Chebanne, Anderson. 2015b. The lack of multilingual education in Botswana – Tragic consequences for the Khoisan Languages. In Peter Sköld, Moa Sandström & Maitseo Bolaane (eds.), *Under the same sun:Parallel issues and mutual challenges for San and Sami peoples and research*, 133–145. Vaartoe: Center for Sami Research (CeSam).
Chebanne, Anderson. 2010. The Khoisan in Botswana–Can multicultural discourses redeem them? *Journal of Multicultural Discourses* 5(2). 11–29.
Chebanne, Anderson M. 2022a. The prospect of languages in education in Botswana: A critical reflection. *Mosenodi: International Journal of the Educational Studies* 25(1). 1–13.
Chebanne, Anderson. 2002b. Preliminary observations on the socio-linguistic situation of the Cuaa language. In Karsten Legère & Sandra Fitchat (eds.), *Language and democratization in the SADC*, 87–103. Namibia: Gamsberg-Macmillan.
Chebanne, Anderson. 2002. Minority languages and minority people: Issues on linguistic, cultural and ethnic death in Botswana. In Isaac N. Mazonde (ed.), *Minority in the millennium: Perspectives from Botswana*, 47–58. Botswana: Lightbooks/Lentswe la Lesedi.
Chebanne, Anderson & Phemelo Kewagamang. 2020. A model for introducing marginalized indigenous languages in the Botswana education system. *Mosenodi: International Journal of the Educational Studies* 23(1). 4–23.

Chebanne, Anderson & Tshiamiso V. Moumakwa. 2017. Issues of equality and equity in education- the fate of minority languages of Botswana. *Mosenodi: International Journal of the Educational Studies* 20(2). 78–89.

Chebanne, Anderson, J. Tsonope & L. Nyati-Ramahobo. 1993. Impact of language policy on education in Botswana. *Mosenodi: International Journal of the Educational Studies* 1(1). 7–23.

Chebanne, Anderson &Kemmonye C. Monaka. 2005. San relocation: Endangerment through development in Botswana. In Nigel Crawhall & Nicholas Ostler (eds.), *Creating outsiders, endangered languages, migration and marginalizaton*, 101–105. Foundation for Endangered Languages (FEL).

Chebanne, Anderson & L. Nyati-Ramahobo. 2003. *Language knowledge and language use in Botswana* (Seminar presentation). Population and Housing Census Dissemination Seminar, Gaborone.

Chebanne, Anderson & A. Molosiwa. 1997. Research on the teaching of Setswana. In Mmantsetsa Marope & David W. Chapman (eds.), *On teaching and teacher education in Botswana, Vol. 1*, 187–204. Botswana: Lightbooks/Lentswe la Lesedi.

Dipholo, K. 2010. Uneven development and the marginalization of minority tribes? *Sunday Standard*. https://www.sundaystandard.info/uneven-development-and-the-marginalization-of-minority-tribes/

Güldemann, Tom & Rainer Vossen. 2000. Khoisan. In Bernd Heine & Derek Nurse (eds.), *Khoisan Studies*, 99–122. Cambridge, UK: Cambridge University Press.

Good, Kenneth. 1999. The state and extreme poverty in Botswana: The San and destitutes. *Journal of Modern African Studies* 37(2). 185–205.

Hays, Jennifer. 2011. Educational rights for indigenous communities in Botswana and Namibia. *The International Journal of Human Rights* 15. 127–153. https://doi.org/10.1080/13642987.2011.529695

Jotia, Latihi & Dudu Jankie (eds.). *Multicultural education discourses: Breaking barriers of exclusion in selected African contexts*. Namibia: Zebra Publishing.

Kamwendo, Gregory, Dudu Jankie & Anderson Chebanne (eds.). 2009. *Multilingualism in education and communities in Southern Africa*. Botswana: UB-Tromso Collaborative Programme for San Research and capacity Building.

Lauder, Hugh. 1999. Education, democracy and the economy. In A. H. Hasley, Hugh Lauder, Phillip Brown & Amy Stuart Wells (eds.) *Education: Culture, economy, society*, 382–392. Oxford, UK: Oxford University Press.

Livingstone, David. 2006. *Missionary travels and Researches in South Africa*. London: David Livingstone, LLC.

Mazonde, Isaac. 2001. San perceptions. In Linn Cassidy, Kenneth Good, Isaac Ncube Mazonde & Roberta Rivers (eds.), *Regional assessment of the status of the San in Southern Africa: An assessment of the status of the San in Botswana*. Report Series No. 3 of 5, 59–70. Legal Assistance Centre (LAC).

Mazonde, Isaac (ed.). 2002. *Minorities in the millennium: Perspectives from Botswana*. Botswana: Lightbooks/Lentswe la Lesedi.

M'bokolo, Elikia. 1995. Cultural policy: National, regional, and continental. In *Conflict and culture in Africa: Proceedings of an international symposium on the role of culture in the prevention and resolution of conflicts*, 74–94. University of Botswana-National Institute of Development Research and Documentation.

McCarthy, Cameron. 1999. Nonsynchrony and social difference: An alternative to current radical accounts of race and schooling. In A. H. Hasley, Hugh Lauder, Phillip Brown & Amy Stuart Wells (eds.), *Education: Culture, economy, society*, 541–556. Oxford, UK: Oxford University Press.

Moffat, Robert. 1842. *Missionary labours and Scenes in Southern Africa*. Cambridge, UK: Cambridge University Press.

Monaka, Kemmonye Collete & Anderson Monthusi Chebanne. 2019. Setswana and the building of a nation state. *Anthropological Linguistics* 61(1), 75–98. https://doi.org/10.1353/anl.2019.0010

Mooko, T. 2009. Mother tongue education in Botswana: More questions than answers. In Gregory Kamwendo, Dudu Jankie & Anderson Chebanne (eds.). *Multilingualism in education and communities in Southern Africa*, 26–30. Botswana: UB-Tromso Collaborative Programme for San Research and capacity Building.

Motshabi, Kgosi &Sidsel Saugestad. 2004. Research for Khoe and San development. In Kgosi Motshabi & Sidsel Saugestad (eds.), *Proceedings of international conference on San/Basarwa*, 5–18. Botswana: University of Botswana–University of Tromso.

Mulimbi, Bethany, and Sarah Dryden-Petersen. 2018. "There is still peace. There are no wars": Prioritizing unity over diversity in Botswana's social studies policies and practices and the implications for positive peace. *International Journal of Educational Development 6*, 142–54.

Nthomang, K. 2004. From dependency to self-reliance: Piloting a shift. In Kgosi Motshabi & Sidsel Saugestad (eds.), *Proceedings of international conference on San/Basarwa*, 49–51. Botswana: University of Botswana–University of Tromso.

Nyati-Ramahobo, Lydia. 1997. Language in education and the quality of life in Botswana. In Doreen Nteta & Janet Hermans (Eds.), *Poverty and plenty: The Botswana experience*, 251–269. Botswana Society.

Nyati-Ramahobo, Lydia. 1995. *A review of the Setswana program to implement the revised national policy on education for ten years of basic education*. A Report Submitted to Curriculum Development Division.

Nyati-Ramahobo, Lydia. 1991. *Language planning and education policy in Botswana* University of Pennsylvania dissertation.

Nyati-Ramahobo, Lydia. 1987. *Minority language users in a multilingual society and early educational hurdles: A case of Botswana* (Conference presentation). Paper presented to the Second Conference of the Association of University Teachers of Literature and language. Harare, Zimbabwe.

Nyati-Saleshando, Lydia. 2011. An advocacy project for multicultural education: The case of the Shiyeyi language in Botswana. *International Review of Education 57(5–6)*, 567–582.

Nyati-Ramahobo, Lydia. 2004. Language planning and policy in Africa. In Robert B. Kaplan & Richard, B. Baldauf Jr (eds.), *Language planning and policy in Africa*, 21–78. Bristol, UK: Multilingual Matters.

Nayti-Ramahobo, Lydia. 2002. Ethnic identity and nationhood in Botswana. In Isaac Mazonde (ed.), *Minorities in the millennium: Perspectives from Botswana*, 11–28. Botswana: Lightbooks/Lentswe la Lesedi.

Nyati-Ramahobo, Lydia. 2000. The language Situation in Botswana. *Current Issues in Language Planning* 1(2), 243–300. https://doi.org/10.1080/14664200008668009

Nyati-Ramahobo, Lydia. 1999. *The national language. A resource or a problem: Implementation of the language policy in Botswana*. Botswana: Pula Press.

Okombo, D. Okoth. 1999. What space will indigenous African languages have in the global village? (Conference presentation). Paper presented at the Tenth International Conference of the African Language Association of Southern Africa (ALASA), Pretoria, South Africa.

Ramsay, J. 1998. The establishment and consolidation of the Bechuanaland Protectorate, 1870–1910. In Wayne Edge & Mogopodi H. Lekorwe (eds.), *Botswana: Politics and society*, 62–98. South Africa: JL van Schaik. RETENG: Multicultural Coalition of Botswana (n.d.). www.reteng.org.

Saugestad, Sidsel. 2001. *The inconvenient indigenous: Remote Area Development in Botswana, donor assistance, and the First people of the Kalahari*. Sweden: The Nordic Africa Institute.

Smeija, Birgit. 2003. *Language pluralism in Botswana: Hope or hurdle? A sociolinguistic survey on language use and language attitudes in Botswana with special reference to the status and use of English*. New York: Peter Lang.
UNESCO. 2001. *31st Session Universal Declaration on Cultural Diversity, 2001*. United Nation, Geneva, Switzerland.
United Nations. 2002. Office of the United Nations High Commission for Human Rights. *Seminar on Multiculturalism in Africa: Peaceful constructive group recommendation. In situation involving minorities and indigenous Peoples*. Botswana.
Vossen, Rainer. 1988a. Studying the linguistic and ethno-history of the Khoe-Speaking (Central Khoisan) Peoples of Botswana. *Botswana Notes and Records 16. 16–35*.
Vossen, Rainer. 1988b. *Patterns of language knowledge and language use in Ngamiland in Botswana*. Charlottesville, VA: The University of Virginia.
Westphal, Ernst O. J. 1962. An example of complex language contacts in Ngamiland. *Proceedings of the Symposium on Multilingualism (Second Meeting of the Inter-African Committee on Linguistics)*. 205–212. Scientific Council for Africa.
Wookey, A. J. 1913. *Dico tsa Setswana* [History of the Tswana.] South African District Committee of the London Missionary Society.
WIMSA & RDU (UB). 2000. *Education for remote area dwellers in Botswana: Problems and Perspectives*. Report on a three-day conference on the education for remote area Dwellers in Botswana. Research and Development Unit (UB) & Workgroup of Indigenous Minorities in Southern Africa. WIMSA.

Jason A. Kemp
Chapter 8
Using your own language against you: Spanish in U.S. classrooms

Abstract: This chapter explores language weaponization in U.S. classrooms in which Spanish is the language of communication. Ideologies and practices that frame students and their Spanish as deficient or broken are harmful, and they ignore the rich cultural knowledge and linguistic practices Spanish-speaking Latinx students bring to the classroom. Instead of weaponizing Spanish against students, educators, at all levels of instruction, should strive to reduce harm through pedagogies that uplift students' languaging practices. This chapter summarizes 40 years of policies and practices that punish(ed) students for simply using Spanish. Then, the focus shifts to the deployment of language weaponization when students use the "wrong" kind of Spanish in the classroom. A review of a theory for understanding the bilingualism of Latinx speakers of Spanish in the United States leads to a discussion of frameworks that could help remove language weaponization from classrooms. Specifically, expanding care in the curriculum and developing educators' knowledge of critical ideologies and practices can help eliminate language weaponization against Latinx students and their Spanish.

Keywords: caring perspectives, critical approaches, education, Latinx students, Spanish

> *So, if you really want to hurt me, talk badly about my language. Ethnic identity is twin skin to linguistic identity – I am my language.* Gloria Anzaldúa (1987, p. 81)

1 Introduction

In the United States (U.S.), various K-12 language education programs enroll students whose home language is Spanish. U.S. public schools enroll 5.1 million students identified as English learners, and 3.9 million of these students have Spanish as a home language (U.S. DOE, 2021). Some programs aim to foster bilingualism and biliteracy at some point in the curriculum (e.g., transitional bilingual education),

---

Jason A. Kemp, WIDA at the University of Wisconsin-Madison

https://doi.org/10.1515/9783110799521-008

while other models have language development and/or maintenance as a core tenet (e.g., two-way immersion). English as a second language programs have the end goal of helping students learn English so that they can participate in an all-English curriculum—no priority is given to the maintenance of home languages. Furthermore, in K-12 settings, initiatives such as the Seal of Biliteracy aim to promote bilingualism and biliteracy by recognizing "students who have studied and attained proficiency in two or more languages" (Californians Together & Velázquez Press, 2015, para. 1). In higher education, Spanish heritage language programs have extended to new regions of the United States (Beaudrie, 2012). As such, more students have access to first/heritage language classes instead of second language courses. Access, of course, depends on the programs in place at a post-secondary institution. The second language curriculum is designed for students whose home language is English, while first/heritage courses factor students' level of familiarity with their home language into the curriculum.

Despite positive changes such as increased access to Spanish classes designed for Spanish speakers, K-16 classrooms are not always a safe place in which students' varieties of Spanish are respected and nurtured (see examples in the next section). In these K-16 classes, educators and their curriculum often fail to build on students' social and cultural capital, which includes the linguistic toolkits students bring to the classroom. For example, Goulette (2020) commented on how a Spanish teacher ignored students' linguistic practices and ways of identifying by assigning a status of either "Spanish-dominant" or "English-dominant" to her Spanish-speaking students. In this eighth-grade class, the labels dictated the type of instruction students received. The "English-dominant" students received direct instruction, while the "Spanish-dominant" students primarily completed form-focused worksheets to prepare for a state-wide Spanish language assessment. The aforementioned research exemplifies a teacher's questioning of the legitimacy of students' Spanish. The teacher made assumptions about her students in pedagogically inappropriate ways, but she did not use Spanish against them. However, the reality is that in many cases, Spanish is used and weaponized against students to affect their validity, credibility, and well-being.

In this chapter, I explore language weaponization in U.S. classrooms in which Spanish is the language of communication. Messages such as "No saben nada." [Students don't know anything]; "Escucha al bobo. Esto no es español." [Listen to the simpleton. That is not Spanish]; "¿Mesero? Esta palabra es de las telenovelas. La palabra correcta es camarero." [Mesero? That word is used in telenovelas. The correct word is 'camarero'] are a few examples of the disparaging language I have heard educators use to describe Latinx students' Spanish. These kinds of comments, and the ideologies behind them, are harmful and disrespectful of the cultural and linguistic diversity Spanish-speaking Latinx students bring to the classroom. Instead of weaponizing Spanish by framing students and their Spanish as deficient, educators, at all levels of instruction, should aim to reduce harm through pedagogical practices that uplift and place value on students' languaging practices.

I begin by providing a review of the physical and psychological violence Spanish-speaking Latinx students face(d) when they simply use Spanish in the U.S. schooling system. I then shift to the issue at hand: language weaponization. In doing so, I illustrate cases that underscore the inappropriate and misguided practice of using students' own language against them. These examples attempt to capture the gamut of experiences across classrooms in which students' home language practices are delegitimized and labeled as not worthy of existing in academic spaces. I then offer frameworks that could help prevent and remove language weaponization from classrooms. For example, encouraging more care in the classroom and expanding educators' knowledge of critical ideologies and practices can help eliminate language weaponization that frames Latinx students and their Spanish as deficient.

2 A history of violence

Historically, U.S. schools have not been a kind place to minoritized students—be they members of racial/ethnic (Library of Congress, 2004), linguistic (Wiley, 2007), or sexuality minoritized (Wimberly, 2015) groups. As an African American from the South, I grew up with the stories of cruelty unleashed on members of my family and community. These acts of violence were perpetrated by adults and children. Yes, even elementary-aged children were taught that physical and emotional violence against their African American classmates was more than acceptable. Through personal relationships and professional experiences, I have learned that many Latinx communities share similar painful stories of school-based violence linked to simply who they are and their use of Spanish.

In this section, I highlight some salient scholarship from the previous four decades (1980s–2010s) that documents the violence Latinx students face when they simply speak Spanish at school, where English is the de facto language of communication for all interactions. To begin, in her seminal work, Anzaldúa (1987) recalls an instance in which she was "caught speaking Spanish at recess— that was good for three licks on the knuckles with a sharp ruler" (p. 75). During her undergraduate studies, "all Chicano students were required to take two speech classes" (p. 76) in order to erase their accents in English. In other words, their identity as Spanish-speaking students was framed as deficient by their university. In her analysis of linguistic terrorism, Anzaldúa (1987) remarks that, as children, Latinx Spanish speakers "are told that our language is wrong. Repeated attacks on our native tongue diminish our sense of self. The attacks continue throughout our lives" (p. 20). The attacks referenced here come primarily from the dominant society, which includes the U.S. schooling system. These attacks on Spanish that frame it as deficient can cause Latinx Spanish speakers to believe the lies they have been told by the dominant society. In turn, Latinx speakers of Spanish internalize these ideologies of deficiency and then use language differences against one another (Anzaldúa, 1987, p. 80) (see Alfaro & Bartolomé, 2017 for an example of this phenomenon in a school setting and Pentón Herrera, 2019 for a discussion of intergenerational language shift).

Additionally, Hurtado and Rodríguez (1989) researched the idea of language as a social problem via a survey of college students enrolled in a university in Texas. Their findings indicated that 43% of the Latinx students believed their K-12 schools disapproved of the use of Spanish at school. As evidence of this intolerance, some students shared that Spanish was not allowed in classrooms, but it could be used after school, in the hallways, during lunch, and at home. When students violated this rule, they were often reprimanded verbally, forced to pay fines, and made to feel like outsiders/foreigners when educators used phrases like "We're in the United States, and the language used in schools is English, so please speak English while in this class" (p. 411) or "If you want to speak Spanish, go to Mexico (p. 411) in order to promote linguistic assimilation. Also, it was commonplace that all forms of punishment were doled out publicly in order to "educate the rest of the students to the consequences of speaking Spanish" (p. 413). Hurtado and Rodríguez (1989) conclude their analysis with a powerful statement: "Language is a mutable characteristic, unlike skin colour, gender, religion or culture. Of all the distinctive attributes possessed by Mexican descendants, Spanish is not only salient but 'easily' modified" (p. 415). For some people who claimed to be concerned about the academic success of ethnolinguistically diverse students, it was easier for them to blame the Spanish language for students' lack of achievement—and then seek to repress Spanish—instead of interrogating larger social problems like access to high-quality public education for all students (see discussions in Gabriel et al., 2017; Murillo & Schall, 2016).

As Aparicio and José-Kampfner (1995) indicated, the problem of "bodily and psychological punishment" (p. 95), as a response to speaking Spanish, is a centuries-old characteristic of schooling in the United States. This centuries-old problem can be traced to the U.S. occupation of lands in the West and Southwest that were once a part of Mexico. Moreover, Valencia (1997) identified deficit models that explain the lack of academic success of particular groups of children as the oldest and most common ideologies in education. This "dispossession of lands" (Aparicio, 2000,

p. 257) was linked to the erasure of language and culture through educational policies and practices. Aparicio (2000) asserted that schools sought to repress and suppress Spanish through "physical punishments, humiliation, segregation, and intellectual undervaluing" (p. 257) so that students would be discouraged from using their home language on school grounds.

In collaboration with her students, MacGregor-Mendoza (2000) gathered accounts from more than 100 adults who described numerous examples of the ways in which they were reprimanded for using Spanish in school. Some participants remembered forms of physical abuse such as having their fingernails trimmed so low their fingers almost bled, being beaten with a paddle or water hose, or being forced to run laps around the track or run up and down stairs—all for speaking Spanish. Like Anzaldúa (1987), MacGregor-Mendoza (2000) also reported teachers washing students' mouths out with soap and hitting them with rulers. Nonphysical forms of abuse also emerged from the participants' experiences in school. For example, interviewees shared that if they were caught speaking Spanish, they could be "given detention, demerits, extra homework, sent to the principal's office, or sent home" (MacGregor-Mendoza, 2000, p. 360) or forced to pay monetary fines. Public shaming was another means to punish students for speaking Spanish. Some participants recounted being forced to stand in the corner or wear a dunce cap in class. As children, the participants were verbally abused by teachers and administrators and denied access to the restroom if they could not request to go in English. The climate of these students' schools encouraged, and in some cases, dictated that Spanish-speaking children tell an adult if they heard their classmates speaking Spanish. MacGregor-Mendoza (2000) warned readers to not "dismiss these experiences as part of the trials and tribulations of childhood" (p. 363) because of the immediate effect of this abuse on children and its long-term implications on their lives as adults.

The study by Sarmiento-Arribalzaga and Murillo (2009) underlined the potential long-term effects on Latinx Spanish speakers. One of their participants (who were all Mexican and Mexican-American students considering a career in bilingual education) shared that she did not want her children enrolled in bilingual education classes because "no quería que sufrieran como yo sufrí" [I did not want them to suffer like I suffered] (p. 621). The suffering the college student references is tied to her K-12 schooling experience as a Spanish-speaking student. Another participant shared that she was sent to the principal's office every day as a form of punishment until she learned English. This in-school experience made the student feel ashamed of herself and also of her "parents and their language" (p. 624). She did reveal, however, that she was determined to not be like the teachers she had as a child.

Furthermore, LeBlanc (2017), in his collaborative ethnographic work with four adolescent boys, also detailed occasions in which the boys were reprimanded for using their home language (either Spanish or Vietnamese) at school. The boys reported being ridiculed by their classmates if they spoke in Spanish or Vietnamese. The researcher also observed, and later discussed with the student, a teacher yelling "English! You talking about me?!" (p. 495) when he overheard two students speaking in Spanish. LeBlanc (2017) noted that the teacher was smiling while he yelled at the children, but it was not clear that he was joking. Nonetheless, this was one example of the censorship of "nonstandard or multilingual repertoires" (p. 495) invoked by teachers.

In their review of a school district's efforts to center social and emotional learning in their disciplinary policies and practices in order to promote equity, Gregory and Fergus (2017) observed an instance in which administrators at a high school did not make decisions that were sensitive to the needs of diverse groups of students. Administrators at this particular high school decided that all students would need to address teachers using "Ms." or "Mr." plus the teacher's last name. The goal was to foster "more respectful interactions between teachers and students" (p. 130). After the implementation of the rule, Spanish-speaking students in the school were issued "numerous discipline referrals" because they used *maestra/maestro* when addressing their teachers. Gregory and Fergus (2017) noted that this cultural norm of the students signaled respect for their teachers, but the school's policy did not acknowledge this cultural practice. Instead, students were punished for using Spanish in accordance with the enforcement of the new rule.

The aforementioned examples provide a general and unsettling glimpse into the ideologies and practices that influence(d) educating Spanish-speaking students in the United States. These perspectives and actions, in turn, result in physical and/or psychological harm toward Spanish-speaking Latinx students. The abuse exemplifies the consequences children face for simply using their language in a racialized, linguicist (Alfaro & Bartolomé, 2017; Freire & Feinauer, 2020; Skutnabb-Kangas, 1988) school setting that was determined to be an English-only setting. Nowadays, policies in many states have led to the creation of programs that seek to support students' home language(s) through maintenance and development efforts. However, we observe a continuation of abusive practices in these classrooms designed to support the linguistic needs of Spanish-speaking Latinx students. In this next section, I explore language weaponization in classrooms in which Spanish is the language of communication.

3 You don't speak the right kind of Spanish

The U.S. education system has traditionally not provided equitable support for students who speak languages other than or in addition to English despite research that has demonstrated the (developmental and social) benefits of bi(multi) lingualism (Baker, 2014; Bialystok, 2011; García & Baetens Beardsmore, 2009). During the past few decades, K-12 education has continued to experience increases in the number of dual language immersion programs (McKay Wilson, 2011; Roberts, 2021). A primary goal of dual language education is the promotion of literacy in two languages (Gómez et al., 2005; Kennedy & Medina, 2017; McKay Wilson, 2011), and most of these programs aim to achieve this goal by providing content instruction in English and a language other than English. This model strives to foster cultural competence and language acquisition, beginning with young learners of languages and continuing, in some school districts, with older students too.

Furthermore, as noted earlier, Spanish heritage language programs are growing in number. According to Kelleher (2008), a "heritage language program is any language development program that is designed or tailored to address the needs of heritage language learners" (p. 8), and these programs exist as K-16 classes or community-based programs. In some K-12 settings, heritage language education is subsumed by dual language immersion classes, while post-secondary (and some secondary) contexts teach heritage language classes as part of a dual-track approach within world language departments. Dual-track programs offer one set of courses for heritage learners and another set of courses for second language learners. However, as Leeman (2015) reminds us, there is no universally accepted definition of heritage languages and the various heritage language program models. In the United States and other parts of the world, the term heritage language education tends to refer to "language instruction designed specifically for students who have prior home or community-based exposure to this language" (Leeman, 2015, p. 104). As such, more colleges and universities have started to offer courses for students who have a familial connection to the language of study. In particular, Spanish heritage language programs are no longer confined to universities with a large Spanish-speaking Latinx population and/or regions of the United States with historical ties to the Spanish language (Beaudrie, 2012).

Despite the growth in support for home language instruction among some K-16 educators, administrators, and researchers (García, 2014; Moore, 2021), current policies do not always lead to curricular decisions and pedagogical practices that fully respect and leverage students' entire linguistic repertoires (Moll et al., 1992) in the classroom (Ramírez, 2022). As such, contemporary program models for

Spanish classes for Spanish-speaking Latinx students across educational contexts tend to solely support the acquisition of a standard or academic variety of Spanish, while disregarding and dismissing students' home language practices. In contradistinction to the examples described in the previous section, we now turn our attention to instances in which Latinx students are reprimanded for not using the 'right' kind of Spanish. The examples all come from classes in which the Spanish language is the medium for instruction and means of communication among students and teachers.

In their essay, Alfaro and Bartolomé (2017) included an observation of a collaborative science experiment in Spanish in a fourth-grade dual-language classroom:

> Yaniel: Es que tú le meneaste el baking soda antes de ponerle suficiente agua. [That happened because you wiggled the baking soda before putting in sufficient water.]
>
> Mrs. Franco: Cómo que le meneaste, esa es una palabra grotesca, la palabra indicada es mezclar . . . compañeros, por favor, dígale a Yaniel como se dice 'baking soda' en español . . . le dicen, bicarbonate de sodio [What do you mean, wiggled, that is a gross word–the correct word is mixed . . . students, please tell Yaniel how to say 'baking soda' in Spanish . . . they tell him *bicarbonate de sodio*.] (p. 19).

The authors' analysis reveals that Yaniel was both engaged and excited about the project. The teacher, Mrs. Franco, clearly did not approve of Yaniel's languaging practices as she was quick to interrupt and *correct* him. Mrs. Franco believed in language separation and the exclusive use of standard Spanish in the classroom so that Spanish, as she described to the researchers, would remain "pure" (p. 19). Alfaro and Bartolomé (2017) label Mrs. Franco's ideological stance as linguicist, and they believe the teacher's reaction probably discouraged Yaniel from creatively using his dynamic bilingualism in class. Hence, Mrs. Franco latched on to Yaniel's *incorrect* use of *meneaste*, and used Spanish to publicly reprimand him for using *una palabra grotesca* during the science experiment.

In his article about raciolinguistic ideologies and languagelessness, Rosa (2016) shares the story of Yesi, a student he met as part of an ethnographic study at a predominantly Latinx high school in Chicago. As a high school student, Yesi, who immigrated from Puerto Rico at the age of four, took four years of Spanish classes, including an Advanced Placement (AP) Spanish course. Yesi enjoyed her AP Spanish class, and she had a Latinx teacher who affirmed the legitimacy of her students' Puerto Rican and Mexican varieties of Spanish (Rosa, 2016). According to the teacher, she hoped the Spanish class would allow students to build on the skills they brought to the classroom. Yesi earned a 4 on the Advanced Placement (AP) Spanish exam,[1] and she believed the class helped her better communicate with her Spanish-dominant father.

When Yesi enrolled in an elite liberal arts college, she took an intermediate Spanish composition and conversation course during her first semester. Despite regularly attending her professor's office hours, completing all assignments on time, and writing extra credit essays, Yesi only earned a D[2] in the class (Rosa, 2016). Grades in the course were closely tied to success on the writing assignments, and Yesi believed that her "slang" Spanish interfered with her success. Yesi shared that her professor publicly embarrassed her when she used *troque* instead of *camión* (truck) during class as the professor believed *troque* was "a problematic English calque," (p. 175) and he insinuated that Yesi's parents would not use a word like that. In this instance, Yesi's professor shamed her for not using Spanish that was free of "English contamination" (Rosa, 2016, p. 175). He even mentioned Yesi's family and their use of Spanish to further convey the point that Yesi's languaging practices were flawed. For Yesi, this attack "hurt a lot, I felt like he was calling me stupid" (p. 175). Yesi also shared with the researcher that the class made her feel like she could not speak "her language" and that she had "failed her family and herself" (p. 175) because of the grade she had received.

Showstack's (2015) case study research provided several examples of some ways in which an instructor negated students' languaging practices (categorized as Spanglish by the instructor) in favor of standard Spanish as the classroom norm. Layla, the instructor of an intermediate Spanish heritage language course at a large university in Texas, moved from Mexico to the United States before high school, and at the time of the research project, Layla was studying literature as a doctoral student in a Spanish department (Showstack, 2015). Once, while reviewing an activity from the textbook, Layla noticed the phrase *llámame pa' atrás [call me back]*. Layla labeled this common phrase as Spanglish and told her students: Nunca digan [Never use/say] *llámame pa' atrás*, which was followed by a gesture of Layla pretending to stab herself with a knife in order to convey her disdain for this and similar phrases. Additionally, Showstack (2015) observed that Layla *corrected* linguistic forms such as *haiga* and *dijistes*. For example, a student used *haiga* out loud, and Layla responded with: "¿Existe la palabra 'haiga'? ¡NUNCA! (yelling)" [Does the word 'haiga' exist? NEVER!] (p. 350). In agreement with Showstack's (2015) analysis, these words exist because people use them. Additionally, *haiga* also refers to a big, ostentatious car in some varieties of Spanish.

---

[1] In some U.S. secondary schools, students can enroll in AP classes. At the end of the term, students take an exam that is centrally scored. Results of 4 and 5 often count towards credits at U.S. universities.
[2] A grade of D, in most U.S. education contexts, is defined as just above failing.

Furthermore, Showstack (2015) documented a student's recurring use of *agarrar* [to grab] and Layla's responses. In one interaction, Layla overhears her student Sarai use the phrase *agarrar una palabra [to grab a word]*, and she provides the following feedback:

> ¿Agarrar? ¿Puedes agarrar las palabras? ¿O qué se dice? [To grab? Can you grab words? Or what does one say?]
>
> ¿Puedes agarrar una palabra? [Can you grab a word?] (students stop talking or lower voices)
>
> ¿Adónde ibas con esa frase? [Where were you going with this phrase?] (students laugh quietly)
>
> 'Tonces puedes adoptar una palabra. [Then you can adopt a word.]
>
> Ves qué buen vocabulario. [See what good vocabulary.] (p. 353).

Layla positioned herself as an authority on language (Showstack, 2015) during this exchange. As a language expert with a particular ideology about what is and what is not Spanish, Layla had the power to not only *correct* her Latinx Spanish-speaking student Sarai, but she was also able to do so in a way that blatantly ignored Sarai's languaging practices. Like earlier examples, Layla publicly weaponized the Spanish language against Sarai and was able to embarrass her, as evidenced by students' laughter.

During a class discussion about code-switching, Sarai expressed that she disliked code-switching; however, she acknowledged that she does it. Sarai concluded her turn by stating, "so no me gusta hacerlo, pero sí lo hago" [so, I don't like to do it, but I do it] (Showstack, 2015, p. 354). Like the phrase *llámame pa' atrás*, the use of *so* is common among some Spanish–English bilinguals in the United States. Layla negated this truth by asking Sarai if the word *so* existed in Spanish, thus upholding language separation ideologies. Layla also told Sarai that her use of *so* was a *muletilla* [tag] and that she should use Spanish words like *pues* [well] or *entonces* [then]. Another student then asked Layla if *pos* (a common pronunciation in some Mexican varieties of Spanish) was acceptable, and let him know the correct pronunciation of the word is *pues*. Again, Layla dismissed her students' languaging practices and deemed their linguistic repertoires to be deficient in some way.

Moreover, in her 2016 work, Showstack highlighted how Layla's students had started to internalize the ideology of standardized Spanish as the only acceptable way to communicate in Spanish. When visiting family during a break, students had *corrected* their parents or labeled their Spanish as archaic. One specific interaction between Layla and a student exemplifies, I believe, language weaponization against students' families. Julián, one of the students, explained that his father (who grew up speaking Spanish in Texas) would not accept the rules his son had learned about *el estilo indirecto* (indirect speech). Layla confirmed that Julián did not need to worry because " . . . sabes las reglas y sabes por qué existen, ¿no? [you know the rules and you know they exist, no?] (Julián nods in agreement) Y entiendes por qué se hace, ¿o no? [And do you understand why they are done or no?] (p. 280). Layla concludes her response by repeating the rule students had learned earlier in the semester and insisting that, in certain contexts, you have to use *el estilo indirecto*. In addition, a participant in a recent study I conducted shared a similar account from her class. Sara, a Latinx student enrolled in a heritage language course focused on grammar, shared that her professor "kind of explained [that] we're taught how to pronounce certain words at home, but grammatically, it's incorrect" (Kemp, 2021, pp. 7–8). This perspective of the professor and her enactment of this ideological stance functions as a creator of tension and division between students and their families—especially when students internalize these messages about themselves.

I find these examples of language weaponization particularly worrisome. Julián's instructor continued to present the Spanish language as a codified, inflexible entity that follows very strict rules at all times. Layla, in a somewhat sinister way, reminds Julián that if he knows the rules about Spanish, then that is all that matters. In other words, the languaging practices of Julián's family are irrelevant, and he will become a good speaker of correct/standard Spanish as long as he learns and follows the rules of the language. The same can be said for Sara's professor, who negated the relevance and value of Spanish when used to communicate with family, friends, and local community members.

Finally, in their exploration of science education as *nepantler@s*, Aguilar-Valdez et al. (2013) shared their personal stories as a part of their research. Diane, one of the co-authors and a former dual language science teacher, revealed that she spent her summers as a child in a Mexican-American "barrio" in San Antonio. The author used quotation marks around *barrio* because "only in graduate school was [she] formally taught that barrio meant poor and dangerous" (p. 848). Diane had always believed that barrio simply referred to a kind of neighborhood until she was *corrected* by a professor, and she identified this moment in her life as an *arrebato* that she had to overcome. In concordance with Anzaldúa's theorization of borderlands, the authors explain that *arrebato* is a "deep rupture and fragmentation. It is a sudden and shocking disturbance to one's wholeness and peace" (Aguilar-Valdez et al., 2013, p. 829). Diane's professor weaponized Spanish against her in a way that took aim not only at her understanding and use of Spanish, but also at her sense of self and lived experiences as a Spanish-speaking person raised in a Spanish-speaking community in the United States.

The previous review highlights that these examples of language weaponization are not isolated incidents. Spanish-speaking Latinx students at all levels of teaching and learning are subject to having their own language weaponized against them in classes that, in one way or another, have been designed to support Spanish-speaking students. Most of the examples of language weaponization detailed here were delivered via public humiliation. Shaming students in front of their classmates seems to be the weapon of choice. Some educators also weaponized Spanish against their students by framing their families' languaging practices as broken or insufficient. This approach questions both students' language and identity in familial and community groups. I believe one example of language weaponization against a student is one too many, and we need to find ways to eliminate this harmful tactic from all classrooms.

4 Making changes for a more supportive and equitable educational experience

García and Otheguy (2015) proposed a theory for understanding the bilingualism of Spanish speakers in the United States that is "a *speaker-centered* view of Hispanic bilingualism, a disaggregated view of linguistic competence, and a translanguaging view of bilingual practices, all sheltered under what is generally known as a heteroglossic ideology" (p. 639). Heteroglossic theorizing suggests that "structural features of linguistic repertoires have no inherent linguistic affiliation but only external cultural labeling" (p. 644). Hence, it is society and culture that drives these categorizations. García and Otheguy's (2015) theory also resists the idea of 'language boxes' by advancing the idea that bilinguals "have an interconnected whole, an ecosystem of mutual interdependence of possible heteronamed linguistic features forming a single web, where translanguaging is the speech product generated by the web" (p. 646). Moreover, this position challenges notions of additive and subtractive bilingualism; instead, it places emphasis on dynamic bilingualism (García, 2009) that captures the "complex and interrelated" language practices of bilinguals (García & Otheguy, 2015, p. 647). The ways in which bilinguals use language are related to communicative goals, and when language users integrate and appropriate new features "within a singular linguistic repertoire" (p. 648), bilingualism truly emerges.

García and Otheguy (2015) also critique the prestige that is often associated with the "monolingual [English] speaker and setting as ideal, natural" (p. 649) by reminding us that language contact, which includes bilingualism, has been and continues to be the norm in many parts of the Spanish-speaking world (García, 2005; García & Otheguy, 2015)—including the United States. Current trends in education often support monolingual settings and speakers "as ideal linguistic archetypes" (García & Otheguy, 2015, p. 649), and in doing so, these perspectives frame bilinguals as deficient or lacking in some way when compared to monolinguals. Additionally, in their pushback against the monoglossic ideology of current curricular practices, García and Otheguy (2015) noted that the establishment of normative diglossia reinforces the maintenance of a dominant language and situates "the other language to a position of inferiority, of minority status, of being simply part of 'the heritage'" of students (p. 652).

In some contexts, as witnessed in this chapter, language maintenance efforts can result in 'linguistic shame,' and this feeling can produce a language shift. The embarrassment that people experience related to 'limited language' is "an attitude that can only be constructed (and deconstructed) within the bilingual community itself, by educators and sociolinguists valuing their dynamic practices" (García & Otheguy, 2015, p. 651). Instead of promoting language maintenance, we should focus on the sustainability of Latinx bilingualism in the United States, as language sustainability is tied to our interactions with the society and culture(s) in which we live and use our linguistic repertoires. García and Otheguy's (2015) theory underpins my call for educators to better understand the languaging practices of Spanish-speaking Latinx students and for the field of education to do more to prepare and (re)train educators across all educational contexts so that learning is not a subtractive schooling experience (Valenzuela, 1999). In the promotion of a predetermined idea of success, these kinds of experiences can force students to participate in cultural genocide that derides students' sense of belonging to a cultural group and divorce them from the cultural practices of said group.

I propose two broad categories to which the field must dedicate more attention and resources. The first is caring, and the second is criticality. These areas may not seem particularly innovative; however, I believe that both expanding what care looks like in classrooms and raising educators' awareness of critical ideologies and pedagogical practices can improve the experience of Spanish-speaking Latinx students in classrooms in which Spanish is the language of communication. Caring and critical approaches to teaching and learning can help shift current paradigms, so that language weaponization is no longer a tool used in the devaluation of students vis-à-vis their home language practices.

4.1 Care in the classroom

In her review of caring and its effect on teacher efficacy, Collier (2005) described some characteristics of effective teachers as "set[ting] high expectations for student performance, . . . develop[ing] improved instructional strategies to meet their students' needs, . . . view[ing] themselves and their students as partners in the learning process" (p. 352). Students like Yesi (Rosa, 2016) and Lupe (Kemp, 2021) perceived that their educators cared about them. As a reminder, Yesi believed that her high school Spanish teacher affirmed the legitimacy of students' varieties of Spanish, and sought to build on what students already knew (Rosa, 2016). Meanwhile, Lupe echoed this sentiment when she described her Spanish heritage language professor: "I don't think she [the professor] ever made anybody feel like their Spanish was broken at all" (Kemp, 2021, p. 12). The reflections of these students support the idea that caring educators have "better affective responses from their students and have more positive classroom atmospheres" (Teven, 2001, p. 159). I also believe that expressions of care could help combat negative feelings and insecurities Spanish-speaking Latinx students might have about their Spanish. Educators, therefore, should create an environment in which students—and their Spanish—feel welcomed and valued so that students do not feel "marginalized, alienated, isolated, unsupported, and unwelcomed" (Strayhorn, 2008, p. 303) in classrooms where Spanish is the language of communication.

Furthermore, as Antrop-González and De Jesús (2006) suggest, authentic care in the curriculum promotes "a not-so-hidden-curriculum that counteracts the informal and formal practices that marginalize Latino/a students" (p. 419). An acceptance and embracing of students' languaging practices as forms of authentic caring could be transformative for Latinx students, especially when this approach is connected to the fostering of high levels of student engagement and "high academic expectations" (Antrop-González & De Jesús, 2006, p. 429) for all learners. According to Teven (2001), it is important that educators know which behaviors influence students' perceptions of caring and which ones undermine this perception. As such, the identification of educators' behaviors that are markers of care could positively affect students' learning experiences (see Dewaele et al., 2022, for a recent analysis of foreign language enjoyment and attitudes/motivation). A vital aspect of effective teaching is the establishment of "a climate of warmth, understanding, and caring within the classroom" (Teven, 2001, p. 159), and creating such a climate through policies and practices could help reinforce students' self-worth as Spanish speakers in the United States.

Caring in the classroom should also include the application of bilanguaging love (Mignolo, 2012), which is a deep appreciation for existing between languages. This demonstration of care can "serve counterhegemonic ends by elevating the epistemologies and knowledges [of students] suppressed by Western modern/colonial projects" (Pacheco & Hamilton, 2020, p. 551). An application of bilanguaging love would remind educators their students "do not fit neatly into dominant constructions of language proficiency" (p. 551)—this point underscores the genesis of many program models designed to support Spanish-speaking Latinx students. Thus, to best meet the social, affective, and linguistic needs of students, we cannot ignore their prior experiences in Spanish. A caring curriculum considers and responds to the unique needs of students.

4.2 Critical perspectives in the classroom

In their essay on ideological clarity for bilingual teachers, Alfaro and Bartolomé (2017) argue that "teachers, in addition to developing humanistic bilingual pedagogical practices, must learn to identify hurtful dominant culture ideologies and their manifestation in the classroom so they can be prepared to intervene and create optimal learning conditions for all their students" (p. 13). This stance must hold true for all educators who teach in classrooms designed to serve Spanish-speaking Latinx students. The authors relay that successful educators often have "a counterhegemonic ideological orientation that enables them to question unfair and discriminatory practices" (Alfaro & Bartolomé, 2017, p. 18). Hence, the researchers request that the formal study of ideology be integrated into teacher education programs. I would suggest that the field expand this call and apply it to all contexts that prepare, train, and employ educators across all contexts. The questioning and critiquing of ideological perspectives that shape teaching and learning is the responsibility of everyone involved in educating Spanish-speaking Latinx students—especially in classrooms in which Spanish is the language of instruction.

Alfaro and Bartolomé (2017) provide the example of bilingual education as a driving force that obligates students "to leave their nonstandard vernaculars at the door" (p. 20) in order to gain strength in the primary or standard language. Again, this experience of students in bilingual and dual language programs holds true for students in Spanish language classes. The goal of these courses, as evidenced earlier, is to replace students' home language varieties with a standard, elite variety of Spanish. Flores and Rosa (2015) posit that "additive approaches to bilingual education continue to interpret the linguistic practices of bilinguals through a monolingual framework that marginalizes the fluid linguistic practices of these communities" (p. 153). Instead, it is better to describe the languaging practices of students as dynamic and context-specific in order to arrive at a deeper, richer understanding of what students can do with their linguistic repertoires. Flores and Rosa (2015) add that we must "engage with, confront, and ultimately dismantle the racialized hierarchy of U.S. society" (p. 167) in order to improve the quality of education for language-minoritized students. Educators need to be trained in questioning hegemonic ideologies and then equipped to push back against them.

Freire and Feainauer (2020), in their analysis of dual language education, encourage using students' languaging practices as a way to promote critical consciousness. This principle "helps individuals develop a deep understanding of the sociopolitical contexts, realities, and positioning in the world" (p. 10). By taking on a critical consciousness approach, educators can advance equitable pedagogical practices that use students' linguistic repertoire as a resource instead of viewing students' languaging practices as an impediment to success. Clearly, these tenets are applicable to other types of classrooms that serve Spanish-speaking Latinx students. As a part of this endeavor, Freire and Feainauer (2020) ask that educators "examine their own linguistic biases and deficit language ideologies" (p. 11) with the goal of fostering critical consciousness in classrooms.

Finally, in a critical essay on the shift in paradigms in Spanish heritage language education, MacGregor-Mendoza (2020) states that teaching a language is not "apolitical, devoid of prejudice, pretentiousness, or injustice" (p. 23). Based on this argument, I would add that teaching Spanish-speaking Latinx students in Spanish in *any* context, cannot be objective either. Educators and researchers must consider the prominent affective dimension present in the types of classes detailed in this chapter. Students have a familial, personal tie to Spanish. Therefore, students' home varieties of Spanish and their languaging practices cannot be weaponized against them. Language weaponization practices label Spanish-speaking Latinx students' Spanish as broken and in need of remediation. This kind of deficit model of education is demoralizing and offensive to students, and can have long-term effects on their self-esteem, and the familial preservation of the language.

5 Final thoughts

The onus of preventing and removing language weaponization from classes that serve Spanish-speaking Latinx students cannot reside only with teacher preparation programs as there are many pathways to classrooms. University language programs are also responsible for preparing undergraduate and graduate students who might teach one day as K-12 teachers, lecturers, professors, etc. Language programs need to make sure their students graduate with coursework in caring and critical ideologies about Spanish-speaking Latinx students. Furthermore, professional development in the importance of caring and critical approaches to teaching and learning should continue for educators at all levels. For example, school districts should require training in these areas, while postsecondary language departments and language centers should engage undergraduate and graduate students and members of the faculty in critical reflections on their language ideologies and practices. Organizers of national, regional, and local conferences are not exempt from this call, as workshops that provide more guidance and training can be of benefit to all educators.

The entire profession is responsible for ending the harm caused by language weaponization, and a limited scope focused on eradicating language weaponization against Spanish-speaking Latinx students is not going to magically resolve this problem. There are many ideas and approaches not covered in this chapter (see Babino & Stewart, 2018; Carreira, 2018; Cervantes-Soon et al., 2017; Christoffersen, 2019; Domínguez-Fret & Morales, 2021; Flores & García, 2013; Kinsella, 2017; Loza, 2017; Noddings, 1992; Pascual y Cabo & Prada, 2018; Paris & Alim, 2014; Pentón Herrera, 2022; Potowski, 2012; Sayer, 2013; Valdés, 2020). Therefore, the field must make a concerted effort to end the weaponization of students' Spanish against them.

During a panel presentation, Walqui (2022) discussed the importance of respecting multilingual learners' home language(s) and how they use them in and outside of classrooms. She also called on educational institutions to provide students with opportunities to meaningfully engage with the subject matter of a class—be it content or language instruction. Walqui's (2022) message echoes those of Alfaro and Bartolomé (2017) and Freire and Feainauer (2020). Alfaro and Bartolomé (2017) call for placing equal importance on increasing the ideological clarity of bilingual teachers in concert with finding "ways to honor and build on" (p. 25) students' linguistic repertoire that they bring to the classroom, while Freire and Feainauer (2020) favor strategic language policies so that students' home languaging practices are "legitimized for both social and academic purposes in the classroom" (p. 8). In classrooms designed to specifically support Spanish-speaking Latinx students' home language(s), we have to find a balanced approach to instruction. That said, we have to find that balance without weaponizing Spanish against students. Spanish cannot be a tool that is used to shame, belittle, or reprimand students, their families, *and* their collective languaging practices.

References

Aguilar-Valdez, Jean R., Carlos A. LópezLeiva, Deborah Roberts-Harris, Diane Torres-Velásquez, Gilberto Lobo & Carol Westby. 2013. Ciencia en *Nepantla*: The journey of *Nepantler@s* in science learning and teaching. *Cultural Studies of Science Education* 8(4), 821–858. https://doi.org/10.1007/s11422-013-9512-9

Alfaro, Cristina & Lilia Bartolomé. 2017. Preparing ideologically clear bilingual teachers: Honoring the working-class non-standard language use in the bilingual education classroom. *Issues in Teacher Education* 26(2), 11–34.

Antrop-González, René & Anthony De Jesús. 2006. Toward a theory of *critical care* in urban small school reform: Examining structures and pedagogies of caring in two Latino community-based schools. *International Journal of Qualitative Studies in Education* 16(4), 409–433. https://doi.org/10.1080/09518390600773148

Anzaldúa, Gloria. 1987. *Borderlands/La Frontera*. San Francisco, CA: Aunt Lute Books.

Aparicio, Frances R. 2000. Of Spanish dispossessed. In Roseann Dueñas González (ed.) with Ildiko Melis, *Language ideologies: Critical perspectives on the official English movement*, 248–275. New York, NY: Routledge & National Council of Teachers of English.

Aparicio, Frances R. & Christina José-Kampfner. 1995. Language, culture, and violence in the education crisis of U.S. Latino/as: Two courses for intervention. *Michigan Journal of Community Service Learning* 2(1), 95–104. http://hdl.handle.net/2027/spo.3239521.0002.109

Babino, Alexandra & Mary Amanda Steward. 2018. Remodeling dual language programs: Teachers enact agency as critically conscious language policy makers. *Bilingual Research Journal* 4(3), 272–297. https://doi.org/10.1080/15235882.2018.1489313

Baker, Colin. 2014. *A parents' and teachers' guide to bilingualism* (4th ed.). Bristol, UK: Multilingual Matters.

Beaudrie, Sara M. 2012. Research on university-based Spanish heritage language programs in the United States: The current state of affairs. In Sara M. Beaudrie & Marta Fairclough (eds.), *Spanish as a heritage language in the United States: The state of the field*, 203–221. Washington, D.C.: Georgetown.

Bialystok, Ellen. 2011. Reshaping the mind: The benefits of bilingualism. *Canadian Journal of Experimental Psychology* 65(4), 229–235. https://doi.org/10.1037/a0025406

Californians Together & Velázquez Press. 2015. Seal of biliteracy: Frequently asked questions. http://sealofbiliteracy.org/faq

Carreira, María. 2018. *Towards a national strategy for capacity-building in heritage languages and Spanish*: A response to America's languages: Investing in language education for the 21st century. *Hispania* 101(1), 5–9. https://doi.org/10.1353/hpn.2018.0080

Cervantes-Soon, Claudia G., Lisa Dorner, Deborah Palmer, Dan Heiman, Rebecca Schwerdtfeger & Jinmyung Choi. 2017. Combating inequalities in two-way language immersion programs: Toward critical consciousness in bilingual education spaces. *Review of Research in Education* 41(1), 403–427. https://doi.org/10.3102/0091732X17690120

Christoffersen, Katherine. 2019. Linguistic terrorism in the borderlands: Language ideologies in the narratives of young adults in the Rio Grande Valley. *International Multilingual Research Journal* 13(3), 137–151. https://doi.org/10.1080/19313152.2019.1623637

Collier, Marta D. 2005. An ethic of caring: The fuel for high teacher efficacy. *The Urban Review* 37(4), 351–359. https://doi.org/10.1007/s11256-005-0012-4

Dewaele, Jean-Marc, Kazuya Saito & Florentina Halimi. 2022. How teacher behaviour shapes foreign language learners' enjoyment, anxiety and attitudes/motivation: A mixed modelling longitudinal investigation. *Language Teaching Research*. https://doi.org/10.1177/13621688221089601

Domínguez-Fret, Nancy & P. Zitlali Morales. 2021. From English language learner to Spanish teacher: The testimonios of heritage Spanish speakers who became Spanish as a heritage language (SHL) teachers. In Eurydice Bauer, Lenny Sánchez, Yang Wang & Andrea Vaughan (eds.), *A transdisciplinary lens for bilingual education*, 232–256. New York, NY: Routledge.

Flores, Nelson & Ofelia García. 2013. Linguistic third spaces in education: Teachers' translanguaging across the bilingual continuum. In David Little, Constant Leung & Piet Van Avermaet (eds.),

Managing diversity in education, 243–256. Bristol, UK: Multilingual Matters. https://doi.org/10.21832/9781783090815-016

Flores, Nelson & Jonathan Rosa. 2015. Undoing appropriateness: Raciolinguistic ideologies and language diversity in education. *Harvard Educational Review* 85(2). 149–171. https://doi.org/10.17763/0017-8055.85.2.149

Freire, Juan A. & Erika Feinauer. 2020. Vernacular Spanish as a promoter of critical consciousness in dual language bilingual education classrooms. *International Journal of Bilingual Education and Bilingualism* 25(4), 1516–1529. https://doi.org/10.1080/13670050.2020.1775778

Gabriel, María L., Kevin C. Roxas & Kent Becker. 2017. Meeting, knowing, and affirming Spanish-speaking immigrant families through successful culturally responsive family engagement. *Journal of Family Diversity in Education* 2(3), 1–18. https://doi.org/10.53956/jfde.2017.93

García, Ofelia. 2005. Positioning heritage languages in the United States. *The Modern Language Journal* 89(4), 601–605. https://www.jstor.org/stable/3588631

García, Ofelia. 2009. Livin' and teachin' la lengua loca: Glocalizing US Spanish ideologies and practices. In M. Rafael Salaberry (ed.), *Language allegiances and bilingualism in the United States*, 151–171. Bristol, UK: Multilingual Matters.

García, Ofelia. 2014. U.S. Spanish and education: Global and local intersections. *Review of Research in Education* 38(1), 58–80. https://doi.org/10.3102%2F0091732X13506542

García, Ofelia & Hugo Baetens Beardsmore. 2009. *Bilingual education in the 21st century: A global perspective*. Malden, MA: Wiley-Blackwell.

García, Ofelia & Ricardo Otheguy. 2015. Spanish and Hispanic bilingualism. In Manel Lacorte (ed.), *The Routledge handbook of Hispanic applied linguistics*, 639–658. New York, NY: Routledge.

Gómez, Leo, David Freeman & Yvonne Freeman. 2005. Dual language education: A promising 50-50 model. *Bilingual Research Journal* 29(1), 145–164. http://dx.doi.org/10.1080/15235882.2005.10162828

Goulette, Elizabeth. 2020. Heritage language learners in a mixed class: Educational affordances and constraints. *Dimension* 55, 64–81. https://www.scolt.org/wp-content/uploads/2020/04/Dimensions2020_Chapter4.pdf

Gregory, Anne & Edward Fergus. 2017. Social and emotional learning and equity in school discipline. *The Future of Children* 27(1), 117–136.

Hurtado, Aída & Raúl Rodríguez. 1989. Language as a social problem: The repression of Spanish in South Texas. *Journal of Multilingual and Multicultural Development* 10(5), 401–419. https://doi.org/10.1080/01434632.1989.9994386

Kelleher, Ann. 2008. What is a heritage language? In Joy K. Peyton (ed.), *Heritage languages in America: Frequently asked questions about heritage languages in the United States*, 8–11. Center for Applied Linguistics.

Kemp, Jason A. 2021. *Responsibly responding to Latinx college students enrolled in Spanish heritage language classes* [Conference session]. American Educational Research Association Annual Meeting, Virtual.

Kennedy, Barbara & José Medina. 2017. *Dual language education: Answers to questions from the field*. Center for Applied Linguistics. https://www.cal.org/wp-content/uploads/2022/05/CAL-Practitioner-Brief-Dual-Language-Education-Sept2017.pdf

Kinsella, Benjamin. 2017. 'Neither here nor there': An examination of language curriculum and ideology in a New Jersey public school. *Language, Culture, and Curriculum* 31(1), 21–38. https://doi.org/10.1080/07908318.2017.1332073

LeBlanc, Robert J. 2017. Those who know and are known: Students using ethnography to interrogate language and literacy ideologies. *Journal of Adolescent & Adult Literacy* 61(5), 489–499. https://doi.org/10.1002/jaal.710

Leeman, Jennifer. 2015. Heritage language education and identity in the United States. *Annual Review of Applied Linguistics* 35, 100–119. https://doi.org/10.1017/S0267190514000245

Library of Congress. 2004. Brown v. Board at fifty: "With an even hand." Washington, D.C. https://www.loc.gov/exhibits/brown/index.html

Loza, Sergio. 2017. Transgressing standard language ideologies in the Spanish heritage language (SHL) classroom. *Chiricú Journal: Latina/o Literatures, Arts, and Cultures* 1(2), 56–77. https://doi.org/10.2979/chiricu.1.2.06

MacGregor-Mendoza, Patricia. 2000. Aquí no se habla español: Stories of linguistic repression in Southwest schools. *Bilingual Research Journal* 24(4), 355–367. https://doi.org/10.1080/15235882.2000.10162772

MacGregor-Mendoza, Patricia. 2020. Language, culture, and Spanish heritage language learners: Reframing old paradigms. *Dimension* 55, 21–36. https://www.scolt.org/wp-content/uploads/2020/04/Dimensions2020_Chapter2.pdf

McKay Wilson, David. 2011. Dual language programs on the rise. *Harvard Education Letter* 27(2). Harvard Education Publishing Group. https://www.hepg.org/hel-home/issues/27_2/helarticle/dual-language-programs-on-the-rise

Mignolo, Walter D. 2012. *Local histories/global designs: Coloniality, subaltern knowledges, and border thinking*. Princeton, NJ: Princeton University Press.

Moll, Luis C., Cathy Amanti, Deborah Neff & Norma Gonzalez. 1992. Funds of knowledge for teaching: Using a qualitative approach to connect homes and classrooms. *Theory into Practice* 31(2). 132–141. http://www.jstor.org/stable/1476399?origin=JSTOR-pdf

Moore, Sarah C. K. 2021. *A history of bilingual education in the US: Examining the politics of language policymaking*. Bristol, UK: Multilingual Matters.

Murillo, Luz A. & Janine M. Schall. 2016. "They didn't teach us well": Mexican-origin students speak out about their readiness for college literacy. *Journal of Adolescent & Adult Literacy* 60(3). 315–323. https://doi.org/10.1002/jaal.581

Noddings, Nel. 1992. *The challenge to care in schools: An alternative approach to education*. New York, NY: Teachers College Press.

Pacheco, Mariana & Colleen Hamilton. 2020. Bilanguaging love: Latina/o/x bilingual students' subjectivities and sensitivities in dual language immersion contexts. *TESOL Quarterly* 54(3). 548–571. https://doi.org/10.1002/tesq.585

Paris, Django & H. Samy Alim. 2014. What are we seeking to sustain through culturally sustaining pedagogy? A loving critique forward. *Harvard Educational Review* 84(1). 85–100. https://psycnet.apa.org/doi/10.17763/haer.84.1.982l873k2ht16m77

Pascual y Cabo, Diego & Josh Prada. 2018. Redefining Spanish teaching and learning in the United States. *Foreign Language Annals* 51(3). 533–547. https://doi.org/10.1111/flan.12355

Pentón Herrera, Luis Javier. 2019. Explorando el spanglish: Abstrusa tesela del mosaico lingüístico estadounidense. *Hispania* 102(4). 467–472. http://doi.org/10.1353/hpn.2019.0098

Pentón Herrera, Luis Javier. 2022. Is the language you teach racist? Reflections and considerations for English and Spanish (teacher) educators. *International Journal of Literacy, Culture, and Language Education* 2. 58–70. https://doi.org/10.14434/ijlcle.v2iMay.34390

Potowski, Kim. 2012. Identity and heritage learners: Moving beyond essentializations. In Sara M. Beaudrie & Marta Fairclough (eds.), *Spanish as a heritage language in the United States: The state of the field*, 179–199. Washington D.C.: Georgetown.

Ramírez, Pablo C. 2022. Reframing dual language education in the U.S. *International Journal of Bilingual Education and Bilingualism*. 1–5. https://doi.org/10.1080/13670050.2022.2087469

Roberts, Gregg. 2021. *Canvass of dual language immersion programs in US public schools*. American Councils Research Center. https://www.americancouncils.org/sites/default/files/documents/pages/2021-10/Canvass%20DLI%20-%20October%202021-2_ac.pdf

Rosa, Jonathan D. 2016. Standardization, racialization, languagelessness: Raciolinguistic ideologies across communicative contexts. *Journal of Linguistic Anthropology* 26(2). 162–183. https://doi.org/10.1111/jola.12116

Sarmiento-Arribalzaga, M. A. & Luz A. Murillo. 2009. Tell me your story: Language and literacy autobiographies as healing pedagogies for Latino educators. In *Proceedings of the National Association of African American Studies Conference*, 614–630. NAAAS.

Sayer, Peter. 2013. Translanguaging, TexMex, and bilingual pedagogy: Emergent bilinguals learning through the vernacular. *TESOL Quarterly* 47(1). 63–88. https://doi.org/10.1002/tesq.53

Showstack, Rachel E. 2015. Institutional representations of 'Spanish' and 'Spanglish': Managing competing discourse in heritage language instruction. *Language and Intercultural Communication* 15(3). 341–361. http://dx.doi.org/10.1080/14708477.2015.1015350

Showstack, Rachel E. 2016. Stancetaking and language ideologies in heritage language learner classroom discourse. *Journal of Language, Identity & Education* 16(5). 271–284. http://dx.doi.org/10.1080/15348458.2016.1248558

Skutnabb-Kangas, Tove. 1988. Multilingualism and the education of minority children. In Tove Skutnabb-Kangas & Jim Cummins (eds.), *Minority education: From shame to struggle*, 9–44. Bristol, UK: Multilingual Matters.

Strayhorn, Terrell L. 2008. *Sentido de pertenencia* [Sense of belonging]: A hierarchical analysis predicting sense of belonging among Latino college students. *Journal of Hispanic Higher Education* 7(4). 301–320. https://doi.org/10.1177%2F1538192708320474

Teven, Jason J. 2001. The relationships among teacher characteristics and perceived caring. *Communication Education* 50(2). 159–169. https://doi.org/10.1080/03634520109379241

U.S. Department of Education, National Center for Education Statistics. 2021. English learner (EL) students enrolled in public elementary and secondary schools, by home language, grade, and selected student characteristics: Selected years, 2008–09 through fall 2019. *Digest of Education Statistics 2021*, table 204.27. https://nces.ed.gov/programs/digest/d21/tables/dt21_204.27.asp?current=yes

Valdés, Guadalupe. 2020. (Mis)educating the children of Mexican-origin people in the United States: The challenge of internal language borders. *Intercultural Education* 31(5). 548–561. https://doi.org/10.1080/14675986.2020.1794122

Valencia, Richard R. 1997. Conceptualizing the notion of deficit thinking. In. Richard R. Valencia (ed.), *The evolution of deficit thinking: Educational thought and practice*, 1–12. New York, NY: Routledge.

Valenzuela, Angela. 1999. *Subtractive schooling: U.S. Mexican youth and the politics of caring*. New York: State University of New York Press.

Walqui, Aída. 2022. *Assessing multilingual learners for success* [Webinar]. Public symposium at the Center for Applied Linguistics.

Wiley, Terrence G. 2007. Accessing language rights in education: A brief history of the U.S. context. In Ofelia García & Colin Baker (eds.), *Bilingual education: An introductory reader*, 89–107. Bristol, UK: Multilingual Matters.

Wimberly, George L. (ed.). 2015. *LGBTQ issues in education: Advancing a research agenda*. American Educational Research Association.

Burcu Ates and Benita Brooks
Chapter 9
Banned books in K-12 classrooms: Weaponization of children and young adolescent literature

Abstract: On September 2, 2021, the Texas Legislature passed Senate Bill 3 (SB 3), which replaced House Bill 3979, and became law on September 1, 2021. SB 3 restricts classroom learning in all K-12 courses by prohibiting teachers from discussing certain topics related to racism, bias, and disturbing historical facts about the founding of the United States. It furthermore restricts how teachers discuss current controversial events and issues. The Texas Legislatures' long-term efforts have directly impacted the books used in K-12 classrooms and libraries asarious independent school districts (ISDs) across Texas have removed books due to policymakers' and parents' raising concerns and making complaints regarding content. This chapter utilizes critical discourse analysis (Fairclough, 1995) to examine how supporters of banned books have used Pascale's (2019) four interlocking components of weaponized language to have books removed from school libraries and curricula to serve their own personal, social, and political agendas. The chapter further discusses the harm that banning books causes students, the school curriculum, and communities in general. It concludes by highlighting the ways student leaders, schools, and communities advocate opposing both national and local efforts to ban books.

Keywords: Banned Books, K-12, Critical Race Theory, Senate Bill 3, Censorship, Propaganda, Disinformation, Fake News, Mundane Discourse

1 Introduction

Since the start of the COVID-19 pandemic, we have witnessed people pack into town hall and school board meetings to express their opposition to mask mandates, vaccinations, online instruction, and other COVID-19 measures. During this time, there has been a renewed focus on other issues many conservatives claim clash with their values, including aspects of the K-12 curriculum and books that highlight social justice issues, gender nonconformity, sexuality, race, and history. We know

Burcu Ates, Benita Brooks, University of Nevada, Las Vegas

there are a wide variety of political, religious, and cultural reasons for banning books, yet Hiorns (2021) argued that the practice of censorship generally stems from "a desire to silence a perspective of opposition" (para 6). In the context of American history, the decision on what books should be assigned for reading as part of the K-12 classroom curriculum has been controversial since the early 1900s.

Most recently, a CBS poll revealed that 80% of Americans overwhelmingly rejected the idea of banning books about history or race (Backus & Salvanto, 2022). Yet, this continuous fight to ban and challenge readers has reached levels not seen in decades. The Office for Intellectual Freedom (OIF) of the American Library Association (ALA) reported receiving over 300 challenge reports since September 1st, 2021, regarding "problem books" on the shelves of school libraries or within school curricula (Eberle, 2022). While parents, activists, school board officials, and lawmakers around the country are challenging books based on their content, DeWitt (2022) argued that banning books is not about parents protecting children; it is about discriminating against others. To date, 66 gag orders have been introduced in more than 25 states across the country that place restrictions on how American history can be taught or even discussed in classrooms (Robinson, 2022). At least a dozen of these laws went into effect, "broadly censor[ing] conversations about racism by framing the subject itself as divisive and harmful" (Robinson, 2022, para 8). In this case, censorship is being weaponized to exclude, silence, and deny the voices and experiences of Black, Indigenous, people of color (BIPOC), and other historically marginalized groups in the U.S.

In this chapter, we utilize critical discourse analysis (Fairclough, 1995) to examine how supporters of banned books use four interlocking components of weaponized language to remove books from school libraries and curricula to serve their own personal, social, and political agendas. For clarity, in this chapter, we understand the weaponization of language as a process in which words and discourse are being used to harm others, especially BIPOC individuals, and as a process in which educational practices, policies, and curricula are being weaponized to further perpetuate inequity and injustice (Pentón Herrera & Bryan, 2022). In addition, this chapter highlights the ways student leaders, schools, and communities have opposed both national and local efforts to ban books.

2 A historical look at book banning

On October 8, 1919, Mildred L. Rutherford addressed the United Confederate Veterans at its reunion in Atlanta, Georgia. Her speech highlighted "the importance of having the South's history correctly taught in our schools" (Rutherford, 1920, p. 2). After the speech, General C. Irvine Walker of Charleston, South Carolina, described

Rutherford as "an illustrious Southern Historian" whose work was " . . . patriotic, historic, and instructive . . . " (Rutherford, 1920, p. 2). In 1920, Rutherford published *A measuring rod to test textbooks, and reference books in schools, colleges, and libraries* at the request of the United Confederate Veterans. In a call to arms, General Walker instructed the Sons of Confederate Veterans and United Daughters of the Confederacy to urge " . . . all authorities charged with the selection of textbooks for colleges, schools, and all scholastic institutions to measure all books offered for adoption by Rutherford's *A measuring rod* . . . and adopt none which do not accord full justice to the South" (p. 3). Additionally, General Walker demanded, " . . . all library authorities in the Southern States . . . to mark all books in their collections which do not come up to the same measure, on the title page thereof, "Unjust to the South" (Rutherford, 1920, p. 3). General Walker concluded by asking " . . . all scholastic and library authorities, in all parts of the country, in justice and fairness to their fellow citizens of the South, to yield to the above request" (Rutherford, 1920, p. 3).

During the Cold War, books that focused on patriotism and respect for authority were favored, and books that were contradictory to these values were mostly not allowed in classrooms or school libraries (Bobbitt, 2019). However, in the 1960s, more media coverage and concerned parents resulted in "book-banning to become part of the culture wars" (Bobbitt, 2019, p. x). These book and culture wars continued into the new century and are now being manipulated not only by politicians and school leaders but also by parents, religious leaders, and national special interest groups (Bobbitt, 2019). In many cases, the book-banning process begins with an individual or a group submitting a challenge for the book. Lusted (2017) defined a challenge as "an attempt to restrict or remove materials from a library, based on the objections of that person or group, usually on moral or religious grounds" (p. 9). Banning is defined as "the removal of those materials" from circulation (News Staff, Business & Heritage Clarksville, 2017, p. 11). In the support of Confederate sympathizers, Mildred L. Rutherford (1920) published a blueprint on how to restrict literature that did not glorify the South from reaching classrooms and libraries:

> But—reject a book that speaks of the Constitution other than a Compact between Sovereign States.
>
> Reject a textbook that does not give the principles for which the South fought in 1861 and does not clearly outline the interferences with the rights guaranteed to the South by the Constitution, and which caused secession.
>
> Reject a book that calls the Confederate soldier a traitor or rebel, and the war a rebellion. Reject a book that says the South fought to hold her slaves.
>
> Reject a book that speaks of the slaveholder of the South as cruel and unjust to his slaves. Reject a textbook that glorifies Abraham Lincoln and vilifies Jefferson Davis, unless a truthful cause can be found for such glorification and vilification before 1865.

Reject a text-book that omits to tell of the South's heroes and their deeds when the North's heroes and their deeds are made prominent.

Refuse to adopt any textbook, or endorse any set of books, upon the promise of changes being made to omit the objectionable features. (p. 4)

In December 2017, six people representing academic, public, and school libraries updated the Selection and Reconsideration Policy to provide current policies on selecting materials on controversial topics (Dawkins, 2018). A reconsideration policy provide parents a voice to challenge or ban a book. Parents are required to submit a form explaining how much of the book they read and provide examples from the book that they object to, and explain why they object and want the specific book to be removed from the classroom and/or school library. There are informal and formal complaints. In an informal complaint, the librarian responds to questions related to material addressed by the parents, such as explaining the selection process and criteria, the purpose of the resource, and/or alternative resources. In place of a formal complaint, the librarian provides a written reconsideration form to be filled out by the parent (TLA, 2021). ALA states that a formal reconsideration request is a written document that is often reviewed by an assigned library staff member or a committee. According to ALA, in order to maintain a standard method, every library should have a written process for handling complaints as part of the reconsideration policy (ALA, n.d.). It serves as a guideline when reviewing, evaluating, and processing formal reconsideration requests.

Other states (e.g., Wisconsin) have also adopted a reconsideration policy that requires parents and community members to go through an appeals process where they articulate how much of the book they read and outline what they object to in the book. While some teachers and parents understand the importance of keeping graphic literature on school library shelves, the majority of parents align with the growing far-right movement to support state laws limiting the way teachers can discuss race, gender, and sexuality. According to PEN America's report, during 12 months, between July 1, 2021, and June 30, 2022, the Index of School Book Bans listed 138 school districts in 32 districts where book bans have occurred (Friedman & Johnson, 2022). Figure 9.1 below (Friedman & Johnson, 2022) represents the documented cases of book bans that were directly reported to PEN America and//or covered in the media. PEN America argued additional bans could exist that have not been reported. Texas had the most banned books, with 801 bans in 22 districts, followed by Florida, with 566 bans in 21 districts.

PEN America also reported the content of Banned Books. Figure 9.2 below represents various subject matter of Banned Content (Friedman & Johnson, 2022) from July 1, 2021, and June 30, 2022.

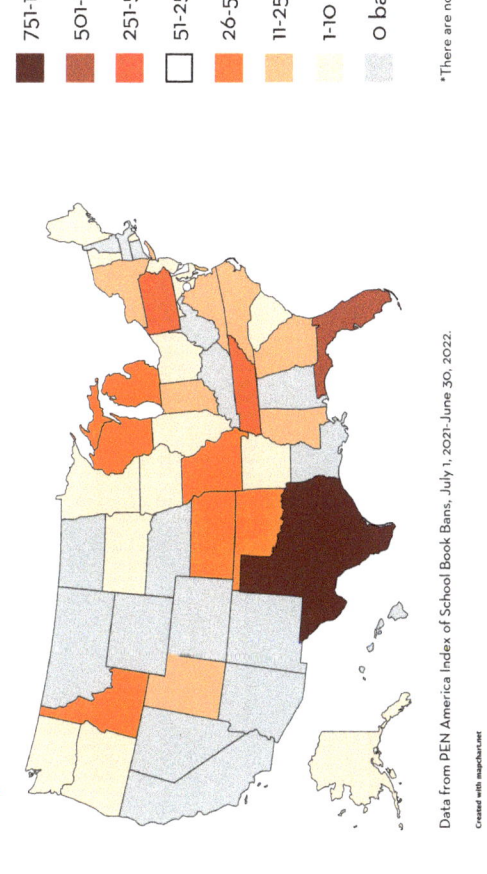

Figure 9.1: School Book Bans by State.
Note: Data from PEN America Index of School Bans, July 2021–June 2022. Used with permission from the creators.

Figure 9.2: Subject Matter of Banned Content.
Note: Data from PEN America Index of School Bans, July 2021–June 2022.

The data revealed that 41% of books, a total of 674 titles, addressed Lesbian, Gay, Bisexual, Transgender, Queer/Questioning, Intersex, Asexual, and more (LGBTQIA+) themes or have protagonists or prominent secondary characters who are LGBTQIA+. Forty percent of other banned books, 659 titles, included protagonists or prominent secondary characters of color.

3 The Texas case

In August 2022, Keller Independent School District (ISD) drew national attention when 41 books that were challenged, then reviewed by a committee of parents and community members, and eventually approved for use were again removed from shelves the day before the school year began (Woodard, 2022). This event did not occur in a vacuum. In April 2022, the Texas Education Agency (TEA), the state agency that oversees primary and secondary public education in the state of Texas, pushed for more scrutiny and parental input in its new policy for school libraries in Texas. While school districts are not required to adopt the agency's recommendations, it is suggested by TEA to use them as guidance as libraries develop new procedures or alter their policies for selecting or removing library books (Lopez, 2022).

Between April and August 2022, Keller ISD elected three new conservative school board members, all recipients of a Christian political action committee's donations, to the district's seven-member board of trustees. Before the election, a school district committee made up of parents, and local community members met last year and recommended that some of the books, including Toni Morrison's *The Bluest Eye* and Anne Frank's *Diary of a Young Girl*, remain in school libraries. Shortly after the election, the school board members approved new guidelines for determining what is appropriate and not appropriate in Keller ISD's school libraries.

Even before Keller ISD made national headlines, the Texas House approved legislation that took aim at limiting teaching about race or racism. In May 2021, the Texas House passed House Bill 3979, which is part of a national effort by red-state legislatures to ban or limit the teaching of critical race theory (CRT), an academic discipline that examines how racism shaped legal and social systems within the United States (Svitek, 2021). On September 2, 2021, the Texas Legislature passed Senate Bill 3 (SB 3), a follow-up to HB 3979, which Governor Abbott signed in May 2021. The Intercultural Development Research Association (IDRA, 2022) described SB 3 as a classroom censorship law that is more restrictive and broader than HB 3979. According to Chute and Mendéz (2021), one change in SB 3 is "the removal of a reference to the Klu Klux Klan being 'morally wrong' from HB 3979" (para. 3). IDRA declared SB 3 to be in stark contrast to a core mission of the Texas public education system, which is to ensure all Texas children have access to a quality education that enables them to achieve their potential and fully participate now and in the future in the social, economic, and educational opportunities of the state and nation. According to the Texas Legislative Education Equity Coalition (2021), SB 3 restricts classroom learning in all K-12 courses by prohibiting teachers from discussing certain topics related to racism, bias, and historical facts about the founding of the United States and by restricting how teachers discuss controversial events and issues.

Additionally, the Texas Legislative Education Equity Coalition (TxTLEEC), a collaboration of organizations and individuals with the mission to improve the quality of public education for all children, with a focus on racial equity, outlined more guidelines K-12 schools are expected to follow after SB 3 went into effect:
1. remove requirements to learn about diverse communities,
2. prohibit students from earning course credit for civic engagement,
3. prohibit schools from using private funding for important programming on curriculum, training, or professional development related to race, racism, and sexism, or diversity, equity, and inclusion,
4. require schools to give parents login credentials,
5. create a civics training program for educator compliance,
6. restrict teacher training on topics related to racism, bias, and historical facts about the founding of the United States,
7. create vague rules about the treatment of student conduct,
8. create Texas Education Agency (TEA) enforcement power, and
9. clarify no private right to sue teachers.

A month later, in late October 2021, Republican Texas state representative and lawmaker Matt Krause launched an investigation into all Texas school districts over books that he assumed included race or sexuality. These books were written mainly by authors of color and/or included LGBTQIA+ characters. Krause, in his letter to Texas Education Agency, targeted 850 book titles. He asked school superintendents to check their inventory and report how many copies of these books existed in their district and how much money they spent on them (Lopez, 2021). Some of the book titles related to race include the 1967 Pulitzer-winning novel *The Confessions of Nat Turner* by William Styron and *Between the World and Me* by Ta-Nehisi Coates. Some of the books that address sexuality and sexual health are, *The Baby Tree* by Sophie Blackall and *It's Perfectly Normal: Changing Bodies, Growing Up, Sex, Gender, and Sexual Health* by Robie Harris (Ellis, 2021). Even though Krause did not specifically mention LGBTQIA+ books in his letter, according to Ellis' (2021) content analysis, more than half of the titles, about 62.6%, contained LGBTQIA+ topics.

Many of the books in this category have been classified under Young Adolescent (YA) and are not 'coming out' stories, but mysteries or adventures that have LGBTQIA+ characters (Ellis, 2021). Overall, about 71.26% of the books to be reviewed are listed as YA, and 17.55% are listed as children and middle grades. Furthermore, about 8.01% address issues related to race and racism, and about 13.55% are related to sex education. This new normal in Texas, where SB 3 and lawmakers put pressure on district leaders to remove books, has led many educators to believe surveillance over what they are teaching is growing (Lee, 2021).

Over one hundred years after the publication of Rutherford's book, we are witnessing how the weaponization of language by far-right political groups relies on "a constellation of tactics that include: censorship, propaganda, disinformation, and mundane discourse" (Pascale, 2019, p. 901). We utilize critical discourse analysis (Fairclough, 1995) as a lens to examine how supporters of banned books use four interlocking components of weaponized language to remove books from school libraries and curricula to serve their own personal, social, and political agendas in Texas and beyond. The data were collected from a myriad of resources such as television, radio, newspaper interviews, articles, author blogs, and editorials. In addition, we highlight the ways student leaders, schools, and communities have opposed both national and local efforts to ban books.

4 Interlocking components of weaponized language: A critical discussion

Pascale (2019) provided a framework of four interlocking components of weaponized language, *censorship, propaganda, disinformation and fake news,* and *mundane discourse*. In this section, we use Pascale's framework to discuss the harm banning books causes to students, school curricula, and communities in general.

4.1 Censorship

> *Access to information is a human right, not to be tampered with or controlled in any way.*
> (DiMarco, 2017, p. 14)

Every year since 1982, Banned Books Week, an annual event dedicated to celebrating the freedom to read, is held during the last week of September in the United States. In 2021, the Banned Books Week theme said it all, "Books Unite Us. Censorship Divides Us." Books help build connections between readers, yet censorship creates barriers (American Library Association, 2021). Books set readers free, yet censorship locks away this freedom. In other words, readers have the right to choose what they want to read, but they do not have the right to censor what other readers want to read. In particular, Murtazashvili and Zhou (2021) argued the limitations and restrictions of censorship. Murtazashvili and Zhou (2021) wrote:

> Censorship can take different forms, but the essence of it is to limit and restrict the information the individuals being ruled can receive and communicate about. Since ancient times, ruling elites have engaged in the practice of banning books. History has also witnessed innumerable criminalization of speech and an endless list of people with heterodox ideologies and beliefs burned or shot as heretics. In the digital age, internet censorship is widespread around the globe. Now that the flow of information is controlled via censorship, ruling elites can feed the masses with filtered or modified information via propaganda. (p. 13)

Furthermore, censorship is about power and control (Knox, 2017). Knox (2017) described active censorship as "four *R*s: redaction, restriction, relocation, and removal" (p. 269). Redaction is when a text or an image is crossed or marked out. Restriction is when a limit is placed on who can use or consume an item (e.g., R-rated movies). Relocation is moving an item (e.g., a book) that is accessible to a not so easily accessible place. Removal is when the book is completely taken out from the library and/or school (Knox, 2017).

National Public Radio (NPR) often covers the impact banned books have on students, authors, and the community. In their November 2021 news coverage with authors of banned books such as Miranda Suarez, Maia Kobabe, and Jacqueline Woodson, Laurie Halse Anderson declared that,

> These books [challenged or banned books] are being used as bricks for a lot of people who don't care what the kids are reading but, see the opportunity to score political points or to get a mob going. The book is the first brick that is being thrown at children because any child who identifies with what's going on in these books, or who has a friend who can see themselves in the stories of these books, they are being targeted for violence. By banning the book, you send a message to kids, "it's okay to reject this kind of person, it's okay, we don't have to pay attention to the victims of sexual violence, or for people who aren't white, or for people who aren't straight or cis [cisgender]". That opens a door to every kind of violence, beginning with bullying and ending with death (NPR, 2021).

Voices and representation of students matter. Yet, due to the ignorance, hate, and fear that exists, it is being silenced or ripped apart. Librarians and educators have often come upon walls, "walls that stand against justice, equality, and kindness" (Pekoll, 2019, p. 10), and walls that are built to utilize weapons of hate and fear (Pekoll, 2019). Pekoll contended that some librarians believe they, "can't overcome the rift between the values of free speech on the one hand, and of furthering social justice on the other; that we can't conquer the walls" yet "can support both principles" (p. 10). Pekoll (2019) further argued that the core "of our professional values embraces equitable access to information for all, including many underserved populations. To provide truly equitable access, we need to also provide an equitable representation of all points of view in all types of content" (p. 11).

Censors from both political spectrums, left and right, are eager for power to control what students view, read, and learn (Scales, 2001). Censors fear the educational system and want to control young minds because "students who read learn to think. Thinkers learn to see. Those who see often question. And, young people who question threaten the "blind" and the "nonthinkers" (Scales, 2001, p. 2). Knox (2020) complements the similar idea that individuals who want to remove books from school curricula and library collections strongly believe in the power of books. They know books change people's minds. Scales (2001) argued, "When adults try to shield students from the "darker side of life" or from ideas that may be controversial, such adults are creating a generation of skeptics and cynics who don't really know the meaning of free speech" (p. xi).

Knox (2020) called people who attempted to censor books challengers. In her research, she investigated the motivations behind why challengers may want certain books to be redacted, restricted, relocated, and removed. Some of the reasons listed are related to their unsuitability for the age group, such as the existence of sexual content and the presence of LGBTQIA+ characters (Knox, 2020). Certain racially diverse books have also been targeted, challenged, or banned due to unsuitability for the age group. Thomas (2020) also agreed that "Sexuality and obscenity, crude language, violence, and religious/political references are the primary reasons for most challenges" (p. 16). Thomas (2020) discussed the motivation behind these actions and concluded that censorship takes place all over the United States; it is not exclusive to southern states and is predominantly based on the protection of identity (p. 16). In her research, Knox (2017) also noted the discourse of censorship centers around three components: power, identity, and the nature of knowledge. Knox (2020) further argued, "Books that do not fulfill their role as a vessel for acceptable ideas are dubbed *trash* or *filth*" (p. 30).

Dr. Tasslyn Magnusson, an independent researcher, has partnered up with EveryLibrary Institute and created a spreadsheet of challenged and banned books in school and public libraries in various states, including Texas, around the United States, starting in the 2021–2022 school year. The spreadsheet data also provides an extensive list of 'status notes' (e.g., banned, challenged filed, restricted permanently, etc.) regarding the books (EveryLibrary Institute, n.d.).

4.2 Propaganda

Propaganda can exert such a strong influence on a person that he loses his ability to see alternative points of view. We have all met zealots who simply will not hear any doctrine other than their own. (McCormick, 1977, p. 35)

Propaganda can take various forms in order to promote and sustain the ruling structures' ideologies. It could be disseminated through school textbooks and curricula (Murtazashvili & Zhou, 2021). The media (e.g., billboards, TV news, and social media) in general has also been widely utilized for propaganda (Bian, 2022; Murtazashvili & Zhou, 2021. In October 2021, Virginia Republican gubernatorial candidate Glenn Youngkin's campaign, and the current governor of Virginia) featured a Fairfax County, Virginia parent on a video where she noted her disbelief regarding the book *Beloved* by Toni Morrison. Morrison's winner of the 1988 Pulitzer Prize for fiction is a novel about slavery and includes depictions of violence, rape, and murder in the aftermath of the Civil War. In the video ad aired, the parent stated, "As a parent, it's tough to catch everything" and further continued,

> So when my son showed me his reading assignment, my heart sunk. It was some of the most explicit material you can imagine. I met with lawmakers. They couldn't believe what I was showing them. Their faces turned bright red with embarrassment. They passed bills requiring schools to notify parents when explicit content was assigned. It was bipartisan. It gave parents a say.

The incident actually happened in 2011 when her son, who was a high school senior at the time, was assigned the reading *Beloved* as part of the Advanced Placement (AP) English curriculum. The mother claimed the book gave her son nightmares (Villarreal, 2021). In August 2022, Keller ISD in Texas also removed Toni Morrison's *The Bluest Eye* along with other book titles.

Pascale (2019) argued that "weaponized language exploits cultural vulnerabilities" (p. 900) and is "used to attack people perceived to be disloyal, to dehumanize minority groups in the service of a mythological homogeneous national state, to discredit known facts, and to strategically manipulate public emotional responses" (p. 900). In May 1933, Nazis burned books by Jewish intellectuals that contained "Un–German spirit" (Engel, 2022, p. 96). In February 2022, a school board in eastern Tennessee voted 10–0 to ban *Maus* by Art Spiegelman from its 8th grade English language Arts (ELA) curriculum due to its concerns over "rough" language (profanity) and (mouse) nudity (Alperstein, 2022; USA Today Staff, 2022). However, Spiegelman's graphic novel is about his parents' experiences in Nazi concentration camps during the Holocaust. Engel (2022) wrote, "Antisemitism is insidious" (p. 96) and further argued, "As literature about the Holocaust continues to be challenged, people lose access to the voices of the oppressed, allowing misrepresentations to seep into popular culture" (p. 96). Banning books like *Maus* minimizes the violence of the Holocaust and validates Holocaust-denial rhetoric (Engel, 2022).

Books such as *Maus* and other commonly banned titles are powerful and crucial to understand the wrongdoings in history . . . (Alperstein, 2022), as the Holocaust did not "start with gas chambers and crematoriums. It started with book-burning, segregation, persecution, and hateful rhetoric from powerful politicians whom some dismissed as harmful buffoons-until it was too late" (Alperstein, 2022, p. 2). Alperstein (2022) reminds the rhetoric during January 6, 2021 insurrection and how some anti-Semitic groups and white supremacists, in a way, wanted to repeat the Holocaust with t-shirts they wore like 'Camp Auschwitz.' It is evident in the examples shared that banning books and banning the discussion of Critical Race Theory in the K-12 educational settings are well-organized propaganda used for political gain.

4.3 Disinformation and fake news

Post-2017, United States presidential elections brought the discussion on fake news that led librarians and other information professionals to take leadership in the wake of the elections (Sullivan, 2019). After the election, it became evident that "access to information in the public sphere would be threatened and that it was important that those on the front lines know how to respond to such threats" (Knox, 2017, p. 268). In late January 2017, American Library Association (ALA) published a *Resolution on Access to Accurate Information,* an extension to the 2005 *Resolution on Disinformation, Media Manipulation and the Destruction of Public Information* to recognize "the contribution of librarianship in informing and educating the general public on critical problems facing society" (Policy, A.1.1). On behalf of its members, ALA (2017) resolved:

1) reaffirms the resolution on Disinformation, Media Manipulation and the Destruction of Public Information approved in 2005 (2005 ALA CD #64).
2) opposes the use of disinformation, media manipulation, and other tactics that undermine access to accurate information;
3) encourages its members to help raise public consciousness regarding the many ways in which disinformation and media manipulation are used to mislead the public;
4) urges librarians and library workers to actively seek and provide sources of accurate information that counter disinformation;
5) supports the critical role of librarians and library workers in all types of libraries in teaching information literacy skills that enable users to locate information and evaluate its accuracy;

6) will pursue partnerships with news organizations, journalism institutions, and other allies to promote access to accurate information and defend the role of journalists and the free press in American society.

The 2005 resolution referred to the "fabrication and deliberate distortion of information used to justify the US invasion of Iraq," and the 2017 version referred to "propaganda campaigns and cyberwarfare operations conducted by governments and non-state actors to influence or disrupt the domestic affairs of adversaries" (Sullivan, 2019, p. 1147). It is important to note that in the 2017 resolution, the notion of fake news has been placed in the larger context of misinformation (Sullivan, 2019).

The weaponized language used to describe the challenged titles by book challengers is central to spreading disinformation. During a school board meeting, one challenger from Iowa regarding the book *Lawn Boy* by Jonathan Evison stated, "Can you tell me: Do equity and inclusion also include incestuous relationships, child-adult sex, and books that promote pedophilia?" (Ockerman, 2021). *Lawn Boy* is a novel Evison partially based on his life experiences and shares the experiences of a Mexican-American boy growing up. It also discusses issues related to race, sex, and sexual orientation. In Leander Independent School District in Texas, a parent at the September 9, 2021 school board meeting also described the content of *Lawn Boy* as depraved and likened some passages to pedophilia (Sanyal, 2021). Comparable disturbing words are often used to demonize other challenged books and their authors to only result in spreading disinformation about the actual content of the book. Evison, the author of *Lawn Boy*, responded in an interview with *Book & Film Globe*, a cultural-review website, that this, "experience has shown him how quickly perception of a book can spread, regardless of accuracy" (Vane, 2021). Similarly, Sherman Alexie's *The Absolutely True Diary of Part-Time Indian*, which deals with racism, poverty, and disability, has been banned for its language and anti–Christian content (Ringel, 2016). *The Hate U Give* (2017) by Angie Thomas has also received various pushback from parents and community members. The book examines the stereotyping that exists for black people to justify violence and racism against them. One supporter for banning books responded to the challenges to ban *The Hate U Give*:

> This is what they are "suggesting "your child read!! Are you going to allow them to teach your kids to hate our police, is this what you really support??! I need all of you any of you to get up make those calls, write those emails demand these books be pulled, you are paying for these books your child is being abused by an organization that wants to control your children!!!! It also entices violence and murder citizens and our police" . . . (Jensen, 2021)

In 2018, after a parent's public complaint at a school board meeting, the superintendent of Katy, Texas Independent School District (ISD) removed *The Hate U Give* from all school libraries in the district. Even after Katy ISD students petitioned and gathered 3,700 signatures for the reinstatement of the book, the decision remained firm for a while. Yet, after a few months, it became available again in high school libraries with parental consent only. Some of the reasons *The Hate U Give* is challenged "include it being "'pervasively vulgar' and because of drug use, profanity, and offensive language" (Jensen, 2021, para. 7).

Sullivan (2019) stated that "Hundreds of studies have shown the ways in which people can be made to recall nonexistent objects, be misled to "remember" events, and have false memories planted" (p. 1150) and further argued, "the real problem of misinformation is not the simple fact that it is "out there," the real concern is this literature is not the fact that people can be misled or made to misremember, but the degree to which false information "sticks' in the face of corrections" (p. 1150). The descriptions shared about the books above and other information shared with challenged books exemplify Sullivan's (2019) point as their descriptions, as portrayed by proponents of book banning, are not the true representations of what these books are actually about.

4.4 Mundane discourse

According to Pascale (2019), mundane discourse is " . . . the linguistic delivery device through which weaponized language enters the mainstream" (pp. 908–909). In mundane discourse, media and social networks are "enlisted to routinize and disseminate disinformation even where outlandish claims and conspiracy theories are repeated, even when they are not plausible" (Pascale, 2019, p. 908). Pascale described how "hate is being mainstreamed through euphemisms and rebranding" (p. 910). For example, white supremacists refer to themselves as alt-right as if they are a legitimate political party with a platform beyond white supremacy (Pascale, 2019). Another example is the creation of the Black Lives Matter movement in response to police violence and armed citizens against Black people. In response, white supremacists sought "to subvert the movement slogan 'Black Lives Matter' by shouting back 'all lives matter[ed]'" (Pascale, 2019, p. 910). Pascale declared rebranding enabled "a range of conspiracy theorists, techno-libertarians, white nationalists, Men's Rights advocates, trolls, anti-feminists, anti-immigration activists, and bored young people to join an organization that has an unchanged core of white nationalism" (p. 910). Finally, Pascale concluded "language is weaponized whenever the politics of hate find expression in the mundane discourse of everyday life. It is most dangerously weaponized when ordinary people can think of no other ways – beyond these framings – to talk about social phenomena" (p. 910).

Godfrey (2020) explained that in mundane discourses, weaponized language normalized hate and hate groups through purportedly organized language. Here in the United States, mundane discourse is not only found in the Black lives matter/all lives matter divide, but it is also found in Trump's branding of the COVID-19 pandemic as the "China" or "Wuhan virus" (DeCosta, Her & Lee, 2022, p. 98). The Far Right in the US is adopting this type of mundane discourse to use to ban books from K-12 school libraries and curricula. It is evident censorship, propaganda, disinformation, and fake news, and mundane discourse are interlocking forms of weaponized language that are powerful forms of symbolic violence (Godfrey, 2020). They have been around since the inception of the American children's literature industry in the 1820s and are still used today to thwart kids from learning how "to navigate imaginary worlds filled with differences" (Ringel, 2016, para. 12).

5 Past and present advocacy groups: Implications for students, librarians, teachers, education preparation programs, and community to continue the fight

In 1931, Ranganathan published his *Five Laws of Library Science* to define a library's function and purpose. Undergirding the five laws was the belief that every book has its reader, and every reader has a book they need. In his timeless rules for librarians, Ranganathan understood that every book did not meet the needs of every young reader, but banning books deprived the reader of the "unsanitized version of history, that diverse books expose[d] them to a variety of experiences and perspectives, that controversial literature help[ed] them to think critically about the world" (The Learning Network, 2022, para. 1). In a recent conversation about current events, The Learning Network (2022) invited students to react to banned books from school libraries. An overwhelming majority of students opposed book banning in any form for reasons detailed below:
1. It is wrong to shield kids from reality;
2. books are meant to challenge and educate;
3. limiting books students can read also limits perspectives students need to access;

4. book bans are not effective. There are better ways to handle sensitive subjects, and
5. parents and lawmakers deciding what students should read is a slippery slope.

In 1975, a New York school board received a complaint from a community group. Parents of New York United submitted a complaint to a New York school board about Kurt Vonnegut's *Slaughterhouse-Five* and Langston Hughes's *Best Short Stories by Negro Writers*. The group argued that the books were "anti-American, anti-Christian, anti-Semitic and just plain filthy" (Bill of Rights Institute, 2022, para. 1). In response, the school district removed the books in February of 1976.

High school senior, Steven Pico, joined with four other students to challenge the school board's decision to remove the books. According to the Bill of Rights Institute (2022), Pico argued that the books were removed because "passages in the books offended [the group's] social, political, and moral tastes and not because the books, taken as a whole, were lacking in educational value" (para. 2). Several libraries and free speech organizations filed briefs on the students' behalf. As a result, the case went to the Supreme Court, and the Supreme Court ruled in the students' favor on First Amendment grounds, declaring that the right to read is implied by the First Amendment.

As book challenges and/or removals take place, students experience the biggest impact during this process. Just as the high school senior, Steven Pico, and other students did to challenge the school board's decision to remove the books in 1976, today's student advocates continue to fight for their rights to access these books in Texas and in other places in the United States.

On April 7, 2022, the United States House Committee on Oversight and Reform held a subcommittee hearing on classroom censorship and book bans. Many student activists, educators, and community members got together for this congressional hearing. The personal stories shared by these students were very powerful; however, the removal of books only reaffirmed that their stories do not matter. The students' effort to make their voices heard is a fight for social justice that all adults could learn from. For example, the high school senior Olivia Pituch from Pennsylvania, who identifies as an LGBTQIA+ member, in her address read:

> It is important to teach inclusion and equality. It is important to have representation. I deserve to walk into my school library and find a book about someone like me . . . This is why education on inclusion is important and necessary. Without it, those kids who come to school for safety and acceptance will no longer have that safe spot (Free speech under attack, 2022).

Christina Ellis, a high school student from Pennsylvania, also discussed her story as an African-American. During the hearing, she shared, "The reason I stood against my school district's book ban was because I didn't want future African American kids to go through some of the things I went through growing up because of lack of cultural sensitivity in my schooling experience" (Free speech under attack, 2022).

Olivia and Christina are just two student examples shared. Yet, they represent many other Olivia's and Christina's and other students from minoritized and marginalized populations. There are so also many other student activists like Olivia and Christina who continually fight for their right to book access. However, they also need to be reminded that they are not alone in this struggle and that there are advocacy groups that support them in this fight. One of the advocacy groups is the National Coalition Against Censorship (NCAC), which serves students, teachers, librarians, and parents who oppose censorship in schools and libraries (NCAC, n. d.). Specifically in Texas, Children's Defense Fund of Texas (see https://cdftexas.org/youthtx/) is one of the advocacy groups that work with young Texans to advocate against book bans and support youth-led advocacy through the state of Texas.

Advocates against book bans take action and often rally to get their voices heard. In December 2021, the National Coalition Against Censorship condemned the recent attack on books in a statement signed by hundreds of authors and national groups. At the local level in 2021, Round Rock Black Parents Association in Texas successfully fought the proposed ban of *Stamped: Racism, Antiracism, and You* by Jason Reynolds and Ibrahim X. Kendi. The association partnered with organizations such as Anti-racists Coming Together (ACT) and worked with local librarians (Morris, 2022). Again, at the local level in Katy and Leander ISD in Texas, students are distributing the challenged books among their peers and/or coming together in banned book clubs to discuss these books (Park, 2022). In February 2022, a Bastrop, Texas, independent bookstore hosted a banned book giveaway through Banned Bookmobile (Aguilera, 2022). In March 2022, 'March for Education' took place outside the Texas State Capitol in Austin, Texas, where advocates gathered for a call to remove censorship. Various student groups from Texas were present at this rally.

Teacher educators also need to be advocates. We, for example, in the fall of 2020, in the midst of COVID-19, invited the author Angie Thomas to Zoom with the teacher candidates in our college to discuss the critical issues portrayed in her book *The Hate U Give*. In another Zoom session, Thomas also talked with the grades 5 through high school students at the Boys & Girls Club in the Huntsville community where our university is located. Meaningful and valuable dialogue took place in both sessions. Lastly, both teacher candidates and the students at the Boys & Girls Club received a copy of the book. However, it should be noted that none of this would have been possible without the support of the College of Education's leadership team.

We firmly believe that it is very important for teacher educators to find means to host banned book authors in their classrooms and communities to show their support for the authors and the issues and topics they discuss in their books. If teacher educators do not have the means (e.g., financial, administrative support, and contact with banned books), they can incorporate the challenged and banned books into their course curriculum and read and discuss the importance of such books with pre- and in-service teachers.

K-12 teachers and school librarians must also be advocates for banned books. They need to advocate for students' rights to read these books in classrooms and school libraries. Access to diverse literature is important for promoting literacy while giving a voice to diverse students. They must also familiarize themselves with school policies for challenged or banned books and provide resources for students and parents if they appeal these decisions. Everyday advocacy groups, locally and nationally, from all ages continue to fight as book banning has become politicized more than ever. It is through collective efforts that society will see positive change.

6 Conclusion

After being disinvited from a planned school talk, Kate Messner, New York Times bestselling author, wrote on her blog, "When we say 'This book is inappropriate,' we're telling those children 'your situation . . . your family . . . your *life* is inappropriate" (as cited in Ringel, 2016). Book banning is detrimental for students who (figuratively) find themselves in books that are removed from school library shelves and classrooms. Godfrey (2020) described weaponized language as "a powerful form of symbolic violence that tills the soil for physical violence." Book banning is symbolic violence and, unfortunately, does not seem like it will end any time soon. As such, It is imperative that librarians, parents, community leaders, and students work together now more than ever to stop this war on truth and diverse perspectives. We must not stand by idly and allow the use of weaponized language to curate a reading list of books devoid of diverse perspectives. In the words of Freire (1985), "Washing one's hands of the conflict between the powerful and the powerless means to side with the powerful, not to be neutral" (p. 122). If we wash our hands of this conflict, then we are participating in this insidious tradition of marginalizing the lives and experiences of young readers, all in the name of protecting them.

References

Alperstein, Olivia. 2022. Banned books should be required reading. *Labor Tribune*. https://labortribune.com/opinion-banned-books-should-be-required-reading/

American Library Association. n.d. *Formal reconsideration*. https://www.ala.org/tools/challengesupport/selectionpolicytoolkit/formalreconsideration#:~:text=A%20formal%20reconsideration%20request%20is,part%20of%20the%20reconsideration%20policy

American Library Association. 2017. *Resolution on access to accurate information*. https://www.ala.org/advocacy/intfreedom/statementspols/ifresolutions/accurateinformation

American Library Association. 2021. *Banned books week to united communities*. https://www.ala.org/news/press-releases/2021/09/banned-books-week-unite-communities

Backus, Fred & Anthony Salvanto. 2022. Big majorities reject book bans. *CBS News*. https://www.cbsnews.com/news/book-bans-opinion-poll-2022-02-22/

Aguilera, Maria 2022. 'Words matter and I think they're important' | Bastrop independent bookshop hosts banned book giveaway. *KVUE*. https://www.youtube.com/watch?v=-Rw2jeeMU-c

Bian, Xu. 2022. The weaponization of Mandarin Chinese. *International Journal of Literacy, Culture, and Language Education* 2, 108–119.

Bill of Rights Institute. 2022. Island Trees School District v. Pico. https://billofrightsinstitute.org/e-lessons/island-trees-school-district-v-pico-1982

Bobbitt, Randy. 2019. *Controversial books in K–12 classrooms and libraries: Challenged, censored, and banned*. Lanham, MD: Rowman & Littlefield.

Dawkins, April. 2018. Introducing the new selection & reconsideration policy toolkit. The Office for Intellectual Freedom of the American Library Association. https://www.oif.ala.org/oif/introducing-new-selection-reconsideration-policy-toolkit/

DeCosta, Peter I., Lee Her & Vashti Lee. 2022. Weaponizing and de-weaponizing antiracist discourse: Some things for language educators to consider. *International Journal of Literacy, Culture, and Language Education* 2, 98–107.

Dellinger, Hannah, Alejandro Serrano & Staff Writers. 2022. Most efforts to ban books in Texas schools came from 1 politician and GOP pressure, not parents. *Houston Chronicle*. https://www.houstonchronicle.com/news/investigations/article/Texas-book-bans-driven-by-GOP-pressure-not-parents-17362170.php

DeWitt, Peter. 2022. Banning books is not about protecting children. It's about discrimination against others. *EducationWeek*. https://www.edweek.org/policy-politics/opinion-banning-books-is-not-about-protecting-children-its-about-discrimination-against-others/2022/02

DiMarco, Scott. 2017. Even librarians ban books. In Marcia Amidon Lusted (ed.), *Banned books*, 14–17. New York, NY: New Greenhaven Publishing, LLC.

Eberle, Holly. 2022. Support #FReadom and support each other. The Office for Intellectual Freedom of the American Library Association. https://www.oif.ala.org/oif/support-freadom-and-support-each-other/

Engel, Angela. 2022. Correcting the distortion of history. *Publisher Weekly* 269(11), 96.

Ellis, Danika. 2021. All 850 books Texas lawmaker Matt Krause wants to ban: An analysis. *Book Riot*. https://bookriot.com/texas-book-ban-list/

Friedman, Jonathan & Nadine Farid Johnson. 2022. Banned in the USA: The growing movement to censor books in schools. *PEN America*. https://pen.org/report/banned-usa-growing-movement-to-censor-books-in-schools/

EveryLibrary Institute. (n.d.). *Book censorship database by Dr. Tasslyn Magnusson*. https://www.everylibraryinstitute.org/book_censorship_database_magnusson

Fairclough, Norman. 1995. *Critical discourse analysis*. London: Longman.

Free speech under attack. 2022. Book bans and academic censorship. Hearing before the House Committee on Oversight and Reform, 117th Cong. https://oversight.house.gov/legislation/hearings/free-speech-under-attack-book-bans-and-academic-censorship

Freire, Paulo. 1985. *The politics of education: Culture, power and liberation*. New Zealand: Bergin and Garvey Publishers.

Godfrey, Neil. 2020. Weaponization of language: Our virus infected speech. *Vridar*. https://vridar.org/tag/pascale-weaponization-of-language/

Hiorns, Celia. 2021. Glenn Youngkin's support for censorship of literature should concern you. *The Badger HERALD*. https://badgerherald.com/opinion/2021/11/05/glenn-youngkins-support-for-censorship-of-literature-should-concern-you/

Intercultural Development Research Association. 2022. *Learn about Texas classroom censorship laws*. https://www.idra.org/education_policy/hb-3979-would-limit-speech-and-engagement-in-texas-classrooms/

Jensen, Kelly. 2021. Anti-critical race theory parents fight the *Hate U Give*. *Book Riot*. https://bookriot.com/the-hate-u-give-challenge/

Knox, Emily J. M. 2017. Opposing censorship in difficult times. *Library Quarterly: Information, Community, Policy* 87(3), 268–276. https://doi.org/10.1086/692304

Knox, Emily J. M. 2020. Books, censorship, and anti-intellectualism in schools. *Phi Delta Kappan* 101(7), 28–32. https://doi.org/10.1177/0031721720917526

Lee, J. 2021. Texas Education Agency as law changing how race is discussed in schools goes into effect. *KVUE*. https://www.kvue.com/article/news/education/texas-education-agency-senate-bill-3-2021/269-13a8c060-7490-4c77-9f3d-83c0d3ccadf5

Lopez, Brian. 2022. Texas Education Agency's new school library standards push for more scrutiny and parental input. *The Texas Tribune*. https://www.texastribune.org/2022/04/11/texas-school-library-standards/

Lopez, Brian. 2021. Texas House committee to investigate school districts' books on race and sexuality. *The Texas Tribune*. https://www.texastribune.org/2021/10/26/texas-school-books-race-sexuality/

Lusted, Marcia Amidon (ed.). 2017. *Banned books*. New York, NY: New Greenhaven Publishing, LLC.

McCormick, Kevin. 1977. Censorship: some philosophical issues. *Index on Censorship* 6(2), 31–37. https://doi.org/10.1080/03064227708532625

Morris, Williesha. 2022. *BIPOC activists consider how to end book bans for good*. Prism. https://prismreports.org/2022/03/08/bipoc-activists-fight-book-bans/

Murtazashvili, Ilia & Yang Zhou. 2021. Ideology, censorship, and propaganda: Unifying shared mental models. *SSRN*. http://dx.doi.org/10.2139/ssrn.3821161

National Public Radio. 2021. *When schools ban books*. https://www.npr.org/2021/11/11/1054798508/when-schools-ban-books

News Staff, Business & Heritage Clarksville. 2017. Banning and challenging are two different things. In Marcia Amidon Lusted (ed.), *Banned books*, 11–13. New York, NY: New Greenhaven Publishing, LLC.

Ockerman, Emma. 2021. *Here are the books parents want to ban in schools now*. https://www.vice.com/en/article/jgm8nk/parents-banning-books-in-schools

Pascale, Celine-Marie. 2019. The weaponization of language: Discourses of rising right-wing authoritarianism. *Current Sociology Review* 67(6), 898–917. https://doi.org/10.1177/0011392119869963

Park, Brooke. 2022. Texas students push back against book bans for censoring LGBTQ, racial justice issues. *The Texas Tribune*. https://www.texastribune.org/2022/03/07/texas-students-banned-books-protest-clubs/

Pekoll, Kristin. 2019. *Beyond banned books: Defending intellectual freedom throughout your library*. Chicago, IL: ALA Editions.

Pentón Herrera, Luis Javier & Kisha C. Bryan. 2022. Language weaponization in society and education: Introduction to the special issue. *International Journal of Literacy, Culture, and Language Education* 2, 1–5. https://doi.org/10.14434/ijlcle.v2iMay.34380

Ranganathan, Shiyali Ramamrita. 1931. *Five laws of library science*. India: The Madras Library Association.

Ringel, Paul. 2016. How banning books marginalizes children. *The Atlantic*. https://www.theatlantic.com/entertainment/archive/2016/10/how-banned-books-marginalize-children/502424/

Robinson, Ishena. 2022. The war on truth: Anti-CRT mania and book bans are the latest tactics to halt racial justice. *NAACP Lega Defense and Educational Fund, Inc*. https://www.naacpldf.org/critical-race-theory-banned-books/

Rutherford, Mildred Lewis. 1920. *A measuring rod to test textbooks and reference books in schools, colleges, and libraries*. New Orleans, LA: United Confederate Veterans.

Sanyal, Pathikrit. 2021. 'Lawn Boy': Texas mom says son found book about 4th graders' sex in school library. *Meaww*. https://meaww.com/lawn-boy-texas-mom-says-son-found-book-about-4th-graders-sex-in-school-library-pedophile

Scales, Pat R. 2001. *Teaching banned books: 12 guides for young readers*. Chicago, IL: ALA Editions.

Sullivan, M. Connor. 2019. Why librarians can't fight fake news. *Journal of Librarianship and Information Science* 51(4), 1146–1156. https://doi.org/10.1177/0961000618764258

Texas Legislative Education Equity Coalition. 2021. Texas' newest classroom censorship bill: SB 3. https://www.idra.org/wp-content/uploads/2021/09/Texas-Newest-Classroom-Censorship-Bill-SB-3.pdf

Texas Library Association. 2021. Reconsideration policies in Texas public school libraries. https://txla.org/wp-content/uploads/2021/12/Reconsideration-Policies-infographic-external-122021.pdf

The Learning Network. 2022. What students are saying about banning books from school libraries. *The New York Times*. https://www.nytimes.com/2022/02/18/learning/students-book-bans.html

Thomas, Daniel. 2020. Book censorship and its effects on schools. *The Torch Magazine* 94(1), 16–20. http://www.ncsociology.org/torchmagazine/v941/thomas.html

USA Today Staff. 2022. They're trying to ban 'Maus': Why you should read it and these 30 other challenged books. *USA Today*. https://www.usatoday.com/story/entertainment/books/2021/09/27/banned-books-week-the-bluest-eye-harry-potter-1984-handmaids-tale-goosebumps-golden-compass/5758877001/

Vane, Sharyn. 2021. Evison, Pérez speak out against censorship. *Book & Film Globe*. https://bookandfilmglobe.com/fiction/evison-perez-speak-out-against-censorship/

Villarreal, Daniel. 2021. 'Son' frightened by Black novel in Glenn Youngkin ad is actually a 27-year-old GOP lawyer. *Newsweek*. https://www.newsweek.com/son-frightened-black-novel-glenn-youngkin-ad-actually-27-year-old-gop-lawyer-1642883

Woodard, T. 2022. Keller ISD adopts new 'library content guidelines' for books. *WFAA News 8*. https://www.wfaa.com/article/news/education/schools/keller-isd-adopts-new-library-books-content-guidelines/287-e3462c7f-dea4-4ff0-ae9d-28e4a2dd75b7

Sandra Descourtis
Chapter 10
French variations and language weaponization in US higher education

Abstract: Despite their widespread presence in French language, language variations and especially slang, are seldom included in the curriculum of U.S. university-level French programs. Instruction is typically oriented towards "standardized" French, creating a gap between formal education and everyday communication (Petitpas, 2010). Variations are often vilified, leading to stigmatization (Silverstein, 1996). Informed by the symbolic power of language (Bourdieu, 1982) this chapter explores the perceptions of undergraduates about learning French slang in U.S. universities. Online surveys and interviews reveal that students' perceptions about French slang are influenced by their primary language and by French language clichés. These clichés, perpetuated by society, institutions, and media, have served as weapons to stigmatize French slang users. Though most participants stated that they would like to learn French slang, they nurture reservations about it. This weaponization of the curriculum (Bryan & Gerald, 2020) has precluded students from learning an important part of the French language and culture and harms the overall view that students have about slang users, reinforcing the stigmatization of those who speak differently.

Keywords: French as a foreign language, language variations, stigmatization, *argot* and *verlan*, standard vs. non-standard language

1 French variation and language weaponization in US higher education

Linguistic variations, the ways that a particular language is used in regional, social, or contextual differences (Nordquist, 2020), are found in most languages and are commonly used and combined by individuals, sometimes without even noticing it. In France, the range of linguistic variations makes French a rich and diverse language. However, some of these variations are viewed negatively, leading to stigmatization toward their users (Bourdieu, 1982; Devereaux & Palmer, 2019;

Sandra Descourtis, Emory University

Lippi-Green, 2012; Metz, 2019; Silverstein, 1996). This statement is especially true for French slang. Even though it is used by most French speakers, it is seen as an informal language mostly used by youth and uneducated people. When, where, and who uses Standard French, as opposed to non-standard French, is an ongoing debate among the French-speaking population and within institutions such as schools and the *Académie Française*.[1] Further, this debate transcends the confines of France, affecting language use and instruction in places where French is taught as an additional language. Indeed, French language programs around the world are often hesitant to include French variations in their curriculum.

Teachers of French as a foreign language have had to consider the pros and cons of teaching linguistic variations in the foreign language (FL) classroom (Fein, 2011). Teaching and learning a foreign language are often viewed as the transmission of linguistic features in order to be able to interact with and understand speakers of the target language. However, the lack of representation of linguistic diversity and variation in the French as a foreign language classroom and curriculum can be problematic for learners once they try to communicate with users across the French-speaking world (Detey, 2017). Hence, many scholars agree that students should be exposed to authentic language, even within the context of the classroom (Auger & Valdman, 1999; Burke, 1998; Detey, 2017; Favart, 2010; Petitpas, 2010; Tomlinson, 2012). Auger and Valdman (1999) argue that "precisely because 'any unfamiliar language sounds strange,' we [French educators] should make sure that students are exposed early to different varieties of French" (p. 408). However, it seems that French variations and slang, especially *argot* and *verlan*, are not yet included in most curricula of higher education in the US.

Argot originated from the *argotiers* corporation, which created this variety of language in order to not be understood by people outside their organization. They were the 'bad' guys, the thugs of the 17th century in Paris (Valdman, 2000). Even though *argot* has now permeated the daily speech of French users (Liogier, 2002; Szulmajster-Celnikier, 1996), this perception of the language from the underworld has somehow remained. Regarding *verlan*, which really emerged in the 1980s in the *banlieues*, it also has a cryptic, but playful function for youth, as a means to express their identity (François-Geiger, 1991). According to Hargreaves (1995), young people from immigrant origins use slang, and especially *verlan,* as a way to reappropriate the French language and a form of contestation as French is

---

[1] Principal French council for matters pertaining to the French language. The *Académie* was officially established in 1635 by Cardinal Richelieu, and comprises forty members, known as *les immortels*. The *Académie* is France's official authority on the usage, vocabulary, and grammar of the French language.

sometimes perceived by immigrants coming from former French colonies as the language of domination.

The lack of representation of French variations and slang in French language education has been used as a weapon to perpetuate the stigmatization of the language and its users, and to maintain the reign of standard French, connoted as the 'good white French.' This exclusion from education harms students as they are not given the opportunity to acquire an integral part of French culture and history that can develop their sociolinguistic competence and their identity as French language users.

In this chapter, I provide an overview of French language variations. I then examine data collected during a qualitative case study where I surveyed and interviewed learners of French at a large university in the US. In the final section of the chapter, I discuss language weaponization as well as the perceptions and attitudes of the participants toward French variations and the implications for teaching French and other foreign languages.

2 Linguistic variations

2.1 Types of variation

Most languages have variations. Language variations can be lexical (i.e., related to the words or vocabulary), phonologic (i.e., related to pronunciation and accent), semantic (i.e., related to the various meanings of words), morphologic (i.e., related to the form of the words) or syntactic (i.e., related to the structure of sentences) (Favart, 2010). Of course, linguistic variation can be seen through the lens of multiple dimensions, as variations have several layers. Moreover, linguistic variations have different dimensions: 1) the diatopic dimension is related to geographical linguistic areas (i.e., dialects spoken in specific regions); 2) the diachronic dimension is related to the temporality and the historical stages of a language; 3) the diastratic dimension is related to the socio-dialects different social groups (regarding individuals' gender, profession, age, etc.) use; and 4) the diaphasic dimension is related to the various levels of style or registers used (i.e., formal/informal, written/oral, etc.) (Detey, 2017). Nevertheless, in order to recognize the linguistic variations, we have to acknowledge the existence of a so-called norm, referred to as the standard language (Favart, 2010).

2.2 Standard and non-standard

As Silverstein (1996) argues, there is a culture of standardization, a desire to have a uniform language, and, thus, a uniform society. Standard French is known as the language that everyone must learn and speak, as opposed to popular and familiar French – *français familier* (familiar or colloquial French). And within the spectrum of familiar French, there are many variations. However, the idea of a 'standard' French remains a myth maintained and entrenched for a long time, from the end of 1789, its linguistic ideal was placed: 'one French for all' (Szulmajster-Celnikier, 1996). This idea of having 'one French for all' is utopic, increasing language ideologies and stigmatization toward speakers of the non-standard varieties.

Moreover, as Valdman (1982) points out, standard French is a norm, and like any norm, it is socially constructed, which makes standard French manufactured. Standard languages are created by institutions that then exercise their power over those who do not use them 'correctly'. This idea of the 'good French,' also referred to as the French of 'quality' by Ager (1999, p. 159), is often connected to a traditionalist idea of France and the French identity. These language ideologies "transfer the issue of language quality to that of the quality of society" (p. 159), giving an ideal picture of French society and of the language that French speakers use. Ager makes the connection between the written language and outdated formality, which conveys again this image of a rigid and static language that is different from the spoken language. But this standardization does not reflect the reality of the French language. There are too many variations in French to reduce the language to just 'standard French.' The reality of the language is very different as the French language is in constant evolution, and many linguistic variations coexist in France.

2.3 Variations in French

Giving an exhaustive depiction of all the linguistic variations in France would be impossible as The General Delegation for the French Language and the Languages of France, which is responsible for leading and coordinating the State's language policy, has listed 82 'languages of France.' However, a tentative overview of the linguistic and dialectal situation in Metropolitan France in the 20th century is provided by the French National Archives (see Figure 10.1).[2]

---

[2] Représentation de la situation linguistique et dialectale de la France métropolitaine au XXe siècle. Archives Nationales de France website: https://www.archives-nationales.culture.gouv.fr/web/guest/cartographie-historique.

Chapter 10 French variations and language weaponization in US higher education — 195

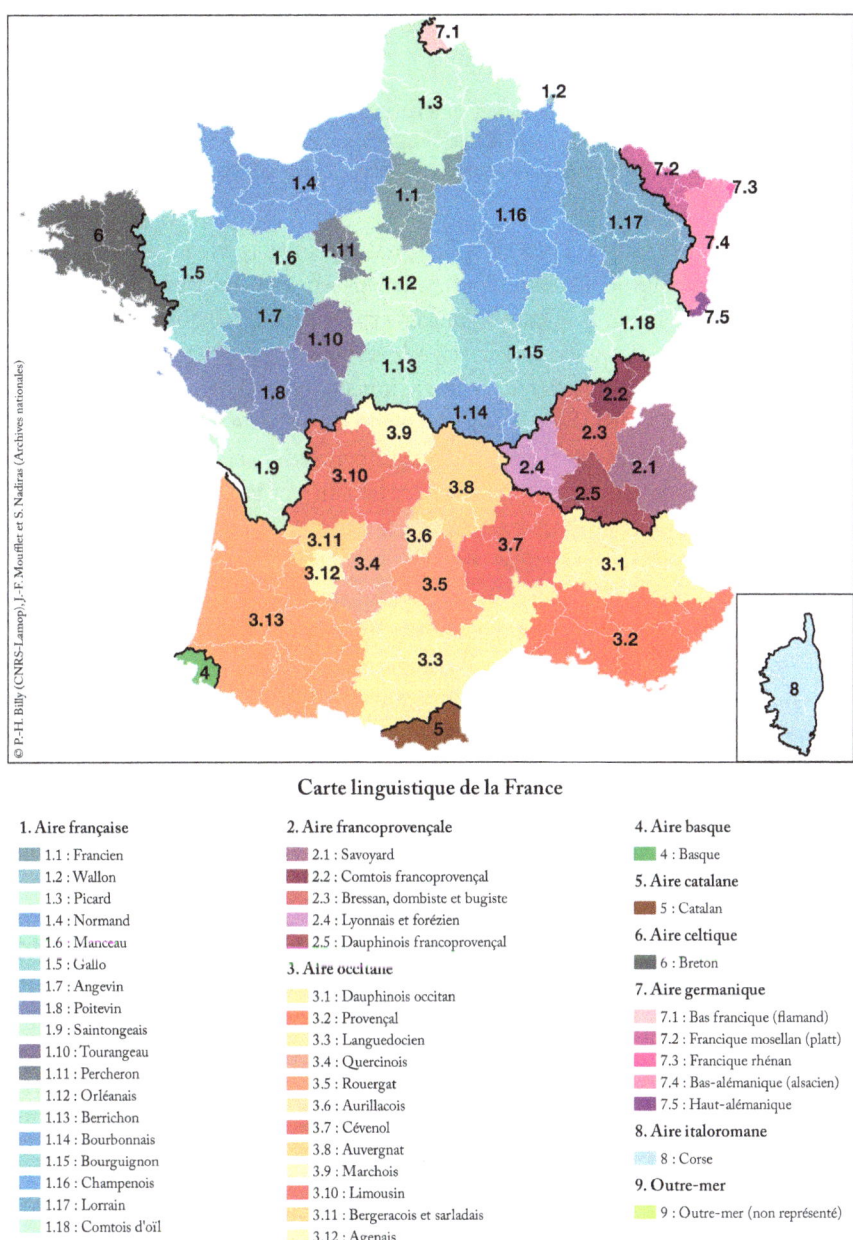

Figure 10.1: Representation of the linguistic and dialectal situation in Metropolitan France in the 20th century (Pierre-Henri Billy (CNRS/LAMOP, Paris), Jean-François Moufflet et Sébastien Nadiras *Archives Nationales de France*, 2019).

It is also important to define and make the distinction between the terms 'dialect' and 'slang.' As Nordquist (2020) explains:

> a dialect is a regional or social variety of a language distinguished by pronunciation, grammar, and/or vocabulary. The term dialect is often used to characterize any way of speaking that differs from the standard variety of a language which is largely considered to be dialect-free (para.1).

On the other hand, slang is defined as "Language of a highly colloquial type, considered as below the level of standard educated speech, and consisting either of new words or of current words employed in some special sense" (Oxford English Dictionary, 1971, p. 2855). However, as Partridge (1940) mentioned, "while slang is essentially part of familiar and colloquial speech, it is not necessarily incorrect or vulgar in its proper place" (p. 179), which places slang as a legitimate variety to use.

Two common types of French slang, *argot* and *verlan*, are not labeled regional languages (or dialects). *Argot* is a set of particular words used by a living social group wishing to protect itself from the rest of the world, and *verlan* is a type of *argot*. *Verlan* is a linguistic process that consists of speaking by reversing the syllables of a word (for example: *lou-che* becomes *che-lou*). However, *verlan* is more complex than this. For the sake of length, the whole process of *verlanisation* will not be developed in this chapter. Historically, even though its use is not clear, the first traces of *verlan* can be found in the 13th century in France (Sloutsky & Black, 2008). *Verlan* reappeared at the end of the 1980s. Initially used by youth from *la banlieue*, this variation kept spreading in French society since, and some words are now in the common speech of everyone in France.

The term *argot* first appeared in 1628, according to Pierre Guiraud (in Valdman, 2000), and came from a corporation of criminals, *les argotiers*. According to the French *Larousse* dictionary, *argot* is defined as "the set of particular words adopted by a social group living on its own, which wants to distinguish itself and/or protect itself from the rest of the society (certain trades, schools, prisons, the world of the underworld, etc.)." For a long time, *argot* has retained this link with the underworld. At the end of the 19th century, the 'traditional *argot*' was spoken by the 'bad boys' of the Parisian surrounding areas, especially those living in the neighborhoods of Belleville, Menilmontant, and Butte Montmartre. For François-Geiger (1991), there are three varieties of *argot*: *l'argot traditionnel* (traditional slang), *les parlés branchés* (trendy speech) and *l'argot commun* (common slang). Today, traditional *argot* is disappearing, but some words still remain in the common language.

Regarding *les parlés branchés* (trendy speech), it is nowadays the most common. It has a playful function and is a mark of identity. As for *l'argot commun* (common slang), it is part of the popular French spoken at the present time and encompasses both *argot traditionnel* (traditional slang), and *parlés branchés* (trendy speech). Some words are completely part of the common vocabulary of most French people, such as *boulot, bosser* or *turbiner*, that are synonyms of "to work." They are used naturally and commonly by most French people in France.[3]

In Liogier's (2002) article, Jean-Louis Calvet mentioned that many words of slang are meant to integrate current French. Indeed, many slang terms have entered the common language. We must therefore be aware that the boundary between slang and the common language is not sealed (Liogier, 2002). Indeed, the two variations are mixed and interwoven, and the distinction becomes more and more difficult to make.

Furthermore, *argot* seems to have been used by societal elites for a long time. Emile Zola used it in *L'Assomoir* (1877), and Victor Hugo even devoted an entire chapter to it in *Les Misérables* (1862). In addition, some words of *verlan* are now so much a part of the common vocabulary that words have entered the dictionary *Le Petit Robert* since 2005 (Sloutsky & Black, 2008). One sees the extent to which *argot* and *verlan* play an important role in the current language. There are words of *argot* which are anchored in the common vocabulary and are thus used by the working classes or the young as well as by the higher classes and the bourgeoisie (Szulmajster-Celnikier, 1996). French slang nowadays is not reserved for the so-called 'unprivileged' people or low-income social class. Slang is now common in the language of many French people. What was considered *argot* a few years ago, is now used as ordinary in a conversation. Some expressions have a functional use in daily life, adopted by individuals, the media, and even literature (Weber, 2013). Thus, while standard and nonstandard varieties of French are very distinct in theory and in teaching, in reality, they are not anymore.

2.4 Spoken *versus* written language

Another recurrent point in the literature is the dichotomy between spoken and written French (Blanche-Benveniste, 1997; Detey, 2017; Favart, 2010; Weber, 2013). Bourdieu (1982) refers to Durkheim's use of the term 'code' when stating that the rules and structures of written language, with its prescriptive convention, take on an authoritative, sanctioned status through the education system. As a result, spoken language is implicitly regarded as informal and inferior. For a long time, teaching French as a foreign language was based on two beliefs. First, oral French must

---

[3] Common *argot* words can be found in various French speaking countries; however, each geographic entity has its own idiosyncratic regionalisms. In this research, I focus exclusively on the *argot* used in France.

be taught through the learning of written language as supported by the grammar-translation method. Second, only a single variety of French, qualified as 'good' or 'standard,' should be presented, following the traditional grammatical norm offered in textbooks.

These teaching methods have changed through the years. Even though the four skills (i.e., listening, speaking, writing, reading) are taught, writing continues to be the main medium through which French is taught. Speaking is also evaluated and explained through the filter of the written language, making spoken French the 'bad French' (Blanche-Benveniste, 1997) as opposed to the 'good' written French.

The question of orality *versus* writing raises questions. Writing is seen as objective, authentic and lasting because words are written down, while orality does not leave any trace (Goody & Watt, 1963). Writing is also anchored in social practices (Miller, 2016; Scribner & Cole, 1981), but orality is also a way to communicate and transmit culture and literacy in general in specific contexts (Heath, 1983). Institutions and education have a role to play in these practices. Literacy is neither neutral nor universal, as there is a "role of power relation in literacy practices" (Street, 2001, p. 430). This power has been used as a weapon to undermine those who use slang and other stigmatized variations, and to perpetuate the hegemony of the 'good' and standard language. Many factors, such as gender, social class, race, community, culture, history, and identity, influence one's literacy and its power, as well as one's interaction and relationships with others. Language can be a powerful weapon (Bryan & Gerald, 2020), and schools and other institutions have the power to change literacy practices. However, the model taught in FL classrooms is often very neat and refined, without any mark of variation.

3 Conceptual framework: Bourdieu, Language and symbolic power

Learning language is a social act. It is thus related to the society of the target language. In the discussion about standard and nonstandard language, the question of social class cannot be ignored. In *Ce que parler veut dire* (What Talking Means, 1982), Bourdieu discussed the concept of language in relation to power and social class. I draw on this concept, as language varieties, such as *argot* and *verlan*, carry out many issues related to power relationships in society, the social classes, as well as questions about language perceptions and one's identity.

According to Bourdieu, the speech of one social class is always compared to another class. Everyone has a variety of schemes and the way one perceives and apprehends the speech of another varies. Thus, Bourdieu develops the concept of 'linguistic market' – *le marché linguistique* – that he defines as a sociolinguistic phenomenon that cannot be understood in the same sense as the language faculty inherent in the brain, as cognitivists view it. The 'market' should be understood in the sense of "any symbolic practice having a social character" (p. 35). "Any linguistic situation therefore functions as a market on which the speaker places his products and the product he produces for this market depends on the anticipation he has of the prices that his products will receive" (p. 35). Hence, the concept of the linguistic market can be seen as a metaphor to portray the competition that exists between languages within a society, as the standard and nonstandard – formal French and familiar French and slang. In fact, language is not neutral. Linguistic competence is a form of capital constructed through relations and interactions in social contexts. Within these contexts, the way one speaks or acts may have more value or be more legitimate than others, which leads to the construction of forms of 'cultural capital.'

Bourdieu also points out that the official aspects of the language are decided by institutions and 'educated' individuals. They have the power to decide what is right or wrong and, thus, to codify and establish the language as a static code. In France, the *Académie Française* has the authority to decide what is valid or not and which word or expression is legitimate to be included in the dictionary and, thus, accepted as part of the French language. The French language has been very static, at least in the written aspect. But language is not static.

> Talking about *the* language without further precision, as linguists do, is tacitly accepting the *official* definition of the *official* language of a political unit: this language is the one which, within the territorial limits of this unit, is imposed to all citizens as only legitimate. (p. 27, emphasis in the original)

Bourdieu argues that there are many variations and differences in languages that are significant and directly related to social disparities. Those disparities might not be taken into account by linguists but are actually relevant for sociologists. Bourdieu claims that speaking is a way to appropriate one or the other expressive styles that already constitute a certain use and is marked by their position in a hierarchy of styles, which articulates the hierarchy of the corresponding groups. The ability to speak *la langue légitime* (the legitimate language), the standard, also depends on the *patrimoine social* (the social heritage). Thus, does being from a lower class reduce the chances of speaking properly? These issues are also discussed by Rosa (2019), who demonstrates that minoritized groups, usually from lower socio-economic classes, are racialized and perceived as non-proficient in any language.

3.1 Education policy and language teaching

Education has played an essential role in the implementation of official languages. By imposing and teaching only the official language, institutions, and especially schools, impose not only a language but a common system and a formatted view of the world. It is a way of 'formatting' children to a unified way of thinking and speaking. Relating to this idea of language variations nowadays, we can wonder if that has really changed. Not allowing the use of language varieties in French schools excludes some students and creates a hierarchy where 'standard' French speakers are at the top, and users of other varieties are at the bottom. Likewise, not including it in FL classrooms makes it irrelevant, not valuable, and not legitimate to be learned. Thus, schools are reproducing the same scheme by promoting an imagined pure and valid language: the official and standard language. According to Bourdieu (1982), the standard language, the norm, makes the language impersonal and not representative of reality. Institutions, such as schools, are used as weapons through which other language varieties and dialects are erased in hopes of the creation of a 'pure' language.

Language is thus weaponized and used as a tool for domination to assert the hegemony of the standard French language in the FL classroom and beyond. Regarding language variation, individuals speaking slang or minoritized languages do not feel legitimate. Some criteria (such as the language, dialect used, or accent) convey mental representations that determine the perceptions that others can have about the speakers. Language becomes a marker of difference, of identity, of belonging to a community.

4 Research design

This qualitative case study aims to explore the legitimacy of language variations. It also intends to document the necessity of deconstructing the cliché of the standard language that has been used as a weapon to stigmatize speakers of language varieties, and create a more diverse and inclusive space in the classrooms and beyond. The data that I share in this chapter is part of a larger study, so only one research question is addressed here: *What are the perceptions of students about learning French variations, and especially French slang, in a foreign language classroom in the U.S.?*

The primary participants in this qualitative case study are learners of French at a large university in the southwest United States. As mentioned before, the data presented is a subset that was collected for a larger study and consisted of online surveys and individual interviews with a language program director, six instructors of French, and learners of French. This chapter will only focus on the data collected from learners of French (see Table 10.1).

Firstly, I analyzed the responses from an online Qualtrics survey completed by anonymous undergraduate students (N=42) enrolled in first, second, third, and fourth-semester French language courses. The questions (open-ended, multiple choice, Likert scale) were related to 1) their background in the French language and its varieties, 2) their knowledge and perceptions about French variations, and 3) whether they would like to learn them. Secondly, I examined the transcripts of two 45-minute-long focus-group interviews with undergraduate learners of French (N=6) conducted on Zoom. All interviews were transcribed with Otter.ai and analyzed qualitatively. Common themes based on participants' quotes were color-coded and categorized using NVivo. The students' survey responses were analyzed both qualitatively with NVivo and quantitatively with SPSS.

Table 10.1: Study Participants.

Participant	French Language Course Enrollment	First Language	Data Collection
Anonymous Students (N=4)	1st Semester	English	Online Survey
Anonymous Students (N=12)	2nd Semester	English (N=11) Navajo (N=1)	Online Survey
Anonymous Students (N=13)	3rd Semester	English (N=12) Spanish (N=1)	Online Survey
Anonymous Students (N=7)	4th Semester	English (N=6) Spanish (N=1)	Online Survey
Jay	4th Semester Study Abroad	Mandarin	Online Survey Focus Group Interview
Jeremy	1st Semester	English	Online Survey Focus Group Interview
Mariella	4th Semester	English	Online Survey Focus Group Interview
Maya	1st Semester	English	Online Survey Focus Group Interview
Natalie	1st Semester	English	Online Survey Focus Group Interview
Vanessa	3rd Semester	Spanish	Online Survey Focus Group Interview

5 Findings

5.1 Perceptions of slang

The perception of slang in general that students have is very personal, even though some aspects might be induced by society. For example, many of the students view slang as an informal way to speak (some even mentioned curse words), more casual, used in private circles, or in different parts of the country. Some added that it is for young people to communicate among each other. It is also seen as a dynamic language that changes across time and varies from generation to generation:

> I consider slang to be driven by the young people and each generation develops its own vocabulary, and once a generation that comes up with a certain set of slang grows up and begins working as adults, that becomes the new standard of vocabulary and the new younger generation begins to create new slang. (anonymous, second-semester French student).

For students, slang is also the language used in text messages and social media, with acronyms and shortened words. A few students associated it with a code that others could not understand and with illicit activities.

For all students, whether on the survey or in the interview, slang is synonymous with informality and varies according to the people we are addressing. Jay (fourth-semester French), whose first language is Mandarin, mentioned that slang in this language is spoken by gangsters and the criminal community: "It's absolutely not for civilized people or educated people." The negative connotation here is striking. Slang in Mandarin is associated with uneducated people and seems inappropriate to use. Thus, Jay makes the connection with slang in general and has a negative perception of it. Similarly, Vanessa (third-semester French), whose first language is Spanish, pointed out the relation to age when using Spanish slang. Using it with someone you barely know or with elderly people will be seen as a lack of respect. The perception of slang in Jay and Vanessa's first languages is interesting as it seems like slang should not be used by everyone and is reserved for circumstances. Slang, then, seems like a more situational practice, and one can decide the time and the context to use it.

The other students also had this idea that slang in English is informal, but not as inappropriate as it is for Jay and Vanessa in their first languages. The representation of slang in the students' primary languages has an influence on their perceptions of slang and its users in other languages as well, which can be problematic for their learning and perceptions of others if they have a negative image. Indeed, the representation of language that learners have can have an impact on their motivation and interests in a language and its culture (Goffin et al., 2009; Perrefort, 1997).

5.2 Perceptions of French slang

After unpacking the perceptions of slang in general, and especially in students' first languages, it was interesting to see the parallel with French slang. As most of the students have been exposed to it, and also have some representation of slang in their primary language, they were able to think about it and, somehow, make comparisons with French.

In the survey, many students (N=15) answered that they did not know anything about French slang, and some of them were not even aware that slang could exist in French. Then, some (N=4) associated slang with the language that the young generation speaks, others (N=4) associated it with a specific region in France, and a few (N=3) considered slang the difference between formality and informality. Slang was also perceived by students (N=5) as an alternative language that is not taught in classrooms: "I think about different phrases and/or words that may not be taught in your typical French class, but that would be used by native speakers" (anonymous, third-semester French student). All these responses show how students' awareness of French slang varies.

In interviews, most students said that mostly the younger generation speaks slang. For Jeremy (first-semester French), Mariella (fourth-semester French), and Jay (fourth-semester French), slang is used by teenagers and high schoolers, which matches their perceptions of slang in their first languages. However, Jay had an interesting comment. He went abroad for one summer to Aix-en-Provence in the South of France and stayed with a host family. His host mother was a professor at the university, and she used French slang sometimes. Jay found it surprising:

> Because my experience, in France, was probably not very typical. But my host mother, she's a professor in university. So, but she . . ., I observed that she speaks French very, very casually. So, she's well educated, but she speaks French very casually, and she probably uses lots of slang.

For him, the fact that someone so educated can use slang might have been something "not very typical" as it does not match his first perception of slang users. He continued:

> I used to believe that most people who use slang very frequently, they should be from some like disadvantage socioeconomic situation. But when I was in France, I found, oh my god, like people just tend to be very . . . . How do I say that . . . active? Interesting? (laughing) And they use slang a lot. I don't know.

His experience abroad with his host mother has somehow changed his belief that slang is spoken by only the young generation and that it is used by uneducated people, which was very surprising to him. This also somehow deconstructed his first perception linked to Mandarin slang use.

This relationship between the level of education and use of slang was mentioned by other participants. For example, Vanessa explained that "from the American perspective, like the French culture is very, like, proper and key part seems to be more formal at least from what I had seen on television and everything." Furthermore, she explained that she thinks that since France is a smaller country than the United States or Mexico (where she is originally from), more people go to school and are more educated. Hence, they are not using slang as much as other countries. That is an interesting point of view. First, she links the size of the country with the number of people who have access to education. It is hard to know why she has this belief. Second, she (as many people) has the idea that French people speak very properly and are very formal. Vanessa said that she gets this picture from television. Her response makes me wonder what type of TV shows and movies she is watching, or what type of exposure to the French language and culture she has had in her FL classroom.

However, it is in line with the perception of an imaginary ideal of the French language that many learners of French have, an idea perpetuated by the media but also by the *Académie Française* that keeps the rigidity of the language. Finally, her comparison with the United States and Mexico tends to suggest that people in these two countries are less educated, and that is the reason why they might use more slang there. Her reflections demonstrate again the strong relationship between education and ways of using the language and how powerful educational institutions are. French people are seen as educated and formal speakers who would not really use slang. These perceptions can impact the motivation and interest of students to learn it but also the way they see the slang users. Minoritized students might feel as if they do not belong to the community of practice of a language spoken formally and highly educated people. This perception of perfect French contrasts with slang users and serves as a strong weapon to marginalize them even more.

5.3 Should slang be taught?

During the interviews, all students except one said that slang should be taught in school. As the exception, Vanessa stated that she would like to have an "educated way of speaking, [. . .] more well-rounded, more formal," so everybody can understand her. She explained that when she moved to the United States from Mexico, people told her that she spoke very formally in English, and she actually liked it. For her, learning slang at school would be "risky" because she might use it, and she wants to speak formally, and maybe learn slang later on. The use of 'risky' seems strong but also understandable. Using non-standard language can be intimidating, and using it the wrong way can lead to uncomfortable situations. This is why Burke (1998) advocates for the teaching of slang to help students avoid these situations. Vanessa's opinion is even more interesting as she is the one who sought interaction with students from France. She said that for her, the best way to learn the language is to interact with target language speakers.

Furthermore, she really wanted to improve her speaking skills, so she interacted as much as possible with students from France to learn how to speak like them and then be able to communicate when she goes to France. Hence, it is paradoxical that she is the one participant who wants to speak more formally but also the one who thinks that communicating with French speakers is the best way to learn the language. When I asked her if they were using slang, she said that if it was a word that she did not know or seemed too familiar, she asked them to reformulate what they were saying in another way. She expressed resistance to slang, stating that she did not want to learn it. Further, Vanessa was very strict about the fact that she should only know standard French.

5.4 Why would students like to learn more French slang in class?

Various reasons were mentioned by students for why they would want to learn more French slang. First, they think that it is a part of the culture and an important component of the language, so knowing slang is a logical continuity in their learning of French. Many of them are considering going abroad and feel like knowing slang will be very helpful in communicating with local people while in France. In general, most of them would like to learn "authentic French" (anonymous, third-semester French student), as seen in the comments below:

> if I was to ever visit a francophone country because if I spoke a language other than English and visited an English speaking country, I would probably not understand what people were saying most of the time because people often don't speak in the proper form of their language all day in their everyday lives and I would want to understand what people were saying to me if they were to talk to me in slang. (anonymous, second-semester French student).

> I would like to be expected to speak the proper French, yet I would like to be aware of the slang. (anonymous, fourth-semester French student)

In the quotes above, the word 'proper' is used in the way that Vanessa used it. It implies that there is a proper and a non-proper way to speak. This language ideology, with the opposition of standard *versus* non-standard, also referred to by

Blanche-Benveniste (1997) as the 'good' and 'bad' French, is very difficult to deconstruct as it seems very anchored in some students' perceptions. But who can decide what is proper or not? The language is a norm (Bourdieu, 1982; Favart, 2010; Valdman, 1982) that is constructed and, thus, it is difficult to deconstruct it–even more so in France, with the hegemony of the standard French, ruled by the *Académie* and French purists. Other students want to learn it to actually speak the 'real' language:

> I believe it is important to learn everyday language rather than too 'posh.' (anonymous, fourth-semester French student)
>
> A lot of people say that the basic level of French you learn in 101 and 102 is just like learning basic elementary French and isn't how the language is actually spoken out in the real world. (anonymous, second-semester French student)
>
> Because I want to sound more casual in my languages, I feel that in French I'm gonna speak "textbook" French and I don't want that. I wanna sound natural. (anonymous, fourth-semester French student)

So, most students are aware that the French that is taught in their classrooms is not the French that is actually used in France (or other French-speaking countries). Of course, standard French is used every day by French people, but depending on the context, many use non-standard French, and especially *argot*, in daily conversations. While many students take French or other languages because it is a requirement for their studies, there is also a great number of students who actually take French for specific goals. Even though their language courses are preparing them to communicate and understand most of their encounters with French in their home country or abroad, it is not preparing them for informal interactions with their peers, for example. They will be able to understand French TV and most media, to read and interact with professors; however, when they want to have more casual conversations with their peers and make friends, they might sometimes feel left out as they will surely encounter slang words.

It seems like there is not a consensus among students on when to start learning French slang. Even though the majority tends toward the third semester, the other levels are fairly close. The interesting part is that there is still this clear dichotomy between standard and non-standard language varieties. Students have it in mind, clearly, and many declared that they wanted to learn the standard before learning the other variations, suggesting that they are very different and should be distinguished and separated. French is thus not seen as a language encompassing multiple variations, but as a single one understood as 'proper' French. This language is an entity on its own and perceived as distinct from any varieties.

We can wonder why some students would like to learn French slang right away and see it as an asset, whereas others would like to learn it later on after being proficient in 'proper' French. What has influenced students in these perceptions? Are these perceptions only about the French language? About slang in general? Or about slang users? Have they been influenced by their previous instructors? We could speculate that students would like to learn standard French first because they wish to be seen as legitimate speakers. Learning slang might seem 'inappropriate' to them, and they do not want to be categorized as non-proficient (Rosa, 2016) and want to be part of the 'proper' French community of practice, demonstrating the hierarchy of language.

6 Discussion

The findings of this study revealed that the majority of students (N=32) would like to learn French slang. They believe that it is an important part of the culture and language and that it would be useful to know in order to communicate authentically and understand French speakers and French media. They are aware that the French they are learning in class is more formal than the one used by French speakers, and they would like to have access to the various registers of the language. As some students and scholars (Burke, 1998; Durán & McCool, 2003; Fein, 2011) mentioned, learners do not want to speak like a textbook; they want to be able to converse naturally with French users.

However, a majority of students (N=23) think that the ideal moment to start is the third semester of French language courses or above. Most of them want to know the 'proper' French first, and some find it confusing to have to learn the standard and non-standard at the same time, while others do not think it is appropriate. Their perception of French slang tends to be close to their perception of their first language (English, Spanish, Mandarin). Slang is informal, mostly used among young people to communicate verbally, by text-messages, or on social media. Thus, why would they know it? Why would they need it to communicate?

The major issue is probably that their perception of slang in both their primary language and French is similar, whereas the reality is different. French slang, and especially *argot* is not used only among the youth or on social media. The misrepresentation of it might skew students' desire to learn it. However, learners of French going to France might surely have trouble understanding their peers if they have not been exposed to at least some slang. Students are projecting their perception of slang in general to French slang; hence, they want to learn the standard language. The supremacy of the standard French language in school has always been the pedagogical norm (Valdman, 1982), influencing not only the way curricula are designed, but also the view of students on the language (and on their speakers). This view has been a weapon that has given students this cliché picture of the French language being sophisticated and romantic; a cliché conveyed by media, touristic experience, and some instructors. Therefore, speaking French using slang does not match the perfect picture, which is nothing but an imagined reality. *Argot* is spoken by a wide variety of French people and is present in the daily speech of the population but also in a large majority of media. The perceptions of educators might also hurt the students' perceptions of slang and their desire to learn it.

Moreover, Vanessa (third-semester French) and Jay (fourth-semester French), would not use slang in public because they think that it is not the proper way of speaking. Vanessa wants to speak the 'proper' French, establishing again this power relationship between the 'good' and the 'bad' French and the people who use one or the other. She and Jay have this conception of slang being inappropriate and reserved for uneducated people based on the language perceptions of slang from their first language (Spanish for Vanessa, and Mandarin for Jay). There is a hierarchy in their image or perception of the French language. The standard language, or the one that is learned in school, is appropriate and used by educated people (implicitly coded as white upper-class); whereas slang is reserved for less educated people or even thieves and bad people (from Jay). If you are educated, you speak properly, and you use the standard language. Then, language has power. Language is a weapon (Bryan & Gerald, 2020). It is a way to discriminate against and stigmatize those who use variations. The standard language dominates the other variations. The education system conforms to the norm and continues to separate standard language from the other forms of language. Bourdieu (1982) gives a clear explanation of this:

> The recognition of the legitimacy of the official language is not an expressly professed, deliberate and revocable belief, nor an intentional act of acceptance of a 'norm'; it is registered in the practical state in the dispositions that are imperceptibly inculcated, through a long and slow process of acquisition. (p. 36)

So, these norms are not even conscious. They are culturally constructed, and people have learned them. The norms are powerful and shape how one might think about languages and their users. They shape the perceptions of a language and, in the context of foreign languages, the way learners envision a language and their motivation for learning it (Goffin et al., 2009; Perrefort, 1997). Therefore, the weaponization of language is affecting the perceptions of learners and shows that there is a power relationship in language.

The opposition between standard and non-standard languages has an impact on individuals and on communities. This dichotomy is anchored in society, perpetuating the power relationship and hegemony of a standard language. The official aspect of the language is decided by institutions and 'educated' individuals with formal authority who have the power to codify language policies (Bourdieu, 1982). And what has been determined as official is what is taught and shown to learners as the correct language to know and use, therefore instilling certain preconceptions about the language in learners. So, who is responsible for not including *argot* and *verlan* in foreign language classrooms? The instructors that are not motivated or simply do not have time to find extra materials to expose their students to them? The textbook editors for not including a section on them? The language program director for not incorporating a module in the syllabus? Or is the issue more profound, stemming from societal norms?

The data collected from learners have shown that the power relationship between standard and non-standard truly exists beyond the borders of France and even within the FL classrooms in higher education in the US. Some participants, like Vanessa and Jay, have drawn a very clear line between standard and non-standard and how these two registers are used, and by whom.

7 Conclusion

In slang, and in languages in general, there is a rapid and constant renewal of vocabulary, which is necessary for encryption and to mislead the novice (Sourdot, 2002). Nowadays, the cryptic function is not as important as it used to be. However, slang is still in constant evolution, representing the image of French society. Thus, the evolution of the language is the mirror of society and culture, and it is essential to be conscious of this evolution as a learner or teacher of foreign languages. Being able to communicate appropriately in French means also knowing which register to use in various contexts.

French slang, including *verlan* and *argot*, have existed in the language for many centuries and have not only been included in classical literature, but are also now incorporated in official dictionaries. Additionally, slang words and expressions are used in common conversation between most French people, no matter their social class, age, gender, etc. A number of factors have led to the valorization of slang: its representation in literature and media, its inclusion in official descriptors (i.e., the Common European Framework of Reference for Languages – CEFRL, and the American Council on the Teaching of Foreign Languages – ACTFL), and a growing recognition of slang as essential to effective communication with French speakers. So why is it still not included in the French language curriculum? Is it because of the representations that slang conveys? Is it because the standard is seen as more legitimate and useful? Or is it a lack of knowledge from educators?

The views that students have about French slang have been influenced by their perceptions of their primary language slang but also by the cliché that is perpetuated about the French language. French language, and especially the French spoken in France, is usually pictured through its users, depicted in movies either as formal and educated and usually white-speaking standard French, or young, coming from lower socio-economic status, often immigrants – using non–standard languages. These clichés, perpetuated by society and the media, have served as weapons to stigmatize French slang users. In FL classrooms in the US, even though most of the participants in this research stated that they would like to learn French slang, they all seem to have some reservations about it. The institutions have served as weapons to preclude students from learning an important part of the French language and culture. Furthermore, it is harming the overall view that students could have about not only French slang users, but potentially about all slang users in the world, reinforcing the stigmatization of those who speak differently. School, and education, in general, should open our students' minds and teach them to become global citizens, and create more diverse and inclusive classrooms. As long as these stigmas persist, students will continue to have these thoughts about language variations (and slang), and the stigmatization will continue.

References

ACTFL (American Council on the Teaching of Foreign Languages). 2015. *Performance descriptors for language learners*. ACTFL.

Auger, Julie & Albert Valdman. 1999. Letting French students hear the diverse voices of Francophony. *The Modern Language Journal* 83(3), 403–412. https://doi.org/10.1111/0026-7902.00030

Billy, Pierre-Henri; Jean-François Moufflet & Sébastien Nadiras. 2019. Carte linguistique de la France. Archives Nationales. https://www.archives-nationales.culture.gouv.fr/fr/web/guest/cartographie-historique

Blanche-Benveniste, Claire. 1997. *Approches de la langue parlée en français*. Paris: OPHRYS.

Bourdieu, Pierre. 1982. *Ce que parler veut dire*. Paris: Fayard.

Bryan, Kisha. & J. P. B Gerald. 2020. The weaponization of English. *Language Magazine*. https://www.languagemagazine.com/2020/08/17/the-weaponization-of-english/

Burke, David. 1998. Without slang and idioms, students are "in the dark!". *ESL Magazine*1(5), 20–23.

Council of Europe. 2018. *Common European framework of reference for languages: Learning, teaching, assessment. Companion volume with new descriptors*. France: Council of Europe.

Detey, Sylvain. 2017. La variation dans l'enseignement du français parlé en FLE: Des recherches linguistiques sur la francophonie aux questionnements didactiques sur l'authenticité. In A.-C. Jeng, B. Montoneri & M.-J. Maitre (eds.), *Echanges culturels aujourd'hui: langue et littérature*, 93–114. Taiwan: Tamkang University Press.

Devereaux, Michelle D. & Chris C. Palmer. 2019. *Teaching language variation in the classroom: Strategies and models from teachers and linguists*. New York, NY: Routledge. https://doi.org/10.4324/9780429486678

Durán, Richard & George McCool. 2003. If this is French, then what did I learn in school? *The French Review* 77(2), 288–299.

Favart, Françoise. 2010. Quels savoirs en matière de variations langagières susceptibles d'optimiser un enseignement du FLE. *Pratiques, Linguistique, littérature, didactique*. 145/146, 179–196. https://doi.org/10.4000/pratiques.1551

Fein, David A. 2011. Promoting vulgarity by teaching slang in the classroom. *Rocky Mountain Review of Language and Literature* 65(1), 97–101. https://doi.org/10.1353/rmr.2011.0008

François-Geiger, Denise. 1991. Panorama des argots contemporains. *Langue française* 90, 5–9.

Goffin, Christelle, Annick Fagnant & Christiane Blondin. 2009. Les langues des voisins: des langues toujours appréciées? *Lidil. Revue de linguistique et de didactique des langues* 40, 17–30. https://doi.org/10.4000/lidil.2897

Goody, Jack & Ian Watt. 1963. The consequences of literacy. *Comparative Studies in Society and History* 5(3), 304–345. https://doi.org/10.1017/S0010417500001730

Guiraud, Pierre. 1966. L'Argot. *Que sais-je? 700*. Paris: PUF

Hargreaves, Alec. 1995. *Immigration,'race' and ethnicity in contemporary France*. New York, NY: Routledge. https://doi.org/10.4324/9780203430187

Heath, Shirley Brice. 1983. *Ways with words: Language, life and work in communities and classrooms*. Cambridge, UK: Cambridge University Press. https://doi.org/10.1017/CBO9780511841057

Liogier, Estelle. 2002. Quelles approches théoriques pour la description du français parlé par les jeunes des cités? *La linguistique* 38(1), 41–52. https://doi.org/10.3917/ling.381.0041

Lippi-Green, Rosina. 2012. *English with an accent: Language, ideology, and discrimination in the United States*. New York, NY: Routledge. https://doi.org/10.4324/9780203348802

Metz, Mike. 2019. Accommodating linguistic prejudice? Examining English teachers' language ideologies. *English Teaching: Practice & Critique*. http://dx.doi.org/10.1108/ETPC-09-2018-0081

Miller, Elisabeth L. 2016. Literate misfitting: Disability theory and a sociomaterial approach to literacy. *College English* 79(1), 34–56.

Nordquist, Richard. 2020. Linguistic variation. *ThoughtCo*. https://www.thoughtco.com/what-is-linguistic-variation-1691242

Nordquist, Richard. 2020. Definition and examples of dialect in linguistics. *ThoughtCo*. https://www.thoughtco.com/dialect-language-term-1690446

Oxford English Dictionary. 1971. Slang. In *The Compact Edition of the Oxford English Dictionary*, 2855.

Partridge, Eric. 1940. Slang. *S.P.E. Tract* 55, 175–196.

Petitpas, Thierry. 2010. Enseigner la variation lexicale en classe de FLE. *The French Review* 83(4), 800–818.

Perrefort, Marion. 1997. "Et si on hachait un peu de paille": aspects historiques des représentations langagières. *Revue Tranel (Travaux neuchâtelois de linguistique)* 27, 51–62. https://doi.org/10.26034/tranel.1997.2648

Rosa, Jonathan Daniel. 2016. Standardization, racialization, languagelessness: Raciolinguistic ideologies across communicative contexts. *Journal of Linguistic Anthropology* 26(2), 162–183. https://doi.org/10.1111/jola.12116

Rosa, Jonathan. 2019. *Looking like a language, sounding like a race: Raciolinguistic ideologies and the learning of Latinidad*. Oxford, UK: Oxford University Press. https://doi.org/10.1093/oso/9780190634728.001.0001

Scribner, Sylvia & Michael Cole. 1981. *The psychology of literacy*. Boston, MA: Harvard University Press. https://doi.org/10.4159/harvard.9780674433014

Silverstein, Michael. 1996. Monoglot 'standard' in America: Standardization and metaphors of linguistic hegemony. In Donald Brenneis & Ronald K. S. Macaulay (eds.), *The matrix of language: Contemporary linguistic anthropology*, 284–306. New York, NY: Routledge.

Sloutsky, Larissa & Catherine Black. 2008. Le verlan, phénomène langagier et social: récapitulatif. *The French Review* 82(2), 308–324.

Sourdot, M. (2002). L'argotologie: entre forme et fonction. *La linguistique* 38(1), 25–40. https://doi.org/10.3917/ling.381.00025

Street, Brian. 2001. The new literacy studies. In Ellen Cushman, Eugene R., Kintgen, Barry M. Kroll & Mike Rose (eds.), *Literacy: A critical sourcebook*, 430–442. New York, NY: Bedford.

Szulmajster-Celnikier, Anne. 1996. La politique de la langue en France. *La linguistique*, 32(2), 35–63.

Tomlinson, Brian. 2012. Materials development for language learning and teaching. *Language Teaching* 45(2), 143–179. https://doi.org/10.1017/S0261444811000528

Valdman, Albert. 1982. Français standard et français populaire: sociolectes ou fictions? *The French Review*, 218–227.

Valdman, Albert. 2000. La Langue des faubourgs et des banlieues: de l'argot au français populaire. *The French Review*, 1179–1192.

Weber, Corinne. 2013. *Pour une didactique de l'oralité: Enseigner le français tel qu'il est parlé*. Paris: Didier.

Juan A. Ríos Vega
Chapter 11
Dismantling weaponizing language in teacher preparation programs

Abstract: Through personal anecdotes and lived experiences in the public school system in the U.S., the author critically discusses how the oppressive language commonly used in social contexts is also used in teacher education programs and textbooks to weaponize the education of students of color. In this chapter, the author argues that the language of weaponization in teacher education programs ill-prepares pre-service and in-service teachers while trying to understand students of color, especially English language learners (ELLs). As such, the author encourages teacher educators, pre- and in-service teachers, and school administrators to treat students of color as cultural and linguistic assets in the classroom. The chapter concludes with the author's reflections on education as "an ethic of love."

Keywords: Latino/Hispanic/Latinx, limited, academic English, at risk, label, stereotype, language barrier, minority

1 Introduction

During the 16-plus years that I taught in the public school system in the United States, I always questioned some of the labels used to stereotype students, especially English language learners (ELLs).[1] Additionally, I noticed that my teacher-colleagues and school administrators used those same labels to create expectations and make assumptions about students. Later, I myself adopted the same terms to refer to my own students without realizing the social and psychological implications behind those labels. Some teachers were not pleased with the academic performance of ELLs and were not happy to have them in their classrooms. At that time, teachers were granted a bonus called ABC ("A" accountability, "B" basics, and "C" control) that was based on the standardized test scores of the stu-

---

[1] For the purpose of this chapter, I will be using the term English language learners (ELLs). I understand that the term Multilingual learners (MLs) is now preferred.

Juan A. Ríos Vega, Bradley University

https://doi.org/10.1515/9783110799521-011

dents they taught. Basically, it was an accountability program that rewarded teachers for student achievement test scores in reading, writing, and math. Some schools and teachers did not get the ABC bonuses due to low test scores and, as a result, teachers often blamed ELLs who were 'not proficient' in English.

I soon realized that the problem was deeper than test scores and language acquisition. I learned that this unwelcoming attitude toward ELLs was not only a school issue, but a social problem that was (and continues to be) perpetuated within the school systems and the classrooms (Motha, 2014; Ríos Vega, 2015a, 2015b, 2020; Solórzano & Yosso, 2009). As a Spanish-speaking immigrant from Panama, who was often mislabeled as 'Mexican' due to my skin tone and 'Spanish accent' while speaking English, I also became a victim of racism and discrimination in the community. I clearly understood that most of the teachers, who happened to be white, had stereotypes toward the new influx of Spanish-speaking immigrants, who were mostly from Mexico and Central America. However, it was not until I pursued graduate studies that I noticed how social layers of oppression (and the language through which it is embodied) position ELLs and other minoritized students as culturally deficient (Solórzano & Pérez Huber, 2020; Valencia, 2010). In a discussion of the role of white mainstream society in perpetuating notions of culture and 'othering,' Gillborn (2009) adds that,

> Whiteness draws much of its power from "Othering" the very idea of ethnicity. A central characteristic of whiteness is a process of "naturalization" such that white becomes the norm from which other "races" stand apart and in relation to which they are defined. (p. 54)

Now, as a faculty member in the department of education, leadership, and counseling at a predominantly white institution of higher education, I realize that the use of weaponizing language in teacher preparation programs, including textbooks, makes it challenging for pre-service teachers to have a real understanding of students from diverse backgrounds. Marx (2006) quotes, "Because contemporary white Americans have been conditioned not to think about race and, especially, not to talk about it, facing the topic can be a challenging, frustrating, and even a frightening experience for many" (p. 21). I never realized how the weaponization of certain academic language in teacher education programs and schools in the United States dehumanizes students of color, especially ELLs. It has been through my critical analysis of the language used by my colleagues, current students, and my critical educational background that I have understood how this idea of learning and teaching English to ELLs to become successful, while devaluing their heritage language(s), was a form of linguist racism (Bryan & Gerald, 2020). Now, I clearly understand how this false idea of pushing my former ELLs to learn English as soon as possible was an exercise to normalize inequity and injustice.

2 Stereotypes & (over)generalizations as language weaponization

Language weaponization is usually taken for granted and not even discussed in teacher education programs. In my role as a faculty member, I have witnessed colleagues, usually white, pre-service teachers, replicating the use of an oppressive discourse that normalizes stereotypes, prejudices, and linguicism. As a former teacher in a predominantly white high school, I also internalized the use of a weaponizing language (i.e., academic English) as the norm. As a critical race scholar (Dixson et al., 2006; Solórzano & Delgado Bernal, 2001; Villenas & Deyhle, 1999) and post-ethnography-qualitative researcher (Noblit et al., 2004), I draw from the critical thoughts of Paulo Freire (1998a, 1998b) and bell hooks (2001) about educating as a love ethic throughout this manuscript.

For the purpose of this chapter, I will focus on some of the commonly used forms of language weaponization shared by colleagues and pre- and in-service teachers, some of which can also be found in teacher preparation programs' textbooks. I will discuss how the misuse and overuse of some labels become stereotypes used to identify and define students of color, especially ELLs, and how these stereotypes hinder their education. I will also share some of my personal anecdotes as a former English as a second language (ESL) high school teacher in the Southeast. First, I will unpack some stereotypes about students of color within the United States. Then, to discuss the use of weaponizing language in teacher education programs and schools, I will analyze some of the most common stereotypes that I have heard and continue hearing in my teaching journey to reflect on how educators have been complicit in weaponizing language to the detriment of communities of color. Finally, I will reflect on bell hooks' (2001) "ethic of love" in education.

3 Unpacking the language of stereotypes

3.1 We are NOT all Hispanic/Latino!

It is definitely true that most Spanish-speaking countries have similar histories with European colonialism and U.S. imperialism. Most Latin American countries share the same mother tongue, foods, music, and traditions; however, there are many characteristics that make us Latinx different, especially when it comes to becoming immigrants in the United States. For instance, many Latin American immigrants do not speak Spanish as their first language. As a teacher, I had students from Mexico and Guatemala whose first languages were not Spanish but Tarasco (Purépecha language) and Q'eqchi' (a Mayan language) (Pentón Herrera, 2021; Ríos Vega, 2020). Due to poverty, lack of opportunities, persecution, communism, discrimination, wars, and natural disasters, these people decide to adopt the United States as their new home. There are others who overstay their tourist visas without understanding how the oppressive systems of racism and classism challenge the everyday lives of communities of color in the United States. In addition, others do not get to understand how society functions and why we are still talking about racism and discrimination in the Land of the Free.

I have previously written about these two categories, as many other scholars have in the past (Ríos Vega, 2015a). "Latino/Hispanic" can be an umbrella term used to silence and stereotype a diverse population. For instance, Clara (pseudonym), whose U.S. citizen parents came from Puerto Rico to live in New Jersey, or as is Juan (pseudonym), who belongs to a Mayan tribe in Guatemala, moved to North Carolina with his uncle when he was eight years old, are both labeled either Latina/o or Hispanic. However, Clara and Juan have two different personal experiences regarding immigration, language, culture, gender, class, and familial expectations. My point is that whenever teachers, school administrators, and staff use the terms Hispanic and/or Latino to define or to understand students like Clara and Juan, chances are that both students will be understood the same way. When we refer to students from Latin American countries or Latinx students born and raised in the United States, we cannot define them based on their skin color, names, or their English pronunciation. Instead, we need to get to know them and their families. Ultimately, students like Clara and Juan want to feel recognized and valued for being who they are as Puerto Rican and Guatemalan, respectively. Motha (2014) argues that since the term Hispanic and Latino were created in the United States as separate categories to differentiate individuals, it has developed "a border, a demarcation" between an "us" and a "them" (p. 95).

Another group of Latin American immigrants is the ones labeled as Blacks or whites due to their skin color. Black Latinx or Afro-Latinx and indigenous immigrants experience double racism, first in their countries of origin for being Black and/or indigenous, then in the United States for being Black, Spanish, and/or indigenous language(s) speakers, and sometimes for being part of the lesbian, gay, bisexual, and trans (LGBT+) community. However, white Latinx immigrants benefit from this racist system since they experience the same privileges as most white middle-class Americans (Bonilla-Silva, 2010; Pentón Herrera & Bryan, 2022). As an anecdote, I had a colleague, whose ancestors came from Italy to Venezuela, and then he moved to North Carolina, but he refused to be referred to as a person of color. The point that I want to make about Latinx stereotypes in the U.S. is that there is not a single story. Some of us internalize what it means to be labeled Latino and/or Hispanic in this country. Others, like me, challenge those labels since they do not define me at all. The umbrella of Latino and/or Hispanic are filled with prejudices and assumptions about us. It also erases our languages, histories, cultures, beliefs, and the reason why we decided to leave our homelands behind. Motha (2014) argues, "Ignoring differences allows us to construct a narrative of power neutrality, in which everyone is assumed to have received equal treatment and opportunity" (p. 82).

It is crucial that student teachers, current teachers, and school administrators, listen to the stories of immigrant students and their families. As a former English as a second language (ESL) teacher, I realized that most of my students and their families were my biggest inspiration and hope to become a more critical teacher, an advocate for social justice, and to treat them as my own children. Learning how most of them came to this country after being separated from their parents for a long time, risking their lives while walking a desert with strangers, or starving for days to reunite with their parents, allowed me to teach my students with love and care. My argument is that even though most Latin American immigrants share similar histories with white European colonization (language and Catholicism), some of us arrive in this country with different forms of privileges or none. Some of us were fortunate to come to this country due to our middle-class status, while others have to flee poverty, corruption, persecution, and drugs. Most immigrant families, especially those who come from rural areas and low socioeconomic status, come to this country looking for a promising future for their children through their education. It is a disservice if those who decide to teach, inspire, and protect our students define them by the label Latino/Hispanic that then becomes a stereotype that weaponizes their education.

3.2 Minority students

This term, minority, makes students feel they are worth less than the rest. It is interesting to check statistics to find out if students of color are classified as a minority, especially in schools where Black and Latinx students are the majority. Wingrove-Haugland & McLeod (2021) argue that,

> The original and literal definitions of "minority' or "minority group" were based on numerical size: these terms referred to members of groups that have distinctive practices or characteristics and that are smaller in number than the majority group that does not share these practices or characteristics (p. 2).

Although there is a historical record of the term minority in relation to numerical size, society and school systems tend to associate minority students with issues of race, ethnicity, and class, leaving out other social categories that also shape students' educational experiences, such as gender, sexuality, immigration status, and languages, to name a few. I still recall when I was doing my practicum to become a certified teacher school administrator. I was sent to a predominantly white middle school where Black and Latinx students were bussed every day. Most of the students of color who attended this school came from low socioeconomic backgrounds and lived in government housing. For me, it was very interesting to witness how these students of color learned to navigate this oppressive space.

During my practicum, I joined an after-school program for Black boys. Most of the students in this program were referred by their teachers for having some behavioral problems in the classroom. Something positive about this group was that its leader was a young Black man who used this program to empower these young Black boys and to teach them how to navigate society as men of color. Honestly, in the beginning, it was not easy for me to be in that space since the students did not know me, and it took them a while to open up and welcome me. I learned a lot from this experience, especially when I helped organize a community event where these boys' parents were invited to attend. The event took place in one of the government housing buildings, and it was a rich professional experience since it allowed me to understand these students in their environment. Also, I had a chance to meet their parents and siblings.

One of the people I met during the event was Taylor (pseudonym), a highly-educated African parent. While I listened to his story and why he and his family moved to America, I realized that he and his son were amazing human beings. Taylor shared with me that he was waiting for his Canadian visa to be approved, so he and his family could finally move. He also shared with me that he did not know why his son was referred to this after-school program since he seemed to be a good child. It broke my heart to realize that Taylor's son was labeled for having behavioral problems based solely on the school culture and teachers' expectations. I wonder how many teachers, usually white, labeled Taylor's son as a troublemaker just by looking at his skin color and gender (Fergus et al., 2014).

Wingrove-Haugland & McLeod (2021) suggest using the term "minoritized" instead of "minority" or "minority group" as being minoritized has been done by the dominant group. They claim that, "being minoritized merely involves being suppressed, that is, prevented from gaining equal power and socioeconomic equality (p. 7). Although I use the term "minoritized group" in some spaces and courses, I critically analyze it as another form of labeling. What happens when oppressed individuals internalized the label "minoritized group"? What happens when marginalized and oppressed individuals play the victims by misinterpreting being "minoritized" and accept inequity and inequality as the norm? Instead, we need to counteract these discourses of "minority" or "minoritized group" related to issues of race, ethnicity, and class. "Minority" has connotations that weaponizes students' education, especially students of color. These students and their families need to become aware of the implications behind these terms in order to challenge them. When students of color, especially, start hearing the term "minority," they tend to behave based on those expectations. Some of them have to give up their cultural wealth and adopt a dominant (usually white) definition of what a successful student means.

Unfortunately, some teachers and school administrators misuse the term "minority" to develop low expectations of students of color and their families. Students of color cannot be compared to their white counterparts by using the term "minority" since it perpetuates the assumption of being culturally deficient. Consciously or unconsciously, the label "minority" is to define students of color in this country. This assumption that students of color represent a "minority" pushes teachers, administrators, and staff to develop stereotypes based on personal anecdotes (socialization) and prejudices against students of color. It is the use of those stereotypes, like "minority students," that weaponizes students' of color education. Instead of stereotyping students based on their skin color, teachers, school administrators, and staff need to discuss how labeling students of color as "minority students" weaponizes their education and what the implications are behind being labeled "minority."

3.3 I have brown skin, but I'm NOT "Mexican"

While teaching high school, I deeply analyzed and reflected on the word Mexican. Soon I realized that being referred to as Mexican implied different connotations and meanings depending on its context and who said it. Since most of my former high school students came from Mexico, it was easy for me to understand and to make them feel proud of their country. It was so beautiful to witness how every time we engaged in an art activity where they had to share part of their culture, all of them colored or cut out their Mexican flag. From my students, I learned about the meaning of the three colors in the flag. I learned the history behind the eagle, the cactus, and the snake. However, I also learned how being called Mexican had some prejudicial, racist, and xenophobic meanings (De Genova & Ramos-Zayas, 2003). I quickly learned that being Mexican also meant 'illegal, wetback, drug dealer, macho, and school dropout.' I also remember one day, one of my students shared with me how one of his teachers asked him to stop speaking Mexican in the classroom. I listened to my student and told him that Mexican was not a language but a nationality. There were instances where I also had to remind my Mexican students that being Mexican did not mean that they came from a different race since they tended to translate the term "raza," which has a different connotation for Mexican, Mexican-Americans, and the Chicano Movement (Contreras, 2017) than for other Latin American immigrants within the United States. "Raza" means that we come from the same ethnic group instead of a different race.

Another insightful example happened this semester in one of the ESL practicum courses. Maria (pseudonym), was born and raised in Chicago, one of her parents was born in the United States, and the other one came from Mexico. As Maria presented her final project, she introduced herself as Mexican. After her presentation, I brought Maria's pride in having Mexican heritage. However, I reminded students that students like Maria claim Mexico as their homeland, although they are born and raised in the United States. I told my students that most students, like Maria, do it as a sense of cultural pride. Finally, I used Maria's comment to highlight that although some students are proud of their cultural heritage, they cannot be stereotyped as foreigners and/or ELLs. Instead, first, teachers need to get to know their students' cultural and family history. I have found that there is a huge misunderstanding between what our Mexican and Mexican-American students define by being self-identified as Mexican and how teachers, school administrators, and staff understand the word Mexican as a stereotype.

3.4 "I am NOT at risk"

Who is at risk? The school, teachers, administrators? What are the implications behind the term "At risk"? Unfortunately, I have witnessed how students are stereotyped as at risk from pre-K all the way through high school. Also, I noticed how some teachers based their assumptions on students who have been labeled 'At risk' (Valencia, 2010). Students of color are most likely to be referred to as 'At risk.' Pica-Smith & Veloria (2012) argue that the term 'At risk' "ignores institutionalized structures of inequality and a systemic analysis of what places youth at risk" (p. 2). Before having all of this academic/critical knowledge about how oppressive language could be while trying to understand other people's children, especially students of color, I recall believing the idea of students being 'At risk.' In 2003, I worked as a family service coordinator for a non-profit organization in North Carolina. One of my roles was to help Latinx families find daycare services for their children, visit newborn Latinx babies, and to translate documents into Spanish.

One morning I was asked to interpret for a child who was taking a screening test to assess whether he could be accepted into a pre-K program. I was delighted to support this child. It was very interesting to meet and observe this boy's interaction and behavior in the classroom. While most (white) kids were on the floor listening to the teacher reading a children's book aloud, Carlos (pseudonym) was mesmerized by the colors, shapes, and puzzle boxes in the classroom. Carlos could not stay still like most of the other children. For a moment, I thought Carlos was deficient. Pica-Smith & Veloria (2012) claim that "deficit theories assume that some children, because of genetic, cultural, or experiential differences, are inferior to other children" (pp. 2–3). It was my internalized prejudice that did not allow me to understand Carlos. It was the language learned at work that did not push me to critically see Carlos' behavior as all he knew from his personal experience with the real world. Instead, I stereotyped him as an 'at risk' student.

Today, I feel guilty for my lack of understanding about children who come from low socioeconomic backgrounds and who live in segregated neighborhoods where the lack of resources deprives them of experiences that prepare them for school. Now, I use that particular experience to teach my students that students like Carlos should not be defined as 'At risk.' Instead, teachers need to work along with parents, so students like him can be ready to succeed academically. Students of color, especially those who come from low socioeconomic backgrounds, should be taught by skillful teachers who understand how social issues such as racism and classism shape a child's education. Teachers need to learn about first-language learning and new language acquisition. It is also important that teachers, school administrators, and staff remind parents about the importance of talking to their children in their heritage language(s), and name things when they go to the supermarket, park, and other social settings. Children of color should not arbitrarily be labeled "at risk."

3.5 "Is my heritage language a barrier?"

The language barrier is probably one of the most common terms my student teachers use in the classroom. Most of the time, I challenge them to become critical thinkers about this term and what it entails. Language cannot represent a barrier, especially for teachers. Instead, teachers must become creative and skillful with pedagogical strategies to support their students. A barrier has negative effects on students. Students at my institution, who are studying to become elementary and middle school teachers, graduate with an ESL endorsement as well. Other students pursuing teacher degrees in Math, Science, or English have the option to add this endorsement to their major. As part of the endorsement, student teachers are required to complete one hundred hours at a local school (i.e., teacher practicum), supporting their cooperating teacher and ELLs.

One of the biggest highlights of these ESL programs in the district is that it provides Spanish immersion programs in elementary schools, so students can reinforce their heritage language before they transition to English. However, the most interesting aspect of the teaching practicum is that some of my students are placed in these spaces where Spanish is the dominant language. Being immersed in a language besides English is always a challenge for my students. Some of them complain about it since they cannot interact with the students, or sometimes they do not know what is going on in the classroom. Others feel they do not need to be there, and others ask to be placed in an English-speaking environment. I feel certain that my students' reactions to these spaces are closely related to their prejudices and stereotypes about ELLs. However, as their instructor, I use their experiences to challenge the idea of language as a barrier. I encourage them to think critically about their thoughts and behaviors in a space where their language is not the dominant one, how they feel, and what crosses their minds. Then I ask them to understand that they will have ELLs in their classrooms (whether they like it or not) who will feel uncomfortable in an English-dominant space. In addition, I remind them that foreign languages in the classroom are always good opportunities for learning.

When teachers encounter students whose first language is not English, they need to use their creativity and pedagogical skills to transmit knowledge, inspiration, and trust. Motha (2014) cites, "When teachers are inadequately prepared to meet the special needs of second language speakers, they are naturally reluctant to work with them" (p. 69). ELLs see their teachers as role models, whether they do a good job or not. I share stories about ELLs using the same weaponizing language as some teachers to make other students stop using their heritage language. This can make ELLs internalize that in the United States, people speak only English or that in order to succeed in this country, they need to speak English. Language is not a barrier but an opportunity for learning about the Other. Heritage languages should become assets in the classroom and schools. As teachers, it is important to understand all of the hidden implications underneath the "language barrier." When teachers, school administrators, and/or staff use the phrase "language barrier," it sends the message that students have a problem since English is the dominant language or the language of instruction. The "language barrier" discourse weaponizes ELLs' education as they see themselves as culturally deficient or unintelligent and cannot communicate with their teachers and English-only peers.

3.6 Who is illiterate?

Nobody is illiterate. When immigrant parents, especially those who do not have a formal education from their home country, arrive in this country, they are most of the time referred to as illiterate. When literacy skills focus only on reading and writing, immigrant parents and relatives are seen as less than literate (Cortes Santiago & Arvelo Alicea, 2015). However, literacy is more than that. In my journey as a teacher in the public school system and community college, I met immigrant parents and students who were very skilled in many things. For instance, I met Ethiopian mothers who were excellent cooks. I met Mexican parents who taught me how to set up a Day of the Dead altar at the local library. I had Latinx high school students who knew how to perform folk dances and cook authentic traditional foods. Additionally, I had Pakistani families who invited me to their houses to eat a traditional meal. Although my students' parents did not speak English, they taught me much about their culture. I felt uncomfortable when they asked me to serve my food first while they waited. Later, I understood that it was a sign of respect.

Linville and Pentón Herrera (2022) agree that "transformative learning" (p. 64) means that teachers need to assume their roles with a positive attitude, focusing on minoritized students' cultural wealth as an asset, instead of as being culturally deficient. It is the teachers' and administrators' responsibility to reach out to immigrant families and learn from them, and send the message across that their funds of knowledge are assets in the school.

> Transformative learning begins when educators create spaces for students with limited or interrupted formal education (SLIFE) to explore how they learn best and use their abilities to shape meaningful learning: learning that applies to their immediate context and contributes to their academic, social, and linguistic growth. (Linville & Pentón Herrera, 2022, p. 64).

Literacy goes beyond the ability to communicate verbally in a language since there are multiple ways to send a message. Immigrant families come to this country with a wealth of knowledge (González et al., 2009) that must be used in school with respect. When immigrant students and families are stereotyped as illiterate, it erases and devalues their assets in schools and the community. As a weaponizing term, illiterate also perpetuates the assumption of being culturally deficient. When issues of immigration, language, race, and ethnicity intersect multiple layers of oppression, such as xenophobia, linguicism, and racism, being stereotyped as illiterate makes an individual's everyday experience extremely challenging. It is important to highlight that when ELLs understand that their families are defined as illiterate, some of them tend to reject speaking their heritage language and practicing their cultural values, which are necessary for their life success and self-identity as future adults. Teachers, school administrators, and staff need to understand that when immigrant parents do not speak English, it is not an excuse to stereotype them as illiterate or that they cannot contribute to their child's education since there are other social barriers that immigrant families have to face in this country (jobs, immigration, family members back home, housing, etc.).

3.7 I don't have an accent; I speak two languages

Who does not have an accent? How do individuals use the term accent to define the Other? How hurtful is it to remind the Other that they have an accent? I have always found that this term is a form of microaggression, especially in the United States. I associate this term with acculturation and assimilation, which I challenge and discuss with student teachers. Instead of reminding individuals whose first language is other than English, that they have an accent, people need to validate that people speak more than one language and encourage them to preserve it as part of their linguistic capital. As a former public school teacher and English language learner myself, I can share how this constant reminder that "We have an accent" hurts and makes us feel unsmart or incapable of having a conversation with native English speakers. 'Having an accent' is that constant reminder that English is not our native language, and we wonder if people will be able to understand us or not. Also, we are always aware that mainstream individuals will define us not only based on the way we look but also by the way we sound in English. In a pluralistic society, the term accent should not even be mentioned.

Another issue I have encountered is how the term *accent* within mainstream English speakers is utilized to oppress and marginalize people based on their race, gender, and/or social status. "Language can achieve legitimacy when it is racialized in certain ways. Discrimination on the basis of language variety and accent has received attention from researchers looking at language attitudes" (Motha, 2014, p. 116). Individuals who live in the suburbs of Chicago sound different from individuals who were born and raised in rural Illinois. Also, communities of color, especially African Americans and Latinx families who live in segregated neighborhoods and schools speak differently than white families that live in upper-middle-class neighborhoods and attend well-equipped schools.

Using "accent" as a form of stereotype weaponizes ELLs' opportunities to become successful in schools. Teachers, school administrators, and staff need to understand that learning a new language might be challenging for some individuals. Pre-K through elementary school children might be able to sound or imitate native English speakers' oral language; however, ELLs attending middle and high school for the first time in this country, might not be able to sound like native speakers due to the fact that they started learning the English language later in life. It does not make them less smart than those students who started school in an English-speaking setting and who sound words and phrases as native English speakers. When ELLs start hearing "you have an accent" as a form of stereotype, it becomes weaponizing. ELLs internalize that they do not sound like mainstream English speakers, and some of them refuse to talk, afraid of being made fun of by their peers, or ridiculed by their teachers, school administrators, and/or staff. Some others, especially high school students, end up dropping out of school. Others still recall how they were singled out or laughed at for sounding different (Ríos Vega, 2020).

3.8 Academic English

While trying to understand the use of the phrase *academic language*, I also struggle to understand how this phrase silences communities whose English is not considered academic enough. I think about African American communities, students who come from Jamaica, Panama, Barbados, India, or any African country where English is spoken. Are we pushing our students to assimilate into a middle-class (white) American culture? Motha (2014) argues, "Whiteness and nativeness in English (whatever these might mean), while sometimes ambivalent or unconscious or inconsistent, are present in our English language classrooms" (p. 92). Sarah (pseudonym), a Black student teacher whose parents immigrated from Belize, referred to her parents' English as "broken." After I heard her talk about her parents as culturally deficient, I had a long conversation with her about the phrase "broken English." I talked to her about her parents' linguistic wealth, the history of her parents' country, and how different languages (a Mayan language, English, and Spanish) make her parents' language a resourceful asset (González et al., 2009). Then she talked about how her parents are building a house in Belize since they want to return to their homeland. I hope that Sarah understood that her parents' heritage language is not "broken," but it is a language filled with the history of different cultures (Howard, 2010).

It is important to understand how the term "academic English" is related to issues of race and class in this country. Who speaks "academic English?" It is probably a white and middle-class individual. When students of color or students who come from low socioeconomic backgrounds understand how "academic English" refers to whiteness, they tend to refuse using their own forms of *Englishes* to adopt a dominant way of producing language. This idea of adopting "academic English" leads some students to be questioned and sometimes rejected by their own groups after they have internalized the use of "academic English" as a form of academic success. Other students who refuse to conform to this form of language weaponization become oppressed and marginalized after they perceive the message that their English is not academic enough.

3.9 Limited English Proficiency (LEP)

The word *limited* has a negative connotation. Although some new textbooks have changed this term, which I consider a form of microaggression, I still find it in current research studies. English language learners are not limited. Instead, they are learners of a new language, and their proficiency level in the target language is based on biased standardized tests (Giroux, 2012). Those standardized tests are then used to label students' language proficiency and literacy expectations. Language learning is a very complex process, especially in the U.S., where students are tracked from day one based on culturally and linguistically biased forms of assessments (Au, 2019). We need to understand that when teachers and school administrators label a student as 'limited,' that student ends up internalizing the meaning behind that word (Browder et al., 2022).

In my experience, it was very common to hear teachers saying, "Marta is LEP," "She is LEP," or "How many LEP students do we have?" Soon I learned that the ELL students were no longer individuals, but labels and those labels became stereotypes. This stereotype of being referred to as "Limited" weaponized instruction (quality, value, etc.) toward ELLs. For instance, I witnessed how school counselors placed ELLs in courses where they were taught by unskilled teachers or courses that did not prepare students to become college bound. Also, I remembered advocating for some of my students after being ignored by their content area teachers after assuming that being labeled "Limited" meant being ignorant or stupid. It was how my ELLs felt after they came and shared with me what was happening in their classrooms. Instead of finding ways and pedagogical strategies to support ELLs, some teachers went by the stereotype "Limited English Proficiency" to weaponize my former students' education.

4 Final thoughts

I look back and sometimes wonder why I left the public school system since I loved teaching middle and high school students so much. First, I think about my academic journey to earn a doctorate in education. Then I think deeply about the injustices that I witnessed as an immigrant and as a queer person of color in the

United States. Also, I realize that there were many times when I felt more oppressed than my students since I could not speak my mind about inequity and inequality in education. I could not talk about how racism, classism, gender discrimination, and linguicism are embedded in the educational system since I was also part of the same system. As much as I wanted to help every single student, I understood that my role is to educate those who want to become teachers. However, I promised myself that I would bring my former students and their families to my teachings. I cannot separate my former ESL students and their families from my lessons and anecdotes. I cannot move away from those students whose lives shaped mine, as a man and as a teacher.

It is important to highlight that as individuals, we are all born and raised in communities where the same values and beliefs are taken as the norm. This first socialization phase pushes us to develop stereotypes about those who look and behave different from us. For students of color, especially ELLs, being seen as the Other at school represents a nightmare as they do not critically analyze issues of inequality and injustice in education. The use of those stereotypes to identify the Other has permeated our white Eurocentric educational system (textbooks, tests, standardized assessments). Also, most of the school teachers are white middle class women with little or no knowledge about how issues of race/ethnicity, class, and gender intersect multiple systems of oppression that weaponizes communities of color in this country (Sensoy et al., 2017).

Although some individuals can refer to the terms addressed in this essay as categories to identify and support students, I argue that more than categories, these are labels that then become stereotypes that weaponize, students of color, especially ELLs educational journey. Once that label is internalized consciously or unconsciously, it becomes a stereotype, which is almost impossible to be erased. When students are not understood as unique individuals as owners of a rich cultural and linguistic wealth, but as "at risk," "minority," "LEP," "illiterate," and/or "having an accent," those stereotypes become forms of language weaponization since those in positions of power (i.e., teachers, school administrators, and staff) use their prejudices and sometimes other forms of oppression (i.e., racism, linguicism, xenophobia, classism, etc.) to define and to interact with students of color. Additionally, students of color internalize those stereotypes as the norm since they are vulnerable to the system and adults at school. Students of color have to decide whether to conform to the school expectations (being seen as culturally deficient) or to become defiant to the system while becoming disposable.

As an academic, I have had the privilege to meet other scholars who think and look like me, whose experiences with different forms of oppression are similar to my former students and mine. As a university instructor, it is my responsibility and moral obligation to better equip future teachers. Some of them might understand the reason why I expose them to my former students' experiences, while others might never understand. As a teacher, I understand that some students might need more time to process the information while others will never understand it, but it is still fine with me. As a critical and post-ethnography scholar, it is important to challenge the weaponizing language that is still used in some teacher preparation programs in this country.

I urge school of education programs, instructors, student teachers, as well as school administrators, in-service teachers, and staff, to reflect on the use of stereotypes as a form of language weaponization and how that type of language harms students of color and their families. Instead of stereotyping students of color based on their language(s), skin tone, names, and spoken English, we need to become better listeners and learners of our students. We need to send the message to our students that they also have something important to share that is worth listening to instead of using stereotypes that weaponize their education. ELLs cannot be treated as empty buckets that need to be filled in with new (academic) knowledge. ELLs must be treated as valuable assets who bring funds of knowledge and previous lived experiences. It will allow teachers and mainstream students to dismantle and unlearn how those stereotypes learned from their parents, relatives, and social media can lead mainstream society to marginalize and to oppress the Other.

In closing, bell hooks (2001) invites us to practice an "ethic of love" (p. 87) in everything we do and to embrace change. Teaching must be an act of love, connectedness, and humanness. Being back in the classroom and after teaching for almost two years, hybrid and online due to COVID-19, I have realized how much I love being a teacher and how I see teaching as an act of love. hooks (2001) argues that individuals who choose to love have the ability to share people's lives "in ways that honor the primacy of an ethic of love" (p. 87). She continues,

> To live our lives based on the principles of a love ethic (showing care, respect, knowledge, integrity, and. The will to face our fears is one way we embrace love . . . Those of us who have already chosen to embrace a love ethic, allowing it to govern and inform how we think and act, know that when we let our light shine, we draw to us and are drawn to other bearers of light. We are not alone. (p. 101)

At the beginning of every semester, I show my students part of my vulnerability by telling them that my teaching performance comes from a space of love. I also clarify that my "ethic of love" comes from Freire's (1998b) and hooks' (2001) theories of teaching as an act of love. I read aloud part of hooks' definition of love in the classroom. Additionally, I instill in them that their "ethic of love" while teaching their future students should become the springboard to engage their students in lessons where their funds of knowledge and language(s) should represent forms of linguistic capitals in the classrooms. I encourage them to use their "ethic of love" to embrace differences with care, respect, and courage. I hope this essay serves as a springboard for more critical discussions about the weaponizing language used in teacher preparation programs and textbooks and how they harm the educational experiences of minoritized students, especially ELLs.

References

Au, Wayne. 2019. Racial justice is not a choice: White supremacy, high-stakes, testing, and the punishment of Black and Brown students. *Rethinking Schools* 33(4), 34–41. https://rethinkingschools.org/articles/racial-justice-is-not-a-choice/
Bonilla-Silva, Eduardo. 2010. *Racism without racists: Color-blind racism & racial inequality in contemporary America* (3rd ed.). Lanham, MD: Rowman & Littlefield.
Browder, Christopher, Luis Javier Pentón Herrera & José Franco. 2022. Advancing the conversation: Humanizing and problematizing the conversation about the students we call SLIFE. In Luis Javier Pentón Herrera (ed.), *English and students with limited or interrupted formal education: Global perspectives on teacher preparation and classroom practices*, 9–21. Singapore: Springer.
Bryan, Kisha C. & J. P. B Gerald. 2020. Weaponizing of English. *Language Magazine*, 1–8. https://www.languagemagazine.com/2020/08/17/the-weaponization-of-english/
Contreras, Russell. 2017. AP explains; Why term 'la raza' has complicated roots in US. *AP News*. https://apnews.com/article/9572a239f3e441b6a0c33f18255b10e9
Cortes Santiago, Ileana & Zaira Arvelo Alicea. 2015. A conversation with Latino/Latina families and its implications for teacher beliefs about cultural and linguistic diversity. In Luciana C. de Oliveira & Mike Yough (eds.), *Preparing teachers to work with English language learners in mainstream classrooms*, 59–76. Alexandria, VA: Information Age Publishing Inc. and TESOL Press.
De Genova, Nicholas & Ana Yolanda Ramos-Zayas. 2003. *Latino crossings: Mexicans, Puerto Ricans, and the politics of race and citizenship*. New York, NY: Routledge.
Dixson, Adrienne D., Celia K. Rousseau Anderson & Jamel K. Donnor. 2006. *Critical race theory in education: All God's children got a song*. New York, NY: Routledge.
Fergus, Edward, Pedro Noguera & Margary Martin. 2014. *Schooling for resilience: Improving the life trajectory of Black and Latino boys*. Boston, MA: Harvard Education Press.
Freire, Paulo. 1998a. *Teachers as cultural workers: Letters to those who dare to teach*. Cambridge, MA: Westview Press.
Freire, Paulo. 1998b. *Pedagogy of freedom: Ethics, democracy, and civic courage*. Lanham, MD: Rowman & Littlefield.
Gillborn, David. 2009. Education policy as an act of white supremacy: Whiteness, critical race theory, and education reform. In Edward Taylor, David Gillborn & Gloria Ladson-Billings (eds.), *Foundations of critical race theory in education*, 38–72. New York, NY: Routledge.
Giroux, Henry A. 2012. *Education and the crisis of public values: Challenging the assault on teachers, students, & public education*. Washington, D.C.: Peter Lang.
González, Norma, Luis C. Moll & Cathy Amanti (eds.). 2009. *Funds of knowledge: Theorizing practices in households, communities, and classrooms*. New York, NY: Routledge. hooks, bell. 2001. *All about love. New visions*. New York, NY: Harper Collins Publishers.

Howard, Tyrone C. 2010. *Why race and culture matter in schools: Closing the achievement gap in America's classrooms*. New York, NY: Teachers College Press.

Linville, Heather &Luis Javier Pentón Herrera. 2022. Why, how, and where to advocate for English language learners with limited or interrupted formal education. In Luis Javier Pentón Herrera (ed.), *English and students with limited or interrupted formal education: Global perspectives on teacher preparation and classroom practices*, 61–82. Singapore: Springer.

Marx, Sherry. 2006. *Revealing the invisible: Confronting passive racism in teacher education*. New York, NY: Routledge.

Motha, Suhanthie. 2014. *Race, empire, and English language teaching: Creating responsible and ethical anti-racist practice*. New York, NY: Teachers College Press.

Noblit, George W., Susana Flores & Enrique Murillo Jr. 2004. *Postcritical ethnography. Reinscribing critique*. New York, NY: Hampton Press.

Pentón Herrera, Luis Javier. 2021. "Me gustaría que habláramos también de mi cultura": A yearlong case study of two Maya English learners. *Journal of Language, Identity and Education*. Advance online publication. https://doi.org/10.1080/15348458.2021.1988606

Pentón Herrera, Luis Javier & Kisha C. Bryan. 2022. Language weaponization in society and education: Introduction to the special issue. *International Journal of Literacy, Culture, and Language Education* 2, 1–5. https://doi.org/10.14434/ijlcle.v2iMay.34380

Pica-Smith, Cinzia & Carmen Veloria. 2012. "At risk means a minority kid:" Deconstructing deficit discourses in the study of risk in education and human services. *Pedagogy and the Human Sciences* 2(1), 33–48. http://scholarworks.merrimack.edu/phs/vol2/iss1/4

Ríos Vega, Juan. 2015a. Ni Latino, ni Hispano: A journal of resiliency and social justice. In Regina Williams Davis & Andrea Patterson-Masuka (eds.), *Intercultural communication for global engagement*, 317–324. Dubuque, IA: Kendall Hunt Publishing Company.

Ríos Vega, Juan. 2015b. *Counterstorytelling narratives of Latino teenage boys: From vergüenza to échale ganas*. New York: Peter Lang.

Ríos Vega, Juan. 2020. *High school Latinx counternarratives: Experiences in school and post-graduation*. New York: Peter Lang.

Sensoy, Özlem, Robin DiAngelo & James A. Banks. 2017. *Is everyone really equal? An introduction to key concepts in social justice education* (2nd ed.). New York, NY: Teachers College Press.

Solórzano, Daniel G. & Dolores Delgado. 2001. Examining transformational resistance through a critical race and LatCrit framework: Chicana and Chicano students in an urban context. *Urban Education* 36(3), 308–342. https://doi.org/10.1177/0042085901363002

Solórzano, Daniel G. & Lindsay Pérez Huber. 2020. *Racial microaggressions: Using critical race theory to respond to everyday racism*. New York, NY: Teachers College Press.

Solórzano, Daniel G. & Tara J. Yosso. 2009. Critical race methodology: Counter-storytelling as an analytical framework for educational research. In Edward Taylor, David Gillborn & Gloria Ladson-Billings (eds.), *Foundations of critical race theory in education*, 130–147. New York, NY: Routledge.

Valencia, Richard R. 2010. *Dismantling contemporary deficit thinking: Educational thought and practice*. New York, NY: Routledge.

Villenas, Sofia & Donna Deyhle. 1999. Critical race theory and ethnographies challenging the stereotypes: Latino families, schooling, resilience and resistance. *Curriculum Inquiry* 29(4), 414–445. https://doi.org/10.1111/0362-6784.00140

Wingrove-Haugland, Erik & Jillian McLeod. 2021. Not "minority" but "minoritized". *Teaching Ethics* 21(1), 1–11. https://doi.org/10.5840/tej20221799

Sender Dovchin
Afterword
Language weaponization and its harm

This edited volume examines how an individual's fundamental human rights are violated and how they are deprived of education, well-being, life, and social opportunities based on their use of language and communicative practices (Dovchin, 2020). Integrating these various social and linguistic justice perspectives breaks new ground in applied linguistics by fully disclosing the sociolinguistic realities by acknowledging ongoing, often profoundly entrenched, local socio-political constraints (Tupas, 2015). It is almost impossible to develop a thorough analysis of people's apparent linguistic choices without acknowledging how ongoing communication is always associated with the dehumanization of others. That is, according to the editors of this volume, the multilayered dehumanization processes by assigning labels to groups, solidifying a culture that these groups are *something* (i.e., not human) rather than someone (i.e., *human*), and, consequently, causing physical and psychological harm by disrupting those groups of people who are dehumanized (Bryan & Pentón Herrera, in this volume).

The central ethos of this book is to apply the concept *of language weaponization* or the *weaponization of language*—to investigate the practices and processes in which linguistic resources in any form may have the potential to inflict harm on others (Bryan & Gerald, 2020; Pascale, 2019; Rafael, 2016). The main ethos of the term *language weaponisation* covers most recent studies in applied linguistics embedded within frameworks such as 'raciolinguistics' (Rosa & Flores, 2017), 'linguistic racism' (Dovchin, 2020 (Wang & Dovchin, 2022)), 'unequal Englishes' (Tupas, 2015), 'linguicism' (Uekusa, 2019), 'linguistic incompetence' (Canagarajah, 2022), 'translingual discrimination' (Dovchin, 2022), 'linguistic microaggressions' (Piller, 2016), 'accentism' (Dryden & Dovchin, 2021), 'linguistic citizenship' (Williams, Deumert, & Milani, 2022) and so on. The concept *of language weaponization* integrates the ever-growing scholarship on linguistic injustice and inequality while specifically unpacking the term *'harm,'* which is of crucial importance, as it highlights how minoritized language users' language, identity, and cultures are negatively affected by dominant ideologies and practices that standardize and normalize injustice in their given contexts. *Language weaponization* addresses injustice not only based on minoritized language users' specific linguistic and communicative repertoires that are (il) legitimized by the popular language ideologies but also adds intensity to the

Sender Dovchin, Curtin University, Australia

knowledge of psychological well-being and vulnerabilities seeded within the individuals and communities (Tankosić et al., 2021). People's quality of life, including their mental and physical health, is harmed by the negative impacts of *language weaponization*, as the minoritized language users tend to develop foreign language anxiety (Dryden, et al., 2021), linguistic inferiority complexes (Dovchin, 2020), depression and suicidal thoughts (Piller, 2016). *Language weaponization*, therefore, reminds us of Pennycook's argument on language – language is a discursive social act (Pennycook, 2007), which is continuously 'dis-invented and reconstituted' (Makoni & Pennycook, 2007), as it may (re)invent and de(construct) the linguistic ideologies of native speakerism, prestige, and prominence from the lens of the ruling authorities, who lead the narratives (Dovchin, 2022).

The different contributors to this volume articulate in their respective chapters various external and internal factors that (re)invent and (de)construct the ideologies and practices of the *linguistic weaponization* of communities that they have investigated. The attention is drawn to a fundamental aspect of *language weaponization*: that which applies in our daily interactions with each other, the exchange of ideas and points of view certainly involves *linguistic weaponization*, notwithstanding that of idiolects. There is certainly harm that constrains how the interaction and communication develop. *Language weaponization* has been operationalized in terms of the intersectionality of the socio-economic, racial, ethnic, gendered, linguistic, cultural, and political marginalization based explicitly on the systematic exclusion of minoritized language users from fully participating in society (Deumert et al., 2021). Many minoritized language users' experience *language weaponization* in the varied local contexts stamped with the systematic marginalization, precarity, and reduced emotional well-being conditions (Dovchin et al., forthcoming).

One of the most dominant paradigms in current language studies of globalization – the standard language norm or 'linguistic purity,' which tends to reinforce the idea of native speakerism, seems to be the center of this book. Linguistic purity sees 'monolingualism as norm' and 'one country equals one language' (Kelly-Holmes, 2010, p. 489). It has been noted throughout this book that this ideology of standard language norm, and like any norm, is socially and discursively constructed and is created by dominant institutions who exercise their power over those who do not use them 'properly.' The idea of this 'proper language' is often connected to traditionalist and purist ideas emerging from guarding one's national language and identity against foreign contaminations (Descourtis, in this volume; Dovchin, 2018). These language ideologies seem to reinforce the idea of *language weaponization* as they systematically marginalize the linguistic and communicative practices of minoritized people while giving an ideal picture of a particular society and of the language that mainstream society (Bryan & Pentón Herrera, in this volume).

Nevertheless, as many scholars note in this edited volume, this standardization of language does not necessarily reflect the sociolinguistic reality of that particular society. This is a problem because 'such a mythically homogeneous community depends in part on the exclusion or suppression of populations and characteristics which do not fit into its ideal self-definition' (Doran, 2004, p.93). As Busch (2010, p. 193) acknowledges, 'Homogenisation in language use is much more difficult to implement today, under the conditions of globalization, where communication and media flows have become more diverse and multi-directional than in previous times, when communication was organized around a national public sphere.' In fact, it is unlikely that every human being speaks purely any particular language (Pennycook, 2007). There are too many variations, dialects, accents, vernaculars, and creoles in any language, and to reduce this language to just 'standard language' seems over the top and unrealistic The reality of any language is very different as language is in constant relocalization, reformation, evolution, and many linguistic variations coexist in any society (Tankosić & Dovchin, 2022).

The chapters in this book further reveal that there is often a disconnect between privilege and harm as the discourses and languages allowed in communities occur when mainstream society allows that particular discourse to dehumanize or exoticize minority groups. In particular, pedagogical and educational contexts may often articulate policies and/or practices, privileging the linguistic purity, native speakerism, and monolingualism of the ruling class (Fang & Dovchin, 2022). In many cases, marginalizing the diverse linguistic repertoires of minoritized language users such as Indigenous Peoples and migrants' heritage languages seems to occur worldwide in multiple educational contexts (Bryan & Pentón Herrera, in this volume; Tankosić et al., 2022). *Language weaponization* causes unequal power relationships in educational contexts between ideologies and practices such as so-called native or non-native, first or second language teachers or students, shifting the central role that language plays in the enduring relevance of race/racism, stereotypes & (over) generalizations, institutional/interpersonal discrimination in the lives of racialized or ethnic minorities in the highly diverse transnational host societies of the twenty-first century, and what it means to speak or communicate as students or teachers with diverse identities (Steele et al., 2022).

The contributions to this volume show the various ways in which the notion of *language weaponization* provokes us better understand the manifold aspects of linguistic injustice in educational contexts, from Bangladesh to Taiwan, to Puerto Rico, to Botswana, and Spanish-speaking immigrants in the USA, from autoethnographic, ethnographic and critical discourse analysis perspectives. The discussions on how various implicit and explicit factors to *language weaponization* may influence the behaviors of teachers, educators, students, and learners, and what effects these adaptations of language users exert on the structures, practices, and ideologies of the relevant languages are thought-provoking. The edited volume further reveals how certain educational institutions promote Anglo-normative practices by weaponizing the native-speaker English mode (Saleh, in this volume), and teachers and students in that particular context are negatively affected by the linguistic, cultural, and ideological dimensions of weaponization (Wu et al., in this volume). *Language weaponization* further perpetuates the rural/urban divide, racial disparity, and, ultimately, socio-economic inequality (Wu et al., in this volume). The identities and positionalities of English as second language learners have become more attuned to the oppressive effects of the power of English (Tupas, 2015).

How can such harm be overcome? Contributors in this volume collectively note that the socio-political voices of minoritized language users and language learners are inadequate. This lack of voice renders them invisible in policy-making processes. It is essential that while *language weaponization* is an outcome of structures, order, and policies in the ruling society, it could also act as a potent catalyst for resistance to challenge the dominant policies of language ideologies and practices of which *language weaponization* is symptomatic (Bryan et al., in this volume). Contributors suggest multifaceted recommendations to improve linguistic and cultural inclusivity (Saleh, in this volume; Chebanne & Monaka, in this volume), gain a complete understanding of why the policy has the effects it does, and, in particular, the dynamics within global English learning in the particular historical, social and cultural contexts (Ates & Brooks, in this volume; Descourtis in this volume), and to treat students and educators of color as cultural and linguistic assets in the pedagogical contexts – as 'an ethic of love' (Vega, in this volume).

The harmful impacts of *language weaponization* are particularly noteworthy, as they are influenced by colonial politics (Deumert et al., 2021). This is a thought-provoking edited volume that calls for actions to turn our attention to volatile conditions that are profoundly affected by the legacy of the colony. Therefore, I ask applied linguists to pay more attention to *language weaponization* because the ethics of applied linguistics is one of the social justices.

References

Bryan, Kisha C. & J. P. B. Gerald. 2020. The weaponization of English. *Language Magazine*, 1–8. https://www.languagemagazine.com/2020/08/17/the-weaponization-of-english/

Busch, Brigitta. 2010. New national languages in Eastern Europe. In Nikolas Coupland (ed.), *The Handbook of language and globalisation*, 182–200. West Sussex: Wiley Blackwell.

Canagarajah, Suresh. 2022. *Language incompetence: Learning to communicate through cancer, disability, and anomalous embodiment*. New York, NY: Routledge.

Deumert, Anna, Anne Storch & Nick Shepherd (eds.). 2021. *Colonial and decolonial linguistics: Knowledges and epistemes*. Oxford, UK: Oxford University Press.

Doran, Meredith. 2004. Negotiating between bourge and racaille: Verlan as youth identity practice in suburban Paris. In Aneta Pavlenko & Adrian Blackledge (eds.), *Negotiation of identities in multilingual contexts*, 93–124. Bristol, UK: Multilingual Matters.

Dovchin, Sender. 2022. *Translingual discrimination*. Cambridge, UK: Cambridge University Press.

Dovchin, S. (2018). Dissatisfaction and Dissent in the Transmodal Performances of Hip-hop Artists in Mongolia. In: Ross, A. & Rivers, D. (eds), *The Sociolinguistics of Hip-hop as Critical Conscience*. Palgrave Macmillan, Cham. https://doi.org/10.1007/978-3-319-59244-2_8

Dovchin, Sender. 2020. The psychological damages of linguistic racism and international students in Australia. *International Journal of Bilingual Education and Bilingualism* 23(7), 804–818. https://doi.org/10.1080/13670050.2020.1759504

Dovchin, Sender, R. Oliver & Li Wei. forthcoming. *Introduction Translingualism: Playfulness and Precariousness*. In Sender Dovchin, R. Oliver & Li Wei. (eds), *Translingualism: Playfulness and precariousness*. Cambridge, UK: Cambridge University Press.

Dryden, Stephanie & Sender Dovchin. 2021. Accentism: English LX users of migrant background in Australia. *Journal of Multilingual and Multicultural Development* 1–13. https://doi.org/10.1080/01434632.2021.1980573

Dryden, Stephanie, Ana Tankosić & Sender Dovchin. 2021. Foreign language anxiety and translanguaging as an emotional safe space: Migrant English as a foreign language learners in Australia. *System* 101, 102593.

Fang, Fan & Sender Dovchin, S. 2022. Reflection and reform of applied linguistics from the Global South: power and inequality in English users from the Global South. *Applied Linguistics Review*. https://doi.org/10.1515/applirev-2022-0072

Kelly-Holmes, Helen. 2010. Languages and global marketing. In Nikolas Coupland (ed.), *The Handbook of language and globalization*, 475–492. West Sussex, UK: Wiley-Blackwell.

Makoni, Sinfree & Alastair Pennycook. 2007. Disinventing and reconstituting languages. In Sinfree Makoni & Alastair Pennycook (eds.), *Disinventing and reconstituting languages*, 1–41. Bristol, UK: Multilingual Matters.

Pascale, Celine-Marie. 2019. The weaponization of language: Discourses of rising right-wing authoritarianism. *Current Sociology Review* 67(6), 898–917. https://doi.org/10.1177/0011392119869963

Pennycook, Alastair. 2007. *Global Englishes and transcultural flows*. New York, NY: Routledge.

Piller, Ingrid. 2016. *Linguistic diversity and social justice: An introduction to applied sociolinguistics*. Oxford, UK: Oxford University Press.

Rafael, Vicente L. 2016. *Motherless tongues: The insurgency of language amid wars of translation*. Durham, NC: Duke University Press.

Rosa, Jonathan & Nelson Flores. 2017. Unsettling race and language: Toward a raciolinguistic perspective. *Language in Society* 46(5), 621–647. https://doi.org/10.1017/S0047404517000562

Steele, Carly, Sender Dovchin & Rhonda Oliver. 2022. 'Stop measuring Black kids with a White stick': Translanguaging for classroom assessment. *RELC Journal* 53(2), 400–415.

Tankosić, A., & Dovchin, S. (2022). Monglish in post-communist Mongolia. *World Englishes, 41*(1), 38–53.

Tankosić, Ana, Stephanie Dryden & Sender Dovchin. 2021. The link between linguistic subordination and linguistic inferiority complexes: English as a second language migrants in Australia. *International Journal of Bilingualism* 25(6), 1782–1798.

Tankosić, Ana, Sender Dovchin, Rhonda Oliver & Mike Exell. 2022. The mundanity of translanguaging and Aboriginal identity in Australia. *Applied Linguistics Review*. https://doi.org/10.1515/applirev-2022-0064

Tupas, Ruanni (ed.). 2015. *Unequal Englishes: the politics of Englishes today*. London: Palgrave Macmillan.

Uekusa, Shinya. 2019. Disaster linguicism: Linguistic minorities in disasters. *Language in Society* 48(3), 353–375. https://doi.org/10.1017/S0047404519000150

Wang, M., & Dovchin, S. (2022). "Why Should I Not Speak My Own Language (Chinese) in Public in America?": Linguistic Racism, Symbolic Violence, and Resistance. *TESOL Quarterly*.

Williams, Quentin, Ana Deumert & Tommaso Milani (eds.). 2022. *Struggles for multilingualism and linguistic citizenship*. Bristol: Bristol, UK: Multilingual Matters.

Editors

Kisha C. Bryan is an Associate Professor of Education and Chairperson in the Department of Teaching & Learning at Tennessee State University in Nashville, Tennessee. She has served on the editorial advisory boards of the *TESOL Journal*, *Literacy Research: Theory, Method, and Practice Journal*, and the *Caribbean Educational Research Journal*. In addition, she is an English Language Specialist for the U.S. Department of State and current director on the TESOL International Association Board of Directors. Dr. Bryan identifies as a public scholar and advocate for marginalized peoples around the world. Her research focuses on minoritized adolescents' intersectional identities and the role of language, literacy, and racial ideologies in identity construction. The scholarship for which she is most proud has been published in *Teachers College Record*, *TESOL Journal*, *English Journal*, and *Language Magazine*. A native of St. Helena Island, South Carolina, her linguistic background and schooling experiences were the impetus for both her career choice(s) and unyielding advocacy for marginalized populations. In her free time, she enjoys listening to podcasts, shopping, and hanging out with her teenage daughter, Ryann.

Luis Javier Pentón Herrera is Full Professor at Akademia Ekonomiczno-Humanistyczna w Warszawie, Poland, the Coordinator of the Graduate TESOL Certificate at The George Washington University, United States, and Co-Editor of *Tapestry: A Multimedia Journal for Teachers and English Learners*. In addition, he is a Fulbright Specialist and an English Language Specialist with the U.S. Department of State. Previously, he served as the 38th President of Maryland TESOL from 2018 to 2019, and earned the rank of Sergeant while serving in the United States Marine Corps (USMC). Two of his professional accolades include the '30 Up and Coming Emerging Leaders in TESOL', awarded by TESOL International Association in 2016, and the J. Estill Alexander Future Leader in Literacy Award, awarded by the Association of Literacy Educators and Researchers (ALER) in 2018 when his dissertation was chosen as ALER's 2018 Outstanding Dissertation of the Year. Dr. Pentón Herrera's current research projects are situated at the intersection of identity, emotions, and well-being in language and literacy education, social-emotional learning (SEL), autoethnography and storytelling, and refugee education. His books can be found in Routledge, Springer, Brill/Sense, TESOL Press, and Rowman & Littlefield. Originally from La Habana, Cuba, Dr. Pentón Herrera enjoys creative writing, playing with his two doggies, Virgo and Maui, and running in his free time. To learn more about Dr. Pentón Herrera, please visit his website https://luispenton.com/

Contributors

Gabriel T. Acevedo is an Assistant Professor in English Education in the English Department at Arizona State University. His identities as a Latinx, Bilingual, and Queer educator in Puerto Rico and the United States inform his research. He utilizes critical and social justice frameworks, along with qualitative methodologies, to interact with and understand the world around him. Acevedo is fascinated by the expansive possibilities that diversity and social issues bring to conversations in the classroom, especially in English Language Arts and Teacher Preparation. He is ever curious to understand how such conversations help in attempts to make sense of each other, as teachers, and as students. In his teaching and research, Dr. Acevedo seeks to advocate for positive change among educators. Acevedo prides himself on having interdisciplinary interests when it comes to teaching and research. He has done work in Teacher Education, Second Language Acquisition, Bilingualism, Queer Studies, Pop-Culture, Multimodal Literacies, Masculinity Studies, and others.

Burcu Ates is a Professor of Bilingual/ESL Education in the School of Teaching and Learning at Sam Houston State University in Huntsville, Texas. Some of her research interests include culturally and linguistically responsive pedagogies, cultural narratives, international service-learning/study abroad, refugee student education and concerns, and online teaching. Her research has been published in *Language and Education, Reflective Practice, Journal on Excellence in College Teaching*, and *World Englishes*. Burcu centers her overall research on diversity, equity, and inclusion.

Benita R. Brooks is an Associate Professor at the University of Nevada, Las Vegas. After serving as the Assistant Dean of Diversity, Equity, and Inclusion and as an Associate Professor of Literacy in the College of Education at Sam Houston State University for several years, she decided to return to her alma mater in Nevada. She co-founded the Diversity Engagement, Education, Development, and Support (DEEDS) Certificate Program for faculty, staff, and graduate students. The American Association for Colleges and Universities (AAC&U) considered the DEEDS Certificate Program "of significant academic merit." She has received numerous awards and recognition for her academic and community engagement work. Her research interests include cultivating culturally responsive and sustaining practices through critical service-learning in teacher education programs, developing culturally proficient leaders in K-12 and higher education, and re-thinking diversity, equity, and inclusion to obtain justice.

Andy Chebanne is a professor of linguistics and languages at the University of Botswana. He has researched and published on African languages of Southern Africa, particularly on Botswana languages. He has actively participated in matters of language documentation revitalization, especially for endangered languages of the Khoisan. As a language rights advocate, he is currently involved in the local language medium of instruction policy elaboration for Botswana. The policy seeks to integrate the use of local languages in early primary, and the development of materials in the mother tongue for literacy for eely primary school learners.

Sandra Descourtis (she/elle) is an Assistant Teaching Professor of French at Emory University. She is an interdisciplinary scholar-practitioner. Her research focuses on French language variations (especially *argot*) and teaching practices. She also works on multilingual language awareness and translanguaging in K-5 education. More broadly, her research interests include sociolinguistics, plurilingualism, as well as language ideologies and raciolinguistics.

Contributors

Sender Dovchin is an Associate Professor and a Director of Research, and an Australian Research Council Fellow at the School of Education, Curtin University, Australia. Dovchin is an Editor-in-Chief of the *Australian Review of Applied Linguistics*. She was identified as the *"Top Researcher in the field of Language & Linguistics"* under The Humanities, Arts & Literature of The Australian's 2022 Research Magazine and Top 250 Researchers in Australia in 2022.

Renee Figuera is an Assistant Professor of Linguistics and TESOL at the University of the West Indies, St Augustine. She is a Fulbright Hubert Humphrey Fellow for TESOL 2022-2023, and has published work with *New West Indian Guide, Caribbean Quarterly, The Africa Knowledge Project, Sage Methods Online, Translation and Translanguaging in Multilingual Contexts,* and *Research in Comparative and International Education.* Her latest project (in press with Routledge) examines the Politics of Internationalization of World Englishes from the Anglophone Caribbean.

Daphne Germain is an eleven-year veteran of the Boston Public Schools Office of English Learners, leading program planning and implementation. She has in-depth experience in how collaborative relationships with Black immigrant communities can develop to create new and innovative programs such as one of the first-in-the-nation Haitian dual language programs, formally named the Toussaint L'Ouverture Academy. She is a member of the Massachusetts Association of Haitian Parents.

Susan Githua is an Academic Success Coach in the College of Education at Tennessee State University in Nashville, Tennessee. Some of her research interests include educational experiences and career pathways of international students, students' performance, and female students studies. Her research has been published in *Online Journal for Workforce Education and Development* and *Journal of Consumer Protection and Food Safety* and is a co-author of a chapter in the *Handbook of Research on Innovative Digital Practices to Engage Learners*.

Ming-Yao Hsiung serves as an English EFL teacher and the Director of the Resource Center for English teaching and learning at Taipei Wanfu Elementary School. In addition to her teaching and administrative roles, she holds several certifications and leadership positions, including Microsoft Innovative Expert, Google Certified Level educator, Wakelet Community leader and Ambassador, Flipgrid Ambassador, Adobe Creative Educator, Humane Happiness Ambassador, and World Wide Green Program Taiwan Coordinator. Ming-Yao Hsiung holds a Bachelor's degree in Journalism with a minor in English Literature and a Master's degree in TESOL.

Denise Ives is an Associate Professor in the Teacher Education and Curriculum Studies department in the College of Education at the University of Massachusetts, Amherst. She earned a PhD in Curriculum, Teaching and Education Policy from Michigan State University and has extensive experience in the fields of literacy and teacher education. Denise uses ethnographic methods and critical discourse analysis to study multiliteracies in classrooms with a focus on culturally responsive pedagogies and supporting diverse learners. Her work has been published in *Linguistics in Education, Research in Teaching English* and the *Journal of Literacy Research*.

Jason A. Kemp is an Assessment Researcher at WIDA at the University of Wisconsin-Madison. He participates in projects that support multilingual learners and their educators. He taught Spanish in K-20 contexts and trained future world language educators. He serves on the WIDA Social Justice Change Team and leads the Assessment Task Force that aims to better apply a social justice lens to WIDA test development processes. He is on the Editorial Board of *Dimensions*, published by the

Southern Conference on Language Teaching. His research interests include critical care in language instruction and equity and inclusion in language proficiency assessments.

Ching-Ching Lin is a faculty member at Adelphi University, specializing in working with culturally and linguistically diverse populations. She was President of NYS TESOL from 2022-2023. Her research is dedicated to using diversity as a means of social transformation. She is a co-editor and contributing author of the following edited volumes, *Inclusion, Diversity and Intercultural Dialogue in Young People's Philosophical Inquiry* (Brill Publishers, 2017), *Internationalization in Action: Leveraging Diversity and Inclusion in the Globalized Classroom* (Peter Lang, 2020), *Supporting Student Success through Community Asset Mapping* (NYS TESOL, 2022) and *Reimagining Dialogue: Identity, language and Power* (Multilingual Matters, forthcoming).

Raouf Mama is a graduate of the University of Michigan with an M.A in English and a Ph.D. in English and Education, and is currently a professor of English at Eastern Connecticut State University, where he holds the title of CSU Professor He is an award-winning author, storyteller and motivational orator of international renown, the only one in the world today who tells in English, French, Yoruba and Fon indigenous tales from his native Benin and multicultural tales from around the world. He performs peace tales, spiritual tales, as well as humorous tales in a style that is a blending of storytelling, poetry, and music. He is an English Language Specialist and the author of numerous books, including *Why Monkeys Live In Trees*, winner of the National Multicultural Children's Book award in 2008, *Why Goats Smell Bad*, the French version of which is a national bestseller in Benin and required reading in the country's high schools, and La Jarre Trouee (The Jar With A Myriad Holes), winner of Benin's Grand Prix Litteraire in 2021, the country's equivalent of the Pulitzer Prize.

Po-Hui Min is a public school teacher and administrator in Taiwan. With her dedication to promoting international and bilingual education, she works with teachers in her school and beyond on curriculum development and teacher training. She works a lot with non-English subject area teachers and parents as she wants to ensure that they can reach out to as many students as possible when it comes to providing students with an opportunity to learn about the world.

Kemmonye Monaka is an Associate Professor of Linguistics at the University of Botswana. She co-authored the first Shekgalagari Grammar, has published in local and international journals, edited and co-edited *Pula: Botswana Journal of African Studies*, *Mapping Africa in the English-Speaking World*, and is currently the Chief Editor of *Mosenodi: International Journal of Educational Studies*. She advocates for marginalized languages and is collaborating on the translation of the Bible into Shekgalagari. She also researches on Khoesan languages. She is a member of the RETENG: *The Multicultural Coalition of Botswana*, which is in the forefront of language development, advocacy, and representation.

Juan A. Ríos Vega is an Associate Professor in the Department of Education, Leadership, and Counseling at Bradley University in Peoria, Illinois. He earned his doctorate in Philosophy in Educational Studies, Cultural Studies Concentration from The University of North Carolina at Greensboro (2014), Women's and Gender Studies Certificate (2014). His research focuses on multilingual learners, critical race theory, queers of color epistemologies, and social justice education. In 2020, Dr. Ríos published *High School Latinx Counternarratives: Experiences in School and Post-graduation*. This book was selected as one of the 2021 Critics Choice Awards Books by the American Educational Studies Association (AESA).

Abu Saleh Mohammad Rafi is an Assistant Professor of Linguistics at the University of Liberal Arts, Bangladesh. He is also an adjunct lecturer in the College of Arts, Society and Education, and a member of the Language and Culture Research Centre at James Cook University, Australia. Dr Rafi has published articles on translanguaging pedagogical approaches in top-tier journals, such as the *International Journal of Multilingualism*, *Language, Identity & Education*, *Teaching in Higher Education*, *Classroom Discourse*, and *Critical Inquiry in Language Studies*, as well as invited chapters in edited collections published by Springer, Routledge, and Vernon Press. He is a co-editor of the 2023 *Critical Inquiry in Language Studies* special issue, and an invited reviewer for two anthologies for *Applied Linguistics*.

Ming-Hsuan Wu is an Associate Professor in the TESOL and Bilingual program at Adelphi University in New York and directs two NYSED funded Clinically Rich Intensive Teacher Training programs for in-service teachers pursuing their ESL or bilingual certification. Her research examines Asian American students' heritage language learning experiences, their interracial friendships, and Asian Americans' work trajectories as English teachers in Asia. She serves as a consultant to the Fulbright office in Taiwan and offers teacher training workshops to English teachers in Taiwan. Her research has been published in the International Journal of Bilingual Education and Bilingualism, Journal of Language, Identity & Education, and Urban Education.

Xinyue Zuo is a Doctoral Candidate in Teacher Education and Curriculum Studies at the University of Massachusetts Amherst, with a Master of Arts in Teaching. Her research interests include instructional design and technology, bilingualism, and interpreting in educational settings. She has conducted research projects on multilingual speakers and linguistic and cultural support services using ethnographic methods and critical discourse analysis. Xinyue has published in the *Journal of International Students* and *Başkent University Journal of Education* and is the co-editor of the 2025 *Advances in CALL Research and Practice* Book Series.

Index

AAVE (African American Vernacular
    English) 67–68, 72, 76–77, 84
Aboriginal education 11
Abu Saleh Mohammad Rafi 8, 13–34
Academic English 225
Académie 192
Acevedo Velázquez, Gabriel T. 109–24
ACTFL 209–10
Adai 116–18, 120
African Americans 76–78, 149, 186, 225
African American Vernacular English. See AAVE
African diaspora 8, 63–64, 66–67, 84–85
African Language Association of Southern Africa
    (ALASA) 145
African languages 65, 75–76, 78, 145
ALA (American Library Association) 170, 172, 178,
    181, 188
ALASA (African Language Association of
    Southern Africa) 145
Alfaro, Cristina 154, 161, 163
American Educational Research Association 167
America's languages 164
Anzaldúa 149–51, 164
AP (Advanced Placement) 154–55, 180, 229
Aparicio, Frances 150–51, 164
AP Spanish class 154
Arab World English Journal (AWEJ) 60
argot and verlan 191–92, 196–98, 209
Aria 90–91, 95–97, 99–101
arrebato 157
Ates, Burcu 9, 169–90
At risk 220–21, 227
Austin 65, 86, 94, 97–98, 104, 186
Austronesian languages 39
autoethnographic, collaborative 36

Bangla 14, 16–22, 25
Bangladesh 8, 13–16, 18–22, 23–29, 31–33, 233
Bangladeshi English 8, 13, 15, 23–24, 26–27,
    29–31
Bangla Language Movement 17, 22
banned books 169, 172, 175, 177–79, 184, 187–89
banned books, supporters of 9, 169–70, 177
Banned books in K-12 classrooms 169–89

Bantu language family 74
Batibo 128–29, 136–38, 140–42
Batswana 127, 130, 132
Batswapong 136
Belize 225
Beninese Indigenous languages 69
Beninese people 80, 85
bilingual education 35, 47, 55, 57–58, 67, 73, 151,
    161, 165, 167
bilingual education policy 36, 46–47
bilingualism 147–48, 158, 164–65
bilingual policy 35–36, 39–40, 46–48, 57
Black English 63, 66–67, 84
Black Language 66
boarding schools 1, 4, 10–11
Botswana 7, 9, 127–35, 137–46, 233
– multicultural coalition of 136, 145
Botswana Constitution 130, 143
Botswana Daily News 137, 142
Botswana Democratic Party 137, 143
Botswana education system 137, 143
Botswana's language policy 142
Bright, Anita 7
Bristol 32, 87, 145, 164–67
British educational system 21
Brooks, Benita 9, 169–90
Brown, Phillip 144
Bryan, Kisha 1–2, 4, 6, 8, 10–11, 31, 38, 61–88,
    124, 229–30, 234

CAE 36, 40–41, 43
Cambridge 10, 31, 60, 106, 144, 211, 229
caring perspectives 147
Carlos 109, 115, 117, 119–20, 123, 221
critical discourse analysis (CDA) 8–10, 109,
    112–15, 124–25, 169–70, 177, 189
censorship 82, 152, 169–70, 177–79, 184, 186,
    189–90
CGPA (Cumulative Grade Point Average) 20
Chebanne, Anderson 65, 128–31, 133–41,
    143–44
Chicago 105, 154, 190, 220
Ching-Ching 40, 42–44
colonial language 4, 38

communication, cross-cultural 89, 91, 100, 102, 104
country, multicultural 128–29
CP (cooperative principle) 93, 95, 105
critical approaches 147, 159, 162
critical discourse analysis. *See* CDA
critical discourse studies (CDS) 5–6, 10, 125
Critical language education 11
critical race theory (CRT) 66, 87–88, 124, 169, 175, 181, 189, 229–30
cross-cultural interactions 93, 104
cross-cultural learning 104
cultural inclusivity 13, 234
cultural weaponization 29
culture wars 171

Davis 93, 97, 105
Descourtis, Sandra 9, 191–212
Dhaka 17–21
Dhaka College 20
discrimination, linguistic 64, 81–82, 91
disinformation 169, 177, 181–82, 184
Dovchin, Sender 231–32, 234

East Pakistan 16–18
education 3–4, 7, 16, 18–20, 27–29, 36–37, 60–61, 65–66, 87–88, 124–25, 127–28, 133–47, 158–59, 161–62, 164–67, 204, 213–15, 217, 219, 226–31
Education Act 21
Educational values 135, 185
Education and Training Sector Strategy Plan (ETSSP) 139
Education for All (EFA) 19, 133, 150, 176
education policies, neoliberal language 58
education programs, dual language 77
education reform 46, 229
EFA. *See* Education for All
Ellis 176–77, 188
ELLs (English language learners) 9, 47, 164, 213–15, 220–24, 226–30
ELT (English language teaching) 14, 22, 24, 33, 37, 86, 230
EMI (English-Medium Instruction) 38, 57
Engel 180–81, 188
English education in Taiwan 36, 41–44, 53

English language and pedagogical practices 22
English language learners. *See* ELLs
English language learning 23, 26, 39, 45
English language proficiency 20, 36
English language teaching. *See* ELT
English-Medium Instruction (EMI) 38, 57
English studies 13, 24
Ethno-cultural barriers in education 140
ETSSP (Education and Training Sector Strategy Plan) 139
Europe 210
European Languages 65, 71

Facebook 42, 60
Fairclough, Norman 9–10, 109, 112–13, 124, 169–70, 177, 189
fake news 169, 177, 181–82, 184
Favart 192–93, 197, 206, 211
Fergus 152, 218, 229
Figuera, Renee 8, 63
First Amendment 185
FL. *See* foreign language
FL classrooms 198, 200, 204, 210
foreign language (FL) 18, 20, 69, 71–72, 131, 136, 160, 164, 166, 191–93, 197, 200, 208–10
Foucault 99, 105
Foundation for Endangered Languages (FEL) 144
France 27, 85, 164, 191–92, 194–97, 199, 203–7, 209–10, 212
French as a foreign language 191–92, 197
French culture 193, 204
French language and culture 191, 204, 210
French language clichés 9, 191
French-lexicon Creole 71, 75, 82
French slang 191–92, 196–97, 200, 203, 205–7, 209–10
French-speaking countries 69, 206

Germain, Daphne 8, 63, 68
Githua, Susan 8, 63
Godfrey 184, 187, 189
Graduate School Hall 90
Gullah Geechee 67, 71, 76, 86–87
Gullah language 76–77

Haiti 64, 66, 72–73, 84
Haitian-American community 85–86
Haitian Creole language programs 86
HBCU (Historically Black College or University) 68
heritage language education 153, 166
heritage language learners 153, 165
heritage languages 55, 153, 157, 164–66, 214, 221–23, 225, 233
Herrera, Luis Javier Pentón 1, 229
higher education 18, 19, 26, 28, 33, 89, 101–2, 104–6, 148, 191–211, 214
Hindi 71
Hispania 164, 166
Hispanic 216–17
Hispanic bilingualism 158, 165
Holocaust 180–81
homophobic language 109, 111, 115–18, 120–21
homophobic language usage 121
homophobic slurs 8–9, 109–10, 117, 119–21
hooks, bell 215, 228
Hsiung, Ming-Yao 8, 35

independent school districts (ISDs) 169, 175, 183
India 16–17, 21, 32, 190, 225
Indigenous Peoples 4, 11, 18–19, 132, 141, 146, 233
international students 27, 51, 77, 89–91, 95–96, 98–101, 103
ISDs (independent school districts) 169, 175, 183
Ives, Denise 8, 89–106

Jamalcan Lanquage Unit (JLU) 65
Juan A. Ríos Vega 9, 213–30

K-12 64, 137, 147–48, 150–51, 153, 162, 169–89
Keller ISD 175, 190
Kemp, Jason A. 147–66
Kenya 7–8, 63, 74–75, 81–82, 84, 87–88
Khoisan Languages 143

LAC (Legal Assistance Centre) 143–44
language
– advantaged 129
– anti-queer 111
– bastardized 76
– ceremonial 71
– derogatory 81
– dynamic 202
– hybrid 75
– lingua-franca/national 130
– of the Shiyeyi 145
language barrier 213, 221–22
language education 7, 10–11, 25, 39, 77, 84, 87, 164, 166, 188, 190
language education policies 85, 87
language hierarchies 65–66, 84
language ideologies 5–6, 11, 15, 85, 88, 163–64, 167, 205, 211, 232, 234
language policies 64–66, 82, 88, 127, 144
language revitalization 14
language sustainability 159
language use practice 127, 133, 142
language variations 191, 193, 200, 210
language weaponization 1, 4, 6–9, 11–33, 61, 63–64, 66, 75–76, 84–85, 147–49, 156–59, 190–211, 215, 226–28, 230–34
languaging practices 9, 28, 147, 149, 155–62
Latino/Hispanic/Latinx 213
Latinx students 147–48, 150, 154, 157, 160, 216–18
Lawn Boy 182, 190
Leeman 153, 166
Lesbian & Straight Education Network 110
Limited English Proficiency (LEP) 226–27
limited language 159
Lin, Ching-Ching 8, 35
lingua franca 21–22, 30, 33, 38, 130
linguicism 82–83, 215, 223, 227, 231
linguistic imperialism 36–39, 44, 58, 65–66, 84, 86
linguistic market 199
linguistic violence 8–9, 63–87

Mama Raouf 63
maricón 9, 109–25
Mayan language 216, 225
Mexico 10, 150, 155, 204, 216, 219–20
microaggression 104
microaggressions 8, 89, 92, 98, 101–5, 107, 224, 226
Ministry of Education (MOE) 45, 57, 87, 137
minority language 14, 29, 84, 143–44
Minute on Indian Education 21

miscommunication 89–91, 97–99, 102–4
Monaka, Kemmonye 127–46
Morgan, Anne-Marie 23, 33
multiculturalism 135, 137
multilingualism 14–15, 87, 127, 137, 144–46, 167
Multilingual learners (MLs) 43, 163, 213
mundane discourse 169, 177, 183–84

Namibia 127, 143–44
National Coalition Against Censorship (NCAC) 186
National Development Council 36, 39, 47, 55, 57, 60
National Development Plans (NDP) 133
National Education Policy 18
National Public Radio (NPR) 178, 189
neoliberal education policy 47
neoliberalism 28, 35–37, 39–40, 45, 49, 57–58, 60
New York 32, 34, 44, 86–87, 105–6, 123–25, 146, 164–67, 188–89, 211–12, 229–30
Nigeria 70, 79
North Carolina 216, 220
Nyati-Ramahobo 129, 131–33, 135–40, 142, 144–45

Office for Intellectual Freedom (OIF) 170, 188
oppressed language 127

Pakistan 16–17
Paris 166, 192, 195, 210–12
pato 8, 109–25
Pennsylvania 185–86
Po-Hui Min 8, 35
Po-Hui's school 50, 53, 55
Progressive Party 110
propaganda 169, 177–78, 180, 184, 189
Proyecto Dignidad Party (PDP) 110
Puerto Rico 7–8, 109–14, 118, 121, 123–24, 154, 216, 233

Raciolinguistic ideologies 154, 167, 211

secondary school grade 20
second language status 20
Senate Bill – 3 169, 175
Setswana language 127–31

sex education 125, 177
slang, perceptions of 202–3, 207–8
slang words 197, 206, 209
Society for the Promotion of iKalanga Language (SPIL) 136
South Africa 3, 127, 145
Spanglish 155, 167
Spanish 9–10, 65, 67, 69, 71–73, 75, 98, 101, 147–57, 159–67, 201–2, 207–8, 215–16, 220, 222
Spanish heritage language (SHL) 160, 164, 166
Spanish language 7, 69, 150, 153–54, 156–57
Spanish slang 202
speech acts 8, 89, 92–95, 104–6
standard vs. non-standard language 191
stereotype 27, 213, 216–17, 220, 224–27
stigmatization 191, 193–94, 210
Straight Education Network 124
Swahili 70, 74–75, 82
symbolic violence 184, 187

Taipei Wanfu Elementary School 45, 48–49
Taiwan bilingual policy 35
Teaching English to Speakers of Other Languages (TESOL) 44, 60, 67
Texas Education Agency (TEA) 175–76, 189
Texas House 175
Texas Legislative Education Equity Coalition 176, 190
Tobago 7, 75, 82–83, 87
translanguaging 10, 13, 28–30, 32–33, 158, 167
Trinidad 7–8, 75, 82–83, 87
Tswana extraction 127–28

United Nations 69, 75, 132, 146

Walqui 163, 167
weaponization 6–10, 13–14, 16, 24–25, 28, 31–32, 35–39, 45–46, 79–81, 86–87, 89, 188–89, 191, 208, 213–14
weaponizing language 16, 214–15, 222, 228–29
Wu, Ming-Hsuan 8, 35–60

Yoruba 69, 73, 79–80
Young Adolescent (YA) 177

Zuo, Xinyue 8, 89–106

www.ingramcontent.com/pod-product-compliance
Lightning Source LLC
Chambersburg PA
CBHW050521170426
43201CB00013B/2042